The Origins of Justice

Pennsylvania Studies in Human Rights

Bert B. Lockwood, Jr., Series Editor

A complete list of books in the series is available from the publisher.

The Origins of Justice

The Evolution of Morality, Human Rights, and Law

John O'Manique

PENN

University of Pennsylvania Press

Philadelphia

Printed in the United States of America on acid-free paper

10 9 8 7 6 5 4 3 2 1

Published by
University of Pennsylvania Press
Philadelphia, Pennsylvania 19104-4011

Library of Congress Cataloging-in-Publication Data

O'Manique, John.
The origins of justice : the evolution of morality, human rights, and law / John O'Manique.
p. cm.—(Pennsylvania studies in human rights)
Includes bibliographical references and index.
ISBN 0-8122-3706-4 (cloth : alk. paper)
1. Justice. I. Title. II. Series.

JC578 .O43 2003
320'.01'1—dc21 2002032346

To Patricia,
Erin, Colleen, Patricia,
Stephanie, and Juliet

Contents

Preface

In the final paragraph of *The Chalice and the Blade*, Riane Eisler talks of a transformation from our patriarchal, androcratic world to a "gylanic" world of partnership and natural hierarchies between women and men. The myths in this new world will not be about the inevitability of fear and evil, and men will not be honored for violence. There will be "new myths, epics, and stories in which human beings are good; men are peaceful; and the power of creativity and love . . . is the governing principle. For in this gylanic world, our drive for justice, equality and freedom . . . will at last be freed. And after the bloody detour of androcratic history, both women and men will at last find out what being human can mean."[1]

This prediction of a cultural transformation from a patriarchal dominator society to a natural partnership between women and men is the culmination of Eisler's study of human origins based on rigorous analysis of empirical evidence and evolutionary theory. Its vision of a world that is naturally good and caring counters the ubiquitous Hobbesian view of life as nasty and solitary, and sets the scene for the present exploration, which does not predict a cultural transformation but does discover the origins of justice in a past "gylanic world."

The objective of this essay is to find the origins of justice, including the origins of human rights. This will be done through an exploration of our human origins, using neo-Darwinian theory and the results of recent studies of evolution by natural scientists. This exploration of our human origins will take us back a million years or more, when the seeds of humanity began to grow. We cannot put a date on this distant and obscure past, but if we are a part of the evolutionary process, then it follows that the elements of our humanity—self-consciousness, symbolic language, morality, and culture—must have emerged with our primordial ancestors. We will probably never know the details of when and how this remarkable emergence took place. We do, nevertheless, know enough about the dynamics and laws of evolution to enable us to build hypotheses about the origins and development of the qualities that distinguish us as human. My objective is to build such hypotheses and use them to shed some light on the origins and nature of justice.

This exploration into our beginnings will lead to concepts of morality, obligation, rights, and justice that are radically different from those in the dominant Western paradigm.[2] Because of this and the consequent novelty of the study, it will necessarily be an *exploration* that attempts to build new *hypotheses*; there will be no confirmations. The exploratory conclusions of this essay will be contrasted with the main thrust of the dominant Western paradigm and any discussions of Western social, political, and legal theory are for purposes of contrast and illustration; these theories do not provide a foundation for what follows. The foundations for my hypothesis building are from the natural sciences.

My approach is not reductionist, nor is neo-Darwinian theory reductionist.[3] By *reductionist* I refer to the attempt to explain something completely in terms of its elements, to reduce something to the sum of its components. The most obvious case of this within the context of neo-Darwinian theory is the attempt to explain human qualities and behavior in terms only of genetics and natural selection. This is precluded by the transcendence found within the evolutionary process and especially in the emergence of life and of self-consciousness. These two events radically changed the very processes that had conceived them. This view of evolution leads to the hypothesis that humanity has arisen from a physical and biological past, but has also, to a great extent, escaped from the constraints of that past; *we are biologically conditioned, but we are not biologically determined.* I make no attempt to provide a biological explanation for every aspect of moral character and behavior, but rather focus on the essential biological elements that form the foundations for our transcendence and that continue as conditions rather than determinants.

Good theory arises from sound hypotheses. Although I have considerable confidence in my conclusions, I recognize that this exploration of justice is a hypothesis-building exercise and, as such, it is an attempt to advance solid, well-founded hypotheses on the relevant aspects of human development. These hypotheses are based on the recent work of many scientists whose research is relevant to human evolution: biologists, biological anthropologists, primatologists, palaeontologists, evolutionary and social psychologists. I believe that the evidence supporting the neo-Darwinian theory is overwhelming; nevertheless, many facets within the theory, such as some that I will be drawing on, are still cloudy and controversial. What we induce from these about human beliefs and behavior, and about morality and justice, cannot be precise and certain. They are emerging hypotheses.

I am looking for the origins of justice in order to explain justice and its essential elements: morality, human rights and obligations, and law. It is a systematic attempt, based on empirical evidence, to explain justice and so, by definition, it is *a theory of justice.* Those words are the title of the very significant and influential work by John Rawls.[4] I will suggest, however, that Rawls's "theory of justice" is rather a model of what he would like justice to be and that a real theory (at least in any scientific sense) must attempt to understand human rights and justice through their origins. My theory does lean very heavily on origins. In fact, a major difference between my approach and that of others like Rawls and Nozick and Western discussions about justice in general is my search for actual evolutionary origins.

Soon after Rawls's *Theory of Justice* appeared a second major and very influential study of the subject was published by Robert Nozick.[5] Within the dominant Western paradigm the two works were perceived to be poles apart; Rawls represented a liberal view in which the state has some positive involvement in the welfare of its people, whereas Nozick provided further conceptual underpinning for the libertarian, minimal state position of the neoconservatives. Viewed from outside their paradigm, however, the two positions are quite similar. In particular, and of central concern to what follows here, both authors begin with virtually the same assumptions about human nature, both use a *state of nature* approach with similar states of nature, and both tailor their premises and rational argument to their desired conclusions, which vary in degree rather than in kind.

The view of justice I will put forward is very different from that of Rawls and Nozick, and of the dominant Western paradigm to which they belong. Because the central positions of that paradigm are broadly known and taken for granted, I will contrast my hypotheses with them. Rawls and Nozick, as very significant representatives of the central thrust and narrow spectrum of the dominant Western position, make ideal foils to facilitate this contrast and so I will make use of their work as such.

Rawls's first necessary condition for a realistic concept of justice is that it must rely on the actual laws of nature,[6] but Rawls does not investigate or identify these laws of nature. Nor does he consider what natural science might have to say about human nature, but assumes *man*[7] to be, first and foremost, an autonomous rational planner. This is consistent within the dominant paradigm. The autonomous rational planner, or maximizer, is basically selfish. The Hobbesian[8] view of life as nasty and solitary persists, albeit sometimes with modifications. Social, political, and legal theories flow, for the most part, from these kinds of assumptions.

I do not say that our understanding of human nature should come only or even primarily from natural science. I do say that it should take into account what natural scientists, and especially those in the life sciences, have discovered. The view of life, animal nature, primate nature, and human nature that I see in contemporary natural science is quite different from the dominant Western view, and consequently my induced hypotheses on the origins and nature of morals and justice are contrary to those of the Western tradition, from Aristotle to Hobbes, to Kant and Mill, to Rawls and Nozick.

What is as significant as the difference between my hypotheses and the conclusions of the dominant streams of Western thought on the subject is the difference in approach. What follows is not a moral argument; it is not my attempt to persuade others to accept my beliefs about what is good and what justice ought to be. It is, rather, an empirically based exploration to try to discover what morality and justice actually are. So, let us begin to explore.

Chapter 1
Introduction

The Basic Argument

As stated in the Preface, the objective of this book is to find the origins of justice, including human rights. The hypotheses it builds are induced from the natural sciences and they differ radically from the dominant Western views on morality, rights, and justice which are still influenced by their pessimistic and rationalist philosophical foundations. A brief preview of my central hypotheses as they contrast with the dominant position might be useful.

What I call the dominant Western paradigm arises from the liberalism characterized in Max Lerner's classic article:

> Thus the liberal image of the state came to mirror the equilibrium physics that the scientific revolution had made familiar. And the liberal image of the human mind came to stress the primacy of self-interest as a drive (egoism), the primacy of reason as an instrument (intellectualism) and the ultimate value of individual efforts toward self-realization (progress, happiness) or of individual non-efforts (laissez faire, quietism) in a state of nature.[1]

These few lines, whether or not they define the contemporary liberal,[2] capture the essential elements of the dominant Western position. The mechanistic model based on classical physics, in which the primacy of self-interest, instrumental reason, and autonomy are assumed, emerged from seventeenth-century turmoil and science and has changed little since. The foundation of the model is Galileo's point masses moving in space, understood by mapping them onto a Cartesian reference frame and seen most explicitly in contemporary economics. The model I wish to promote in its place mirrors contemporary science, especially biology, rather than sixteenth-century physics and seventeenth-century geometry. It stresses a balance between the self-interest, instrumental reason, and autonomy of the dominant Western position and altruism, other forms of cognition, and relatedness in community, all of which many scientists now see as essential elements of human development.

I must emphasize from the outset that I do not dispute the existence or value of self-interest, reason and autonomy. It is the assumption of their primacy that I argue against. In briefest outline, my approach and argument are as follows:

- My approach is not a rational argument for my beliefs on morality, rights, and justice, but an exploration, based on natural science, of how these arose within our origins and early development. The following hypotheses emerge from this exploration:
- Humans are naturally *both* self-interested (selfish, egoistic) *and* open to others and to the needs of others (altruistic). The mix or balance of these natural characteristics varies over time and space, to a great extent as a consequence of culture.
- Human development is distinguished primarily by self-consciousness and its various cognitive manifestations, including understanding, self-conscious feeling, intuition, and reasoning/rationality (inducing, deducing, calculating). Reasoning is indispensable, but neither primary nor central.
- As an integral and essential part of the evolutionary process, morality emerged as humanity emerged, as the self-conscious capturing of the basic selfish and altruistic inclinations that drive the process. Rights, obligations, and justice are integral parts of this long process of emergence.
- The emergence of justice was determined by the developmental conditions of the origins of humanity and in particular by a developmental balance of the selfish and altruistic inclinations of *social* individuals—not isolated, autonomous individuals, but individuals-in-community—transformed by self-consciousness.
- The continuing evolution of justice, while not determined by the biological conditions that gave it birth, cannot completely escape their influence and so must be understood within the context of these biological conditions. Self-consciousness and cultures join the biological base as determinants of human development, and over eons have become the major determinants.
- Rational choice theory, rational decision theory, images of *man* as *rational animal* and *rational utility maximizer*, utility as identified with the egoistic individual, life as *nasty* and *isolated*, the *autonomous* individual—all these are abstract, partial, and/or exaggerated characterizations

of the human and, if presented as capturing the human reality or even major parts of that reality, become gross distortions that can lead only to misleading or false conclusions.

The exploration that ensues does not always follow a simple, linear path. It is, rather, composed of interrelated parts, reflecting the organic world that it probes, and so, to assist the reader through this iterative and convoluted discussion, I offer now an outline of the inquiry.

Outline

The remainder of this chapter will define the concepts central to my investigation and attempt to contrast my own approach to the dominant Western paradigm.

Chapter 2 sets out the biological "Foundations of Morality," which are also the foundations of human rights and justice. Because I see morality to be a transcendent continuation of the inclinations for development found in all living organisms, I will use the neo-Darwinian theory and recent research on evolution to present these inclinations as naturally both selfish and altruistic.

Chapter 3, "The Evolution of Self-Consciousness," argues that the capacity to reflect—the distinguishing characteristic of human beings—is a radically new and transcendent activity within the evolutionary process. The emergence of self-consciousness is considered, as are the consequences of this remarkable evolutionary experiment to our own beginnings.

Chapter 4 brings the biological base and self-consciousness together in "The Genesis of Morality." It claims that the essential elements of morality, value and obligation, emerge when self-consciousness captures the natural developmental inclinations that drive the evolutionary process. Morality is not a product of reason but rather arises with humanity itself from profound self-conscious feelings of development needs and the inclinations to secure them.

Chapter 5, "Culture: Our Transcendent Environment," presents culture as the transcendent human environment that has, from the early beginnings of humanity, been created/constructed by self-conscious humans. As cultures develop they become an ever greater influence on moral judgments and behavior, creating new needs and transcending our biological foundations.

Chapter 6 brings us to the threshold of the origins of justice itself through an exploration of "The Origins of Rights." Reflections on development needs and on caring and feelings of obligation flow naturally from the beginnings of morality and emerge as the foundations for rights. Within this perspective, the exercise of human rights is human development itself.

Chapter 7, "The Origins of Justice," brings all the above together as the foundations and progenitors of justice. The origins of justice are explored through the use of scenarios but, unlike the fictional "states of nature" from Hobbes to Rawls and Nozick, these are drawn from the natural sciences. They are not confirmed and so remain hypotheses in the scientific sense, but they do at least attempt to get at actual human origins and, thereby, at the real origins of justice.

Chapter 8, "The Origins of Law," is a consideration of law as it arose within systems of justice. Because law is seen to be a further manifestation of self-consciousness capturing developmental propensities, it shares in the positive and developmental character of morality and justice. Law is claimed to be the order required for the just exercise of rights, that is, for human development itself.

Chapter 9 is not so much a "conclusion" but simply "Some Concluding Comments" to help bring all this together.

Definitions

The meanings I attach to the concepts that are central to this study—justice, rights, obligations, moral—will unfold as the work progresses. It may be helpful, nevertheless, to give the reader some preliminary notion of how I use the terms *moral* and *justice* and what I mean by *theory of morality* or *theory of justice. Moral* is the most basic of these concepts, so we will start with it.

The Meaning of *Moral*

Moral refers to beliefs and judgments about what is good (or bad) and about what *ought* to be, to acts or behaviors that can be judged to be good or bad, and to principles or standards, or systems of these, that are intended to elicit behavior that is judged to be good and prevent behavior that is judged to be bad.

The *Oxford English Dictionary* (second edition)[3] defines the adjective moral as:

> **1. a.** Of or pertaining to character or disposition, considered as good or bad, virtuous or vicious; of or pertaining to the distinction between right and wrong, or good and evil, in relation to the actions, volitions, or character of responsible beings; ethical.
> **1. c.** Of knowledge, opinions, judgements, etc.: Relating to the nature and application of the distinction between right and wrong.

Moral comes from the Latin word *moralis*, which comes from the Greek for *ethic*, and both *moral* and *ethical* derive from *custom* or *norm*. They are interchangeable and I will use them as synonyms.

Norm is the root of both words, and *moral* (*ethical*) is normative. *Normative statements* refer to what is believed to be good or bad; they are *value judgments* such as "We ought to help the poor." They state what one *believes* to be *good* and what *ought* to be, not what *is*. No empirical test can confirm a normative proposition. *Empirical statements* say something about the way things are: about what *is*. Their truth can be tested empirically.

The word *ought* contains two elements. First is a belief that something is good or bad; it implies a *value judgment*. But the word means more than that. If I say, "we ought to help the poor," I am saying that helping the poor is good *and* that we *should* do this good thing: we owe it to somebody to do this good thing. I am making a value judgment and I am making a claim about obligations. Morality has to do with what *ought* to be and is, therefore, about *both values and obligations*.

Moral pertains to goodness *and* badness, but it is also used in a specific sense as a synonym for good and *im*moral for bad. I will use *moral* in the generic sense, encompassing *good* and *bad*, as opposed to *amoral*. An amoral act cannot be judged to be *either* good or bad. What is the difference? It would appear that the difference has to do with *responsibility*: the ability to respond consciously and freely to what is going on around us. If I do something as a result of my understanding of a situation and of my own considered decision that I ought to respond to the situation in this particular way, then I am *responsible* for my action. My behavior could, therefore, be judged to be either good or bad. If it is judged to be good I may be rewarded, if bad I may be punished. On the other hand, if my reaction to something is not based on my knowledge of the situation and/or is not something I have thought about and chosen to do, in other words, if it is not something I have freely and knowingly decided that I ought to do, then I am not responsible and the behavior would not be judged to be either good or bad. I will be neither rewarded nor punished. My action would be called *amoral*. Most of human behavior falls between these poles: between free and responsible behavior determined by the person acting for objectives set by that person (self-determination) and behavior determined by agents other than the conscious self.

Should we call all freely chosen behavior *moral*? I would think that any such behavior that is trivial or inconsequential should be called *amoral* and suggest that the test would be whether or not the act has any bearing on human development, of the self or others. I will, therefore, define moral as follows:

Moral pertains to human behavior to the extent that the agent of the behavior is responsible for that behavior and that it is related to human development. If the agent is not responsible and/or if the behavior has no relationship to human development, then it would be termed amoral.[4]

The Meaning of *Justice*

What I mean by *justice* will become clear as my exploration unfolds. The following are some definitions to get us started.

The *OED* defines *just* as

> **1.** That does what is morally right, righteous. **2.** Upright and impartial in one's dealings; rendering every one his due; equitable.

and *justice* as

> **1.** The quality of being (morally) just or righteous; the principle of just dealing; just conduct; rectitude. . . .
> **4.** Exercise of authority or power in maintenance of right; vindication of right by assignment of reward or punishment. . . .

I define a just person as one who responds in an appropriate way to the real needs of others. A just society is one that responds appropriately to the real needs of its members. This appropriate response could be through a system of justice that supports a distribution of resources for an equitable exercise of human rights and provides protection for individual rights. The meaning of this will become clear as this exploration unfolds.

The Meaning of *Theory of Justice*

Using John Rawls and Robert Nozick as foils, I will contrast my concept of *theory of justice* with theirs. Their methods and assumptions are representative of the dominant Western view in general and the contract school in particular.

Although the title of his major work is *A Theory of Justice*, Rawls devotes a section of chapter 1 to the clarification of "moral theory" rather than *theory of morals*.[5] Rawls says that humans have a moral capacity: a capacity to judge things as just or unjust and to support these judgments by reason. Moral theory is not, he insists, a description of this moral capacity, nor is a theory of justice a description of our sense of justice. What moral theory is, he claims, "is a formulation of a set of principles which, when conjoined to our beliefs and knowledge of the circumstances, would lead us to make these judgments with their supporting reasons were we to apply these principles conscientiously and intelligently" (46).

The production of moral theory so defined is a good thing for humans to do. It is what moralists usually do. It is not, however, what I propose to do. I propose to present not a moral "theory," not a set of moral principles, but a theory of morals: a possible explanation of what morality, including justice, is, why it is, what its foundations are, how it works. I believe that a theory of morals or of justice in this sense is not only different from the traditional approach, including Rawls's, but is a prerequisite to that approach.

Rawls reveals key elements of his and the dominant Western view of moral theory in the following:

> A correct account of moral capacities will certainly involve principles and theoretical constructions which go much beyond the norms and standards cited in everyday life; it may eventually require fairly sophisticated mathematics as well. This is to be expected, since on the contract view the theory of justice is part of the theory of rational choice. (47)

Let us consider this statement carefully. Rawls's stated objective is "a correct account of our moral capacities." To achieve this objective, he says, involves the kinds of principles and theoretical constructions that he himself develops. His set of moral principles is to help us to "understand our sense of justice" or our "moral sensibility" (46). Rawls's moral principles are rational principles; they are derived through rational argument from premises that are his assumptions about the nature of *man* and his imaginary original position. He suggests that, because this is based on rational choice theory, "fairly sophisticated mathematics" may be required to go further. This confirms the rational character of his approach, which is also the approach of the utilitarian view and the Western tradition in general.

In his *Anarchy, State, and Utopia*, published in 1974, Robert Nozick also sees humans as rational maximizers, as rational beings who maximize the utility of their actions through *rational* procedures. And, like Rawls, he believes that mathematics can be applied to rational action, including moral action.[6] "The expected utility formula marks an action as best. . . . An action is rational when it is generated by a process that tends to produce the best actions, the ones with maximal DV [decision-value]."[7] Using characters that give the illusion of mathematics, Nozick represents various kinds of utilities. These include symbolic utilities (SU), which encompass ethics: highly valued outcomes or *grand things* such as being rational, caring, unselfish, living in accord with nature, and seeing others as creatures of God (49). To further the illusion he puts these characters into a formula:

$$DV(A) = W_c \times CEU(A) + W_e \times EEU(A) + W_s \times SU(A)$$

This is the decision-value of a rational action.[8] Within this abstraction Nozick deals with morality:

> The moral acts get grouped with other possible events and actions and come to stand for and mean them. Thereby, being ethical acquires a symbolic utility commensurate with the utility these other things it stands for actually have. . . . The utility of these grand things, symbolically expressed and instantiated by the action, becomes incorporated into that action's symbolic utility. Thus, these symbolic meanings become part of one's reason for acting ethically. (29-30)

For Nozick, pseudomathematical rationality is the basis of morality and the way to understand morality. I believe that morals cannot be reduced to rational abstractions and that an understanding of morality requires an empirically based exploration of human beings, their origins, behavior, abilities, cognitive and affective functions, interrelationships and interactions within their communities, needs and wants, objectives and goals. It does *not* involve, as Rawls claims, "principles and theoretical constructions which go much beyond the norms and standards cited in everyday life," but rather requires an understanding of the principles and constructions, the norms and standards of everyday people in everyday life. In no sense do Rawls's or Nozick's principles and theoretical constructions tell us anything about our moral capacities, nor would the most "sophisticated mathematics." What is the moral capacity, the moral sensibility, the sense of justice of six billion people in everyday life? These are questions that demand an empirical investigation of the moral dimension of humanity.

The assumption of the primacy and ubiquity of rationality governs both the image of human nature upon which Rawls's and Nozick's arguments rest and the methods they employ. If this assumption is not an accurate representation of human nature then the conclusions will be suspect. But even if it is accurate, it does not follow that the principles of justice can be discovered without empirical investigation. The dominant Western paradigm sidesteps this requirement with the assumptions of the rational choice model and the further assumption that a rational model conjured up in the mind of a Western philosopher can tell us anything about morality.

According to Rawls, "The rational plan for a person determines his good."[9] If this is indeed the case, then perhaps one could deduce moral principles from it without further ado. Or if some part of it seems a bit distant from reality, that troublesome element can be assumed away, as Rawls does with the additional "special assumption . . . that a rational individual does not suffer from envy" (143). There is no empirical evidence presented to confirm the hypothesis that people are rational planners and that rational planning determines the good.

Indeed, as I will try to show, the foundations of morality are not at all rational, reason emerged along with morality, and perhaps a bit after morality, and *good* was determined by the real and profound self-conscious inclinations and feelings of real, everyday people, without a rational plan.

Nozick goes beyond Rawls in his emphasis on the autonomy of the individual and the individual's right to life and property. Autonomy and these rights appear as virtually absolute. The only requirement in the state of nature, following Locke, is the protection of the life and property of the autonomous individual against transgression (9). This propensity to transgress the rights of others leads to "inconveniences" according to Locke and to war according to Hobbes. For both of these founding fathers of the dominant paradigm, the state is presented as the rationally constructed remedy for aggression and transgression. Nozick follows this pattern, but, having established the need for a state, as did Hobbes and Locke, he occupies himself with arguing from his view of human nature that only the minimal state, whose function is protecting individuals and their property from transgression, is justified.

Nozick presents an extended rational argument to support the position that, because of the extent and absolute character of individual entitlements, any redistribution of wealth by a state is unacceptable and, consequently, only the minimal state function of protection of life and property is acceptable. It has been suggested that, in contrast with the moderate and conventional theory of Rawls, Nozick's theory represents a radical change—a paradigm shift.[10] Nozick's argument supports laissez-faire capitalism with minimal state interference in the market, while Rawls's provides justification for the more liberal version of capitalism, which includes a limited welfare state. The differences are real, but given that both start their arguments from virtually the same premises and use the same method and approach, the difference is not at all radical. These are two sets of rational argument within the same paradigm, with conclusions within the acceptable Western range, each representing a segment of the Western political spectrum.

Nozick bases his argument on a state of nature and, like Rawls, appears unconcerned about its validity. To highlight the contrast to my approach, I will let Nozick explain, with his emphasis:

> A theory of a state of nature that begins with fundamental general descriptions of morally permissible and impermissible actions, and of deeply based reasons why some persons in any society would violate these moral constraints, and goes on to describe how a state would arise from that state of nature will serve our explanatory purposes, *even if no actual state ever arose that way.*
>
> . . . A *fundamental* potential explanation . . . carries important explanatory illumination even if it is *not* the correct explanation. . . . Fact-defective fundamental

> potential explanations, if their false initial conditions "could have been true," will carry great illumination; even wildly false initial conditions will illuminate, sometimes very greatly.
>
> State-of-nature explanations of the political realm *are* fundamental potential explanations of this realm and pack explanatory punch, even if incorrect. (7-8)

Just how "wildly false" can the initial conditions be if the conclusions are to be illuminating? There must be limitations to the liberties one can take with a state-of-nature scenario and still expect it to have explanatory value. A balanced and precise account of what humans are and how they behave would seem to be a necessary condition for such a model to be useful, and although Nozick doesn't appear to be concerned with his model's validity, he seems confident that his view of human nature is accurate. I do not share his confidence.

The approach to the development of a theory of justice used, inter alia, by Rawls and Nozick is as follows. Without any evidence, they present a set of assumptions about the nature of *man* (women are excluded) and the state of nature. Both Rawls and Nozick emphasize that this account does not need to reflect the real world during that period in human development. Nevertheless, they use these assumptions as a basis for rational arguments leading to their conclusions about justice. The hypotheses that flow from my empirical exploration of human origins will suggest that their assumptions about human nature are wrong in that they present only one side of that nature. Half of the human character is missing, as is the female half of humanity.

It appears to me strange to say that the state of nature is not intended to be real, but to claim that it can still lead to reasonable or useful conclusions about reality. (Recall the frugal fellow who baited his mousetrap with a picture of a piece of cheese and caught a picture of a mouse.) In creating any simulation that is to be useful, only those elements that are peripheral to the issues to be explored can be removed; every attempt should be made to retain the relevant central and essential elements as they would be in the real world.

Foundations of the Dominant Western Perspective

What I call the dominant Western perspective has already been introduced, especially in the context of Rawls and Nozick, who are among its most significant contemporary representatives. Because others such as Hobbes, Kant, and Mill have had a major impact on modern Western philosophers and are representative of major streams in the dominant Western paradigm it might be useful also to contrast their approaches with mine to help set the context for this exploration.

For Immanuel Kant, valid moral laws are products of pure reason.[11] They cannot be in the least tarnished by experience and their foundations are not in human nature or natural inclinations. Pure reason, uncontaminated by empirical reality, creates the universal law by which the will determines morality by the conception of rules. Not all philosophers of the dominant Western tradition would go to these lengths to avoid the empirical, but the tendency in Western moral discourse is nevertheless in this a priori direction.

Kant's assertion that morality is a creation of pure reason leads him to his claim that the autonomy of the will is the supreme principle of morality. Kant uses *autonomy* in a very strong sense, claiming that it makes the will a law to itself. Autonomy can also mean self-determination, but as Kant uses the concept the emphasis is on *self* as free *from* constraints: freedom-from rather than freedom-to, and, in the case of the human will, an absolute freedom-from.

In spite of the differences between them, Kant and Hobbes emphasize the same human characteristics as bases for their deliberations on the human: *reason* and *autonomy/isolation*. Indeed, these are the pervasive human characteristics of the dominant Western paradigm, with the tendency to define *autonomy* as freedom from constraints. In this paradigm, reason, as systematic, logical, analytic thinking, as deducing and inducing, as calculating (reason is the faculty of the mind that, in Aristotle's words, "calculates means to an end"[12]) has been accorded the status of *the* activity of the human mind. Other self-conscious activities, such as feeling, intuiting, and understanding, are ignored, marginalized, or classed as subhuman. Autonomy as independence, self-control, freedom from external influence is also a characteristic cherished and exalted in the West, as, indeed, it should be. But autonomy is a relative, not an absolute, quality of human life. We are independent, dependent, and interdependent. We are self-determined and determined. We are immersed in and interacting with our total environment, and although we can be more or less autonomous within this context, we can never be completely autonomous. To be so would require total isolation and hence extinction.

The discourse that follows will counter any undue emphasis on reason and autonomy. While accepting the value of rational method, and indeed using reason throughout this exploration, and emphasizing the importance of self-determination, this essay will unfold from the assumption of a dynamic, ever-changing, interacting, relational world from which humans and human morality emerge. A significant degree of independence will be seen as an essential ingredient of human morality, but not its supreme principle. *Self-determination* will be identified with freedom and presented as a defining principle of humanity, but *self* will not be autonomous or isolated; the Hobbesian individual-in-isolation will give way to the *individual-in-community*.

Within the dominant Western paradigm there are, of course, many different views and emphases. The consequentialist approach, which is itself a broad subgroup within the paradigm, counters the Kantian, deontological school. The emphasis on human rationality is shared by deontologists and consequentialists, the latter, however, showing greater interest in reason as the capacity to calculate rather than to create principles. The consequentialist's criterion for moral behavior, therefore, is not a principle derived by pure reason but rather a calculation of the consequences of the moral act. Utilitarians are the best-known consequentialists, and John Stuart Mill is one of the foremost utilitarians. He said that the foundation and principle of morals "holds that actions are right in proportion as they tend to promote happiness, wrong as they tend to produce the reverse of happiness."[13]

Mill, however, goes beyond this statement on criteria to the question of the origin of justice. Whereas Kant associates morality with pure reason alone, rejecting the intrusion of any inclination into the moral realm, Mill claims that justice is based on both rule, emerging from a calculation of consequences, not principle, and *sentiment*, where sentiment is an *animal desire for reprisal* (79–80). The morality of the sentiment or feeling of revenge comes from the human capacity to extend this feeling to others and/or do it in an enlightened way.

We have now before us two tests of morality. For the deontologist, *good* and *bad* are determined by principles: by maxims derived by reason, a priori. For the consequentialist, *good* and *bad* are determined by a rational calculation or benefit/cost analysis of the consequences of the act, or of the rule that elicits the act. Reason, in both cases, determines morality.

We have also two positions on origins. For Kant, the origin of morality is pure reason; for Mill it is animal feelings of revenge at a self-conscious level.

In *A Theory of Justice*, Rawls presents us with a blend of principles and concern for consequences. He defines *good* as that which the rational *man* chooses. He, in fact, identifies goodness with rationality.[14] Rawls believes that his account of the *original position* improves on Kant's thesis by going beyond Kant's fundamental maxim to show which principles would be chosen by free and rational people. The principles rationally chosen by rational humans to "reveal their independence from natural contingencies and social accident" are the principles "defining the moral law, or more exactly, the principles of justice for institutions and individuals" (255). This, it seems to me, is a statement on the origin of moral law and justice. As in Kant, the emphasis is on principles of reason, although Rawls's rational planner and calculator does consider the consequences of *his* calculation to *his* rational and autonomous life.

Rawls encounters the problem of reconciling the practicing liberal with the Hobbesian assumptions; if the human is, by nature, a self-interested rational maximizer, how can the concern for community of the liberal citizen come about? For the Kantian liberal the problem is solved by the categorical imperative: a purely rational (divine for some) drive toward what is right; but even the rationalists of the later twentieth century have difficulty seeing this mysterious and pure rational faculty of the eighteenth century. Rawls's solution in later writings is to propose special powers and interests that culture induces in the individual to satisfy the communitarian requirements of a liberal society.[15] The other solution within the dominant Western paradigm is a simpler one. Those on the neoconservative side see no need for special powers and interests; the marketplace will ensure that the net consequences of the behaviors of rational maximizers will be for the common good.

We have looked briefly at the views on morals of three very significant and, I believe, representative figures from the modern Western tradition: from eighteenth-century Prussia, nineteenth-century England, and twentieth-century United States. What do they tell us?

First and foremost, morality is associated with rationality. The *good* is determined by principles of reason (Kant), a rational calculation of consequences (Mill), and/or a "rational plan" (Rawls). The association is absolute for Kant, very strong to absolute for Rawls, but weaker for Mill. For Kant and Rawls, reason appears to be not only the criterion for determining what is good or right but also the very origin of morality. For Mill, moral criteria are rational but the origin of morality is to be found in feelings of retaliation that are animal at base, though raised to a self-conscious level in humans.

Put in its simplest terms then, the dilemma confronting the present dominant Western paradigm is this: What keeps *man*, assumed to be naturally a selfish rational maximizer, from a constant state of war. The basic solution, like that of Hobbes, more than three centuries ago, is the state, whose principal function is, through laws and sanctions, to protect *men* and their property from other nasty *men*. Many of today's Western thinkers find this view of society too negative and pessimistic, but they remain wedded to the Hobbesian assumptions about the nature of *man* from which the negative view arises.

Within the dominant Western paradigm there is agreement that *man* is autonomous, selfish, and rational, and that women are irrelevant. There is also agreement that all problems are solved by reason. The debate centers on what rational solution is required to ensure the common good to the extent that a state of war is avoided and some human development will take place. Minimalist state plus the rational marketplace? A free market and somewhat expanded state? Acculturation to produce the special inclinations required to balance the natural inclinations of the rational maximizer? Selfish animal urges are controlled by laws and sanctions, based on reason and enlightened self-interest, and directed by markets. Altruism is reduced to enlightened self-interest, or marginalized. "Homo homini lupus" (Man is a wolf to man); "the life of man [is] solitary, poore, nasty, brutish and short."[16] To what extent do these assumptions capture the full and relevant human reality? To what extent do they apply to women as well as men?—to rural agrarian as well as urban industrial people?—to Africans, Asians, and First Nations as well as Europeans and North Americans?—to the wretched of the earth as well as the dominant elites? It seems to me that the *man* in the dominant Western paradigm is the Western, affluent, urban male—a very small, but powerful proportion of our planet's population.

Virtually all the Western professional thinkers who have sought to solve the question of morality and justice have been men. The evidence I will present is going to raise the strong possibility that they were incapable of seeing the real and natural source of justice because it was not, primarily, within the male community. If morals and justice arise not from fear and reason but from empathy and caring, these qualities are more likely to thrive among the women in a community.

Let us begin, then, to explore the origins of morality

Chapter 2
The Foundations of Morality
An Overview of Our Evolution

Humanity's great diversity is recognized from the outset and throughout this exploration. Different peoples have constructed different cultures with different values and beliefs. Whatever our differences, however, we six billion humans are all members of one species: *Homo sapiens.* We have a common origin.

In biology, a *species* is a set of organisms that can successfully interbreed.[1] Whether or not we belong to the same biological species as our early self-conscious ancestors has no bearing on my argument. A new species does not arise from an existing one in one generation. Significant changes over hundreds of thousands of years could be required to preclude potential interbreeding. *Homo habilis* lived about two million years ago, *Homo erectus* about one million. *Homo sapiens* is a different species from these two species, but there is no point in time at which one became another.[2] Nor does it matter to our exploration whether we descended from Lucy, an *Australopithecus afarensis,* or, also from over three million years ago, from Ken, a *Kenyanthropus platyops.* We need not concern ourselves with such details.

We know that we humans are distinguished from other animals by our self-consciousness, symbolic languages, morality, and cultures, including science, art, and technology. Even if some animals have some of these characteristics, ours are much more highly developed. Within the neo-Darwinian context we claim, with a high degree of certainty, that we and all our distinctive human qualities have evolved in one continuous process. If we trace our lineage back far enough through time we will find hominid ancestors who do not have these human characteristics. It follows, then, that these human qualities must have emerged as integral components of the process. We can say little about the details of this emergence, but we can say with certainty that humanity, with the characteristics or potential for the characteristics we have today, did emerge.

By definition, the emergence of humanity was, *pari passu,* the emergence of human morality. To the extent that we can understand the gestation, birth, and early development of humanity, we can understand the origins of morality and then justice. Within this evolutionary context, therefore, I will explore the emergence of humanity itself, of human characteristics, beliefs, and behaviors, to try to discover the origin of humanity's moral dimension.

The concept of evolution I have drawn from major neo-Darwinian evolutionists itself precludes reductionism. I see within the evolutionary process true novelty: the emergence of qualitative changes. Two of these stand out: the emergence of life and the emergence of self-consciousness. The emergence of life within the process of physical/chemical evolution from basic energy to complex organic compounds initiated a new kind of development: biological evolution. In a similar way, but with much more profound, extensive, and dramatic consequences for us, the birth of self-consciousness was the foundation of human development. These transformations marked new kinds of evolution with new capacities following a new set of laws for their further development.

With life came a capacity for new kinds of development based on reproduction with inheritable change, along with new laws to govern it, understood now to a considerable extent through neo-Darwinian theory. With life also came a transformation of the very environment within which life's evolution continued; life emerged from a reducing atmosphere, which would be fatally poisonous to us, but then began to produce the oxidizing atmosphere in which we now live. Some three billion years ago bacteria began to use the carbon of carbon dioxide for their own development and leave the oxygen for us to breathe; life itself radically changed the conditions for its own continuation.

The emergence of self-consciousness was even more spectacular, not so much in its actuality as in its potential. By self-consciousness[3] I refer to the ability to reflect on one's self, including one's thoughts and feelings, and thereby understand in a new and profound way, distinguish self from other, judge, reason, and create symbols, language, morality, techniques, art, and science. This, like all evolution's remarkable creations, did not arise from a simple, linear process.[4] The process would have been an interactive one, in many communities, over many millennia, in which embryonic capacities to distinguish between self and other, reflect, create symbols, communicate with symbols, would all interact among themselves and with the continuing physiological development of individuals and among individuals-in-community, in a vast and complex dynamic of failed and successful experiments, out of which eventually emerged those characteristics and behaviors that define humanity today.

The part of the process that gave humanity its unique character, at least here on Earth, was the interaction of reflection with the beginnings of language. Because I see reflection to be a requirement for language, I refer to it as the actual beginning of the evolution of the human mind: the cognitive dimension of this development. I hasten to add that language is essential for the development of self-consciousness, and if some claim that language came first, that bothers neither me nor my argument.

I say little about the physiological dimension of these interactions, but nevertheless emphasize that it is a necessary and integral part of this process.[5]

This remarkable evolutionary innovation—the capacity to reflect on what is known and felt, on the *self* and the *other*—emerging from mutations that in themselves were probably no more remarkable than any other mutations,[6] gave rise to new evolutionary paths with new capacities for development following radically new rules. This is not, however, a simple linear process whereby a mutation produced self-consciousness in a human that was then chosen by natural selection.[7] Frans de Waal, who agrees that self-consciousness is "at the core of being human,"[8] presents substantial evidence for the emergence of self-consciousness in other primates and possibly nonprimate animals. Self-consciousness probably emerged among our primate ancestors and evolved along several primate lines, including those leading to contemporary apes.[9] This book's focus on human development, therefore, in no way suggests that we are the only self-conscious beings nor that there has been a single path of self-conscious development leading to us.

Furthermore, my claim that self-consciousness is the foundation of human development—"the core of being human" as de Waal says—does not imply that self-consciousness and our species are coextensive in time. Self-consciousness probably existed long before what we now call *Homo sapiens* emerged. De Waal, Alison Jolly, and others present a very solid case for the hypothesis that the origins of self-consciousness and of morality itself pre-date our species. There is good evidence that *Homo sapiens* evolved from the same ancestors as the contemporary African apes (gorilla, chimpanzee, and bonobo).[10] There is also good evidence that these apes are self-conscious. They are not members of our species and the common ancestor, living about five million years ago, was not a member of our species either. Nevertheless, for the purposes of this exploration it does not much matter whether we contemporary humans could mate successfully with those of our ancestors who gave birth to morality, that is, whether we are biologically the same species. So, rather than make this more complicated than need be, I will talk of those early moralists as if they were human.

The development of our ancestors up to the era during which they became self-conscious was determined by the evolutionary process, but once animals became self-conscious they could themselves, as self-conscious, influence the laws of development and development itself; self-conscious life was, to an at first infinitesimal but ever-increasing extent, in control of the process and of the environment in which it continued to develop. The physical laws that rule the inanimate were still present. The biological laws that govern the evolution of living organisms were still in effect. But a new dimension of the process had emerged in which the evolving self-conscious organisms, while still subject to the natural environment and to the laws of physical and biological nature, were now creators of new environments and their own laws of development. Two essential and extremely important conclusions follow from this:

- Humans determine much of their own development within environments (cultures) that they themselves construct.
- Human self-determination and culture, although constantly transcending their physical and biological foundations, do not completely escape the conditions of those foundations.

Just as life from its beginning altered the environment within which it evolved, so too did self-consciousness. Whereas the transformations effected by organic life are physiologically determined, however, those caused by humans as humans are self-conscious responses that continuously recreate the environment. I will refer to this essential dimension of the environment created by humans as *culture.*

I am obviously using the concept *culture* in its widest possible connotation: *everything* that has been produced (constructed) by humans as self-conscious agents. The other dimension of our total environment, the so-called "natural" environment, is that part of our physical/biological environment that human agency has not modified. It is clear that *culture* and *physical/biological environment* are concepts whose objects overlap and are interrelated and integrated. Culture is constructed from or influenced by our physical/biological environment, and more and more of the physical/biological environment on this planet is modified by human construction.

Discussion of the complex interacting set of environmental conditions for human activity will continue throughout this exploration, but the simplified picture of this in Figure 1 might be useful now. The horizontal arrow in the figure represents human development. This arrow does not imply a linear or teleological process, but simply represents the complex interactive evolution of self-conscious animals over time. This development is influenced throughout and relatively constantly by its biological base, below, and the environment, above. With the emergence of self-consciousness, however, the human community begins to create culture, represented by the space under the exponential curve. The influence of culture increases at an accelerated rate, while the other two influences remain relatively constant and, because of the continuous interactivity among all the dimensions of this process, are themselves influenced by cultures, and cultures by them.

I use the word *creation* metaphorically to emphasize the novelty, the qualitative change, not to suggest any supernatural intervention from inside or outside the process. The seeds of transcendence are contained within the evolutionary process itself. The events that initiated this whole new dimension of the process, a new path, a transformed animal, were probably slight genetically induced changes that were themselves barely noticeable.[11] But once these changes were selected and established there was no turning back; transcendence had occurred.

The concept of transcendence used here is shared by Theodosius Dobzhansky, one of the founders of neo-Darwinian theory.[12] He defines *transcend* as "to go beyond the limits of, or to surpass the ordinary, accustomed, previously utilized or well-trodden possibilities of a system."[13] Dobzhansky sees the origin of life and the origin of the human as cases of evolution transcending itself, but he also sees, with A. I. Hallowell, the

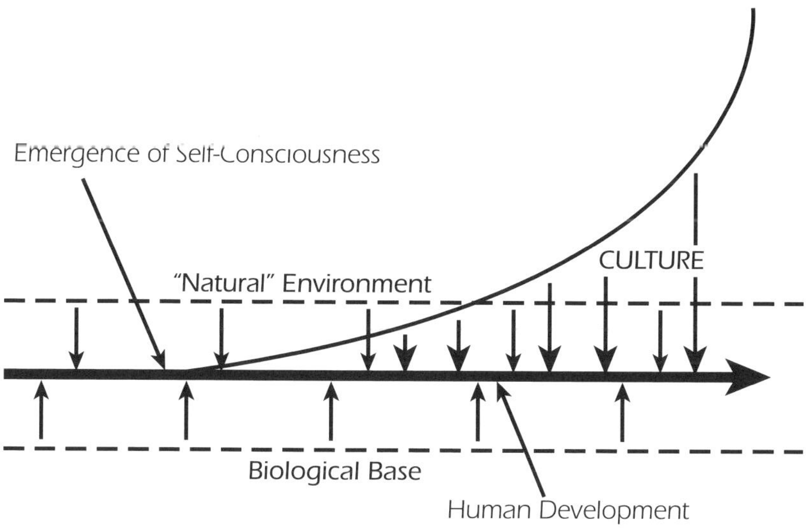

Figure 1.

new, transcendent human as itself constantly transcending itself.[14] The human species is, in other words, a transcendental product of evolution that has powers of creativity whereby it innovates within parameters that it itself constantly pushes outward.

If we do find the origins of morality within this biological evolutionary process, it will not follow that morality can be reduced to and explained by the laws of biological evolution; other more immediate sources of morality are self-consciousness itself and its interaction with the cultures it creates.

Evolution: Some Basic Ideas

Having introduced a view of evolution that should ward off fears that I will reduce morality to genetics, we will explore the theory of evolution to find the source of morality. I will begin with some basic ideas on evolution.

The tendency to survive is the most basic of all the tendencies of living organisms. It is really a set of inclinations to do or get all that is needed for survival—nourishment, shelter from the elements, and refuge from predators, for example. These tendencies arise from a particular genetic structure in the organism. An organism with a genetic structure that does not effect the required inclinations—that does not elicit a search for food, shelter, escape from a predator—will not survive to reproduce. The inappropriate genetic structure will consequently be quickly removed from the community. If, however, this unfortunate creature's siblings do have the appropriate genetic structure, they will eat, seek shelter, and escape; some will live to reproduce, and the genes that contributed to their development to the time at which they reproduce will be passed on.

From the above it is obvious that more than survival is required for evolution to continue. The organism must survive long enough and develop sufficiently to reproduce. The customary focus on survival, which suggests a bare minimum—a subsistence level of life—obscures the more positive and complete *development* within the evolutionary process. The propensity to survive is really a propensity to develop, at least to develop enough to reproduce. The measure of biological success is reproduction. It is through reproduction that genes are passed on and, if the characteristics that they induce help subsequent generations to develop, they themselves survive: they are *selected.*

Focusing on the critical act of reproduction itself, Charles Darwin added to *natural selection* the concept of *sexual selection.*[15] Sexual selection is the choosing of a sexual partner. It is not hard to see that this can have a powerful influence on which genes survive and, therefore, on evolution.

In most cases the female of a species invests much more in reproduction than does the male. Considering our own species from only the physiological perspective, that is, without cultural parameters, a human female who nurses her babies can reproduce about every two or three years. During that period she provides energy for gestation and nourishment for the child and energy and pain at childbirth, and because she has the strongest bond with her progeny, she will continue to bear the greatest burden of responsibility for the child for many years. The male, on the other hand, is physiologically capable of spreading his genes daily, with virtually no physiological cost and no consequent pain, and can divest himself of any responsibility for childcare. The males of nonhuman species, and too many human males, do not know who their offspring are.

The genes of a female who chooses a fit male for a partner will more likely survive than will the genes of a female who chooses a less fit partner. The female, in most species, has a small fraction of the opportunities to reproduce that the male has and makes a much greater investment in reproduction, so she is the one who makes the choice. The male sex, consequently, evolves characteristics that will attract the female. The peafowl is an obvious example of this. The peahen, in choosing a mate, is attracted to a display of bright colors. The peacock who can produce the brightest display is more likely to be chosen and his genes are therefore more likely to be passed on. Over eons this sexual selection has induced the development of a brightly colored train of tail feathers that are longer than the body length. To attract the female the male raises and vibrates his tail feathers in a spectacular sight and sound performance.

The peacock has carried attractiveness to the extreme; the large tail could be an impediment to survival, slowing the bird's escape from predators, for example. This might suggest that in some cases sexual selection runs counter to natural selection, which promotes fitness. It could be, however, that only the most fit peacocks can survive with such a burden of beauty, and so to choose the most beautiful is also to choose the most fit. The males of most species do not go to the extremes of the peacock, and in many cases the attractive features are directly related to fitness: size, strength, endurance, and the like.

Sexual selection can induce change much more quickly than can natural selection alone. If females are attracted to tall males, then tall male genes are more likely to be passed on, and, if the attraction is strong, the height of the male population will increase rapidly in relation to evolutionary time. If, however, tallness is an impediment to survival and the possibility of developing to reproduce is lower for taller than for shorter males, then both the genes for tallness in males and the genes for attracted-to-tallness in females will die out. Natural and sexual selection work together determining what genes continue through the generations.

Geoffrey Miller notes a 1993 Gallup poll showing that almost half the U.S. population accept human evolution, but only 10 percent believe that natural selection can explain the emergence of the human mind. Most think that "the mind's evolution must have been guided by some intelligent force, some active designer."[16] Miller shares these doubts about the efficacy of natural selection but adds, "I think the active designers were our ancestors, using their powers of sexual choice to influence—unconsciously—what kind of offspring they produced." They are conscious of the choice, but not of its influence within the evolutionary process.

The activities required for development have been called a *struggle,* contributing to the rather nasty image that evolution has acquired. Darwin used the phrase "struggle for *existence*" in, he said, a "large and metaphorical sense including (which is more important) not only the life of the individual, but success in leaving progeny."[17]

Struggle for existence or the more popular *struggle for survival* suggests not only a minimalist position but also that the process is a nasty, brutish, Hobbesian affair. This was certainly not Darwin's intention. He used *struggle* to refer to competitive, aggressive behavior, but he also used it in a metaphorical sense, and made this very clear: "Two canine animals, in a time of dearth, may be truly said to struggle with each other which shall get food and live," he says, referring to the nasty, brutish side. "But," he adds, to emphasize a non-Hobbesian side, "a plant on the edge of a desert is said to struggle for life against the drought, though more properly it should be said to be dependent on the moisture" (75). The ecologist would now add that the edge of the desert is also dependent on the plant to resist further desertification, and so *inter*dependence or symbiosis is involved; the plant and soil do not struggle to overpower one another, but each exerts its own power-with in a mutually beneficial process.

We should note that it was a major and influential *social* Darwinist, Herbert Spencer, not Darwin, who coined the phrase *survival of the fittest* and proceeded to use his own distorted Hobbesian view of evolution to support a laissez-faire approach to society—a foundation for today's neoconservatism.[18]

In a most illuminating statement, Theodosius Dobzhansky expands on Darwin's broader and precise meaning of *struggle* as follows:

> natural selection is due to the survival of the fittest in the struggle for life. This terse formula is partly metaphorical, as any reasonably attentive reading of

Darwin's work will clearly show. The "struggle" is not necessarily contention, strife, war or combat. . . . The survival of the "fittest" does not mean that just one fittest variant survives and the rest die; what is fit to survive survives.

In vain did some naturalists point out that success in the struggle for existence is at least as often achieved among animals by co-operation and mutual help as by competition and combat. Many people preferred to take Darwin's metaphors quite literally. The idea that struggle without quarter or mercy is a universal law of Nature and that harsh and ruthless competition results in biological progress and improvement were grasped as ready justifications of power politics, conquest, exploitation of the weak by the strong, child labor, and even of forms of laissez-faire economics. Racism . . . also tries to appear decent and "scientific" in a Darwinian garb.[19]

Following Darwin and Dobzhansky we can, then, more precisely translate *struggle for survival* as *competition and cooperation* for *development.*

This interpretation is supported by the current understanding of the evolution of social behavior, including cooperation and altruism, based to a great extent on the discovery of kin selection and reciprocal altruism and from more recent studies of social behavior among animals and especially primates.[20] This theme has been developed in studies of social behavior in animals and humans and, at the human level in the extensive and often reductionist literature of sociobiology.[21] Because of its central position in supporting my interpretation of "a state of nature," I will introduce the biological bases for social behavior.

Social Behavior and Altruism in Evolution

The major transitions in evolution, the major increases in complexity, all arose from cooperation.[22]

The view of evolution that informs my theory of justice includes both egoism and altruism, competition and cooperation, isolation and communion, as natural and necessary elements of the process. Many if not most students of evolution now accept this view; however, the view that informs the dominant Western paradigm sees only egoism, competition, and isolation/autonomy as natural.

The key to understanding biological evolution lies in a truism: *genes that induce behavior that increases the probability of the survival of those same genes will more probably survive.* This behavior could be directly related to survival—getting nourishment, fleeing from predators, seeking shelter—or to the selection of a mate. Survival is always relative to a specific environment. If Priscilla rabbit has a genetically induced ability to run faster than Peter rabbit, and there is a predator in their environment with a propensity to eat rabbits, then, considering these factors alone, Priscilla is more likely than Peter to live to reproduce, and consequently the genetic base for the faster running will more likely be passed on to the next generation.[23]

Returning now to our truism: *genes that induce behavior that increases the probability of the survival of those same genes, will more probably survive.* The most fit—by definition those whose genes induce behavior most adapted to their environment—will most probably survive. So we have "survival of the fittest" and the images of struggle, conflict, and competition between individuals for their very survival, which Darwin himself and Dobzhansky a century later tried to correct. More recently within science there is increasing evidence that selfish competitive behavior, cooperative behavior and altruistic behavior all arise naturally within the process and all are necessary for its continuation. De Waal argues:

> the very same principle of natural selection that mercilessly plays off life forms and individuals against one another has led to symbiosis and mutualism among different organisms, to sensitivity of one individual to the needs of another, and to joint action toward a common goal. We are facing the profound paradox that genetic self-advancement at the expense of others—which is the basic thrust of evolution—has given rise to remarkable capacities for caring and sympathy.[24]

Applying this view of the process to us humans, he goes on to say, "Instead of human nature's being either fundamentally brutish or fundamentally noble, it is both."

To get some understanding of how "remarkable capacities for caring and sympathy" fit into the process of natural selection, consider a hypothetical case directly involving life and death. An animal is in a situation in which it can save the lives of four of its offspring by sacrificing its own life. If it behaves so as to preserve itself rather than its progeny, then all its own genes survive and can continue in subsequent generations. If, however, it *sacrifices itself* to save the four progeny, each of which has half its genes, then even though its own life and the genes it is hosting are lost, twice as many of its genes survive, thereby doubling the odds of their continuation. From the standpoint of the genes, the sacrificial, altruistic behavior is twice as effective as the selfish behavior; the odds of their survival have doubled because of the altruism of their host, and, of course, so have the odds of survival of whatever genes gave rise to the altruistic behavior. This simple case indicates that increasing the chances of survival of an organism at the expense of its kin can be less effective for gene survival than increasing the odds of survival of the genetically related group, even if the individual is sacrificed. Hence the importance of kin as well as individual selection and inclusive as well as individual fitness—of altruism as well as egoism—for the propagation of the gene.

Expositions such as the above of these processes can be misleading. Simplistic scenarios such as the following can easily emerge: genes control behavior; there is a gene that produces altruism and another that produces egoism; and that's it! But, of course, that's *not* it. The situation is much more complex and subtle than that. I will note what I think are some of the salient points for our purposes. First, the hypothetical example above abstracts from the intricate and enigmatic real world. Even in cases where one life is sacrificed for four immediate progeny, it would not necessarily follow that the odds favor the altruism gene two to one. The environmental interactions are many and complex, and there is normally not a one-to-one correspondence between a gene and a characteristic or subsequent behavior, nor is there a direct causal connection between them. Genes control the synthesis of protein, which is the basis of all the structures and metabolic processes that make up a living organism. Many parts of the integrated organic system are involved in a particular behavior, but the control center is the neural circuitry that the genetic material has already laid down. (I should note that the genetically produced system is not fixed from its inception but can itself change through its interactions with the environment; this very important point will be discussed later.)

How, then, could *an* altruistic behavior be traced back to *a* gene? Most probably it can't be. Structurally it could be traced to complex sets of neural circuits, constructed by genetically controlled protein synthesis. Iterative processes involving many neural networks and many biochemical interactions could be at work, all with different or shared or overlapping genetic origins. Given that organic systems are vast and complex sets of interactions, it is possible that virtually all genes are in some way involved in each behavior. Nevertheless, specific behaviors can be associated with specific genes or groups of genes.

It has been proposed by Ross Buck and Benson Ginsburg that there is no immediate genetic base for altruism as such, but that altruistic behavior is a "derivative epiphenomenon" arising from "spontaneous communication" that *is* genetically based.[25] If so, this would strengthen our position, for the "communication" base is itself associated with the quality of *openness* that will be a central element of my theory and that directly counters the Hobbesian tendency toward egoism and isolation.

More recently, Larry Young and colleagues have identified a link between the genetically determined distribution of a peptide hormone receptor and social behavior.[26] The hormone vasopressin, produced in the brains of most mammals, is associated with a range of behaviors, the variation in behavior across species depending on the distribution of the receptors in the brain. Young et al. located the gene that controls the receptor distribution and inserted this gene from a prairie vole, a social animal, into an antisocial mouse. This genetic manipulation changed the receptor distribution and induced social behavior in the mouse. They refer to this social behavior more specifically as affiliative behavior. They claim that, given the receptor distribution of the monogamous and gregarious prairie vole, vasopressin facilitates social behaviors such as affiliation, pair bonding, and paternal caring, whereas it does not facilitate these social behaviors in the closely related montane vole, which has a different receptor distribution. Vasopressin itself has for some time been associated with communication, social memory, sexual behavior, and aggression, which would appear to link it with a range of social behaviors—both "nice" and "nasty."

What is the point of all this? Simply to present empirical support for our hypothesis that we are naturally nasty and solitary, but also naturally caring and social. If the inclination to communicate, to be open and caring, is facilitated by, inter alia, the genetically determined distribution of hormone receptors, then we can say that in mammals there is a genetic base for social behavior. As I have insisted from the outset, if we self-conscious humans also have these genetically based inclinations we would not be determined by them; we could override them, modify them, and sometimes ignore them. Nevertheless, no matter what we humans do with them, we have inherited natural foundations for open, social behavior.

The hypothesis that life is not just nasty and solitary but also open and social is peripheral at best within the dominant paradigm. We now turn to what I believe to be classic examples of the Westernization and masculinization of scientific theory that support the Hobbesian view of human nature.

Some Patriarchal Myths

Homo homini lupus. (Man is a wolf to man)[27]

Healthy wolves and healthy women share certain psychic characteristics: keen sensing, playful spirit, and a heightened *capacity for devotion*. Wolves and women are *relational by nature*, inquiring, possessed of great endurance and strength. They are *deeply intuitive, intensely concerned* with their young, their mate and their pack.[28]

Freud, like Hobbes and so many other influential Western male thinkers, associated *man*/humanity with a nasty, brutish nature, demonstrating a shallow understanding of humanity and a profound ignorance of nature. Clarissa Estés, a Jungian analyst and naturalist who studied wolves and recognizes their *real* nature, sees in it the opposite to what Freud implies and associates their positive characteristics with women.

For Freud, the wolf epitomizes domination, aggression, power-over: the only power he seems to know; he uses this perception as a metaphor for *man*. For Estés, the wolf is an example of another power: the natural, feminine, symbiotic *power-with*. Rather than dwell on Freud's reinforcement of the myth, however, I will focus on a contemporary and even more fundamental example of seeing nature as nasty or, more specifically, the gene as selfish.

Richard Dawkins explains evolution in a clear and lively manner in his books, one of which is titled *The Selfish Gene*. This title characterizes his view of evolution and his important contribution to the perpetuation of the Hobbesian myth. Because his work is a highly regarded and influential exposition of and contribution to the theory of evolution *and* is also a classic example of male construction, I will make use of it to try to do two things: to develop my own argument that altruism is as real and natural as selfishness, and to present what I see as a classic case of the reinforcement of the dominant Western model through male construction, or myth-making, or viewing from the dominant standpoint, all within otherwise good science.[29]

Dawkins's contribution to clarifying and advancing neo-Darwinian theory is most admirable, as is his effort to rid us of fuzzy, anthropomorphic thinking about the subject. It seems to me, however, that his defense of selfishness to dispel what he calls the myth of universal love—a most *uncommon* myth indeed!—is itself metaphorical, fuzzy, and determined by his subjective standpoint. We have here, within an excellent work by an excellent scientist, what I see to be an unscientific bit of confusion in support of the Hobbesian, masculine mythology that supports the dominant Western system. If I am correct in this view, then this confusion is well worth exploring and exposing.

Dawkins says that "a predominant quality to be expected in a successful gene is ruthless selfishness," and then immediately, "This gene selfishness will usually give rise to selfishness in individual behavior."[30] If the latter sentence means only that the genetically determined behavior of an organism promotes selfishness more often than it promotes altruism, then I cannot contest it since I don't know what the proportions are—nor do I think anyone knows. But that is not his point; he appears to be claiming that the genetic foundation for all behavior is selfishness itself—that the selfishness of the *gene* is passed on to the organism, thereby giving some primordial priority to selfishness. This can be contested.

As noted above, the behavior of an organism, whether selfish or altruistic, is a consequence of neural systems based on genetic templates, not of the "ruthlessly selfish behavior" of genes. Dawkins states that "there are special circumstances in which a gene can achieve its own selfish goals best by fostering a limited form of altruism at the level of individual animals" (2). Dawkins is obviously using metaphors to get his idea across, but his metaphors–that a gene "can achieve its own selfish goals best by fostering"—do seem to influence his view of evolution in a substantive way. Genes don't have goals and don't behave to achieve goals, selfish or otherwise. We get closer to the reality if we replace these teleological and anthropomorphic metaphors with more neo-Darwinian language, as follows: *If a particular genetic arrangement within a genetically related group of organisms elicits altruistic behavior that has the net effect of increasing the chances of survival of the members of that group, then the chances that that genetic arrangement and the consequent behavior will continue will also increase.*

This proposition does not give primacy to selfishness and thereby marginalize altruism, but simply states that altruism is, along with selfishness, a type of behavior that enhances survival prospects and has therefore survived.

Dawkins goes on to emphasize that these instances of altruism are "special and limited" and "that universal love and the welfare of the species as a whole are concepts which simply do not make evolutionary sense" (3). To attack arguments for universal love and welfare, whether based on evolution or not, is to tilt at windmills. This could be ignored as idiosyncratic, but if the tilt includes claims about genes having selfish goals and about selfish genes transmitting selfishness and thereby giving some preeminence to selfish behavior, then it should be carefully analyzed.

Why does Dawkins say that altruism is special and limited? If he is saying that it is special in the sense that it is a specific, identifiable type of behavior, and limited in that not all behavior is of this type, then he is obviously right. But if he is also saying that altruism is special and limited because the gene is selfish, and selfish normally begets selfish—altruism being, therefore, a rare and unusual child, or, perhaps, not a natural child at all—then he is speaking in metaphors.

Dawkins defines *selfish* and *altruistic* as follows: "An entity is said to be altruistic if it behaves in such a way as to increase another such entity's welfare at the expense of its own. Selfish behavior has exactly the opposite effect" (4). These, as Dawkins correctly points out, are behavioral definitions. But it is organisms that behave—"individual animals" as he himself says in the quotation above—not genes.[31] By synthesizing protein, genes are a cause of an organism's propensity to behave in a particular way; the genes do not behave in that way themselves and they certainly do not synthesize protein *in order to* increase the chances of their survival. *Selfish* and *altruistic,* as Dawkins's own definitions directly imply, are labels for different kinds of welfare-promoting behavior, distinguished by whether the object of the welfare is self or other.

If one wished to speak in metaphors, then one could conjure up reasons for "the altruistic gene." But to label the gene either altruistic or selfish is stretching both the analogy and the biology too far. All we should say is that genetically induced behavior that increases the probability that an organism will survive increases the probability that the genes of that organism, and the behaviors induced by those genes, will be passed on. If the behavior increases the probability of the survival of the behaving organism itself, we call the behavior *selfish.* If it increases the probability of survival of another organism, we call it *altruistic.*

Pointing to other misconceptions regarding altruism, Elliott Sober and David Sloan Wilson say that:

> The concept of selfishness that became established in evolutionary biology . . . claims to explain such apparently altruistic traits as the bee's barbed stinger and human morality. These and other characteristics are said to be only apparently altruistic because individuals who help others receive benefits in return or promote their "genetic self-interest" by helping copies of their own genes that are found in the bodies of others.[32]

I have already dealt with "genetic self-interest" above. Two misconceptions remain. First, the idea that human morality is an altruistic trait is contrary to my definition of morality, the standard dictionary definitions, and the concept of morality throughout Western philosophy. It is, however, a common misconception in Western social science, in evolutionary biology, according to Sober and Wilson, and, as Miller notes, in evolutionary psychology: "Most evolutionary psychologists have viewed human morality as a question of altruism."[33]

As defined in Chapter 1, morality has to do with the behavior of a responsible agent acting responsibly, whether good or bad, nice or nasty, altruistic or selfish. To identify morals with altruism is to break with the traditional meanings of both of these terms. "Morality and altruism are sometimes equated, both at the level of action and at the level of motivation. . . . Both these equations are mistaken."[34]

The second misconception identified by Sober and Wilson is that some altruistic behavior is "only apparently altruistic because individuals who help others receive benefits in return." A distinction must be made between an agent who behaves in a particular way only for the purpose of receiving benefits in return and one whose purpose is to some extent to benefit another, at the benefactor's own expense. No matter what they *appear* to be, the former is selfish behavior and the latter, to the extent that the intention is to benefit another, altruistic. We are not interested in the appearance of behavior but in whether the behavior is actually to some extent altruistic. A behavior could be totally for the benefit of another and therefore, by definition, totally altruistic.

This might be rare. A behavior could be for both the benefit of the self and the other, in which case it would be a mixture of altruism and egoism, in any proportion. Cooperative behavior would be an instance of this. To say that these behaviors do not exist is to ignore the evidence.[35]

Throughout the literature that deals with this issue, there is the tendency to take an extreme and absolute *either/or* approach to altruistic behavior: altruism is pure, 100 percent sacrificial behavior. If there is just the least bit of egoism in the act, then it is not altruistic, or it is only apparently altruistic. This view of altruism is of little use; it is like searching for universal love. Our world is not like that; it is made up of blends of openness and isolation, care and aggression, cooperation and competition, altruism and egoism. The proportions vary and there might be cases of 100 percent of one or the other, but the central tendency probably moves back and forth about the 50 percent mark—perhaps moving more into the egoism side in our own patriarchal societies. To say that altruism is a natural and necessary element in evolution is not to say that all is nice and good and beautiful and loving. All it says is that altruism can be found in any population, in any individual, and in any behavior, and it is natural.

One might accept that altruism is as basic and natural as egoism and therefore cannot be reduced to it, but still marginalize it by claiming that it is rare. If, however, there is a basic genetically induced propensity for "spontaneous communication"—a "social cement" at the basis of all social structures and altruistic behavior[36]—then this fundamental characteristic is all-pervasive and tallying up individual accounts of altruism is peripheral to the issue. Reports that genetically based distribution of receptors in the brain induces social behavior[37] confirm further that there are genetic foundations for altruism, without recourse to specific cases, although there are in fact many known instances of altruistic behavior among living organisms. Virtually all animals are to some extent social in that they are aware of others in their community and of the needs of others.

Alison Jolly emphasizes the fundamental importance of cooperation to the process: "Cooperation between entities evolved even before life itself."[38] Richard Fortey sees the very beginnings of life on earth to be an ecosystem in which cooperation and coexistence played a necessary part. "Existence at base can be thought of as reciprocal rather than competitive. If the first living systems worked as teams, by mutual nourishment, it must have been the arrival of animals that hotted up the competitive aspect of evolution,"[39] and, with reference to those early bacteria joining to form more complex life, "This extraordinary development is a kind of symbiosis. . . . It affords the ultimate example of the cooperativeness of early life" (60). Reinforcing this, Lynn Margulis writes: "I believe that most evolutionary novelty arose, and still arises, directly from symbiosis. This is not the popular idea of the basis of evolutionary change in most textbooks."[40]

So if we must assign priorities, social behavior would come first, and individuality would be a later and secondary addition. But I say this only to press my point and counter the dominant view, and not to replace one bias with another.

To add a bit of the real world to this rather abstract discussion, we will briefly consider an actual instance of altruism in a creature that most humans would perceive to be even more nasty than the wolf of Freud's dreams.

The vampire bat will offer a meal of regurgitated blood to a hungry member of its kin.[41] This, in the long run, increases the odds of the genotype continuing because, on average, the increase in the odds of the survival of the recipient is greater than the decrease in the odds of the survival of the donor. This is not always the case, but it is often enough the case that the altruistic behavior itself survives. The efficacy of this behavior is a function of the probability that the recipient of the meal also has the gene that elicits the behavior, as well as of the probability that, after the donation, the net probability of the two bats surviving has increased.

It would appear from the above that altruism could emerge only among closely related members of a species; that is, it is based on kin selection.[42] *Reciprocal altruism*, a concept introduced by Robert Trivers, expands altruistic behavior beyond the bonds of kinship.[43] A behavior that reduces my chances of survival for the sake of increasing the chances of survival of another cannot be explained by natural selection if that other is not closely genetically related to me. As in my example above, an animal that sacrifices its life to save four of its progeny, each having half the parent's genes, saves 200 percent of its genes. If it saves four of its progeny's progeny, who each have 25 percent of its genes, it breaks even. There is evidence, however, of altruism beyond close relatives—not just among humans but throughout, for example, our vampire bat community.

It is possible that the altruistic propensity could be misdirected. If, however, this were to occur too often and if the recipients of the altruism were themselves not altruistic, then the survival rate of altruists would drop and that of the more selfish kin would rise. If, however, the altruism were directed at those in the community who would most likely reciprocate, whether or not closely related, then selection pressure would not reduce the altruistic inclination. Elaborate mechanisms within individuals and within the animal community would be required for reciprocal altruism to work. If altruism was not common throughout all or most of the community, then cognition would have to be developed enough to enable altruists to identify other altruists; they would have to "remember" which of their community had assisted them—who were their "friends." Apes and several other primates would appear to have these abilities, and perhaps other animals as well.[44] I note with emphasis, however, that inclusive fitness (kin selection) and reciprocity are *factors* in the evolution of altruism and must be distinguished from the altruistic inclination itself. We can know that altruism exists without understanding all the factors that cause its existence, and these factors do not diminish the fact of altruism in any way. More will be said about this important point later.

If altruistic behaviors happened only rarely, they would probably not secure their genetic bases and consequently would not continue within that community. The precise proportions of the behavior of organisms that are selfish or altruistic, however, is not really important. The central point is that altruism, like egoism, is a strategy for the survival of organisms and for the continuation of their genes; it is an integral and effective part of the evolutionary process. Furthermore, altruistic behavior is not reducible to egoism. The behavior of the donor bat is truly sacrificial in that the chances of its survival do fall so that the recipient's will rise. Recalling Dawkins's definition—altruism increases the welfare of the other *at the expense of its own*—makes this irreducibility even more explicit.

Further Elaboration on Altruism and Human Behavior

In the light of the analysis above we will explore further the concepts of altruism, egoism, and related concepts and apply them to human development. The concept of *spontaneous communication* introduced above can help us to define altruism more precisely. The communication that would underlie altruistic behavior among animals would itself be based on a capacity and propensity to be aware of others and the needs of others followed by the inclination to react to those needs. We are not discussing self-conscious animals here; these capacities and inclinations are consequences of the long process of natural and sexual selection—of genetic programs selected because they increased the odds of survival of their hosts.

Vampire bats are genetically programmed to be aware of starving members of their colony and to react to their need for nourishment. Their awareness of other and of the needs of other is in no way self-conscious; it is not a consequence of reflecting on or understanding the situation. The genetically programmed biological interactions that cause them to react to the needs of others are basically the same as the ones that effect any other reaction—to others or to the self. They do not decide to be altruistic or selfish. They are determined to behave selfishly or altruistically by their genetic makeup. They are not responsible for these behaviors; they cannot be commended or blamed for them. The fundamental distinction that I would make is that some of these biologically determined behaviors are consequences of awareness of the needs of the self—selfish behavior—and some are consequences of awareness of the needs of others—altruistic behavior. I will refer to the awareness of other and the needs of other as *openness.*

The factors required for the selection of altruistic behaviors—kin selection and reciprocity—are important in understanding the evolution of egoism and altruism, but do not define the basic behavior itself. This point is central to our whole argument, and to the current interpretations of human behavior, and so I will spend some more time on it.[45]

The tendency among those who apply recent theories on the evolution of altruism to human behavior is to put great emphasis on the conditions that induced this evolution—kin selection and reciprocity. To be selected, through sexual and or natural selection, altruism had to increase the probability of survival of the genes of the altruist (whether or not they are hosted by the altruist). As we have seen, this could be done in the following ways: the altruist could risk its own well-being to enhance the survival chances of near kin (kin selection); the altruist could risk its own well-being to enhance the survival chances of members of the community who are more distantly related but will probably return the favor (reciprocal altruism); altruism could be attractive in sexual selection, especially in primates and humans.[46] Reciprocal altruism requires greater cognitive development than does kin selection, but not self-awareness. A natural inclination to assist only close kin would stand a good chance of being selected. The chances of a natural altruistic inclination that was not so selective and spread to more distant relatives would depend on factors such as the frequencies of the less discriminating altruism, the distribution of genetic material within the community, and reciprocation. If altruistic behavior were an attractive characteristic in choosing a mate, then sexual selection could induce a significant development of this propensity.

The discoveries of kin selection and reciprocity as factors in the development of altruism led to claims about the very nature of altruism, including human altruism, such as: that pure altruism exists only within the family; that beyond family, altruistic behavior is no more than an investment in future returns; that pure altruism is just a familial, domestic feeling, an affection; and that reciprocal altruism requires rational calculation: if my cost of helping is x, the return is y, and the chance of getting that return is z, then I will/will not help. Pure altruism is downgraded as a nonrational, domestic behavior. Reciprocity based on a benefit-cost calculation, a selfish behavior, is, within the rational planner/ maximizer model, seen to be the truly human behavior. These interpretations are seriously flawed.

To see the flaw, let us again distinguish clearly between the altruistic behavior itself and the factors that enable its selection. We begin with a behavior that is not self-conscious. An animal helps another to survive in a way that reduces its own chances of survival. The behavior itself requires the following elements, all genetically induced: an awareness of the other; an awareness of the need of the other; an inclination to behave in a way that will satisfy that need, to some extent.

The awareness in this case is not self-conscious. It is the same kind of awareness as the awareness of food, of an obstacle in one's path, of a predator. A vampire bat flying toward a tree receives a signal from its interaction with that tree and its flight path is adjusted accordingly; the bat and its genes fly on. This process is analogous to the adjustment to the flight path of an airplane effected by its radar and computer. Neither bat nor airplane is itself aware of what it is doing; neither is working at a symbolic level; neither can say "there is an obstacle that I ought to avoid by turning to the left." It is in this same programmed way that the vampire bat receives a signal that another bat needs food and its behavior is adjusted according to its genetic program: it provides the food.

The bat's awareness of the tree is a complex interaction (echolocation) between the bat and the tree. The capacity for echolocation has been selected because it prevents disastrous crashes, thereby protecting the bat itself and its genes. The bat's awareness of the other-in-need is also a complex, and less understood, interaction between the donor bat and the other bat. It also has been selected because it in the long run promotes the donor's genes, but by immediately helping the other. The awareness of the tree is an interaction between animal and environment, the immediate consequences of which help that animal to survive. If the obstacle were another bat rather than a tree, the situation would be the same; the first bat would receive a signal of bat-as-obstacle and adjust its flight path, the consequence of which would be that it would survive.

The awareness of other-in-need is an interaction between one animal and another; the first animal's consequent reaction to information from the interaction is a behavior that helps that other and in some cases threatens the survival of the helper. This awareness of other as other-in-need rather than other-as-obstacle, and the consequent behavior that helps the other could be called *social awareness* and *social behavior*. This, I suggest, is the "spontaneous communication," the genetically based "social cement," that Buck and Ginsberg say is at the basis of all social structures and from which altruistic behavior arises, and is perhaps linked to the genetically determined distribution of hormone receptors as described by Young et al.[47] These have been selected within the context of mutuality or social behavior. On the other hand, the awareness and behavior of the bat in the context of confronting an obstacle—whether tree or other bat—has been selected in the context of behaviors whose immediate consequences are for the behaving agent only, isolated from others as members of a community.

Whatever the factors involved in selection in either case, the consequences are instances of altruistic or selfish behavior. In particular, altruistic behavior and its antecedent spontaneous communication are what they are regardless whether the factors of selection are kin selection, reciprocal selection, sexual selection, or whatever.

The denotation and connotation of *social*, as well as of *altruistic* and *selfish*, cause problems here that we should address now. Most of the human cultural meanings and associations of these terms do not apply to the present context. In fact, all that *social* means in a non-self-conscious, noncultural context is that the cognitive and behavioral interactions involve more than one member of the community and have consequences for more than one member of the community. Social behavior is a consequence of natural selection in the same way that more isolated individual behavior is. And that is the important point. Social behavior and altruistic behavior are simply natural parts of the process. They do not arise from self-consciousness, are not motivated, are neither nice nor nasty, deserve neither commendation nor blame. The problem I see in the extrapolation of these behaviors to the human level is that they are usually not stripped of their human denotation and, especially, connotation *before* the extrapolation begins; egoism and altruism evolve from non-self-conscious animal to human, but, obviously, none of the human character of these, which arises from self-consciousness, exists at the non-self-conscious level.

We humans have inherited the basic, biological inclinations for selfish and altruistic behavior, but these biological bases when captured by self-consciousness manifest themselves in new and transcendent ways.

We have inherited inclinations to make sacrifices for our near kin, but in only rare cases are human sacrifices for kin driven only by biological inclination. A human mother has the biological inclination to help her child, and this could at times be the major cause of her caring, supportive behavior. But the integration of self-consciousness and then culture with the biological inclination has changed dramatically even this most basic of basic propensities. Over millennia, biology, reflection, and culture have created new and transcendent interrelationships between mother and child from which the human form of altruism arises. Given such new dimensions of the inclination, it can be directed intentionally beyond kin and even beyond our species.

Because we can calculate and predict, reciprocation can play a significant part in human behavior toward others. Here, however, reciprocation is not a factor in the selection of altruism but rather the reason for a self-conscious decision to help another, not for the sake of the other, but for an eventual return on the investment; it is an *objective* of the behavior. As such, this for a human would be selfish or at least somewhat selfish behavior.

On the other hand, it does not follow that altruistic behaviors that are reciprocated are ultimately based on selfish objectives. If expected reciprocity is the only reason for helping another, then the behavior is selfish, but if reciprocity is not a consideration, then, even if reciprocated, the behavior is purely altruistic.

At the non-self-conscious level, altruism and egoism are no more than consequences of genes and selection, kin, reciprocity, and mating attractions being factors in that selection. Non-self-conscious organisms have no purpose, no objectives, no goals.

We inherit the basic, genetically programmed, naturally and sexually selected biological systems that induce these behaviors, and that is all. The rest, the human dimension, is a human, self-conscious, and cultural construction. To the extent that I help myself or help another for the purpose of getting help in return, then my behavior is selfish. To the extent that I help another for the sake of the other, whether or not there is reciprocation, my behavior is altruistic.

A Word on Selfishness

If I seem to emphasize altruistic behavior, it is because it is the behavior that is usually ignored, marginalized, seen as an anomaly, or reduced to selfish behavior. The consequent emphasis on selfish behavior perpetuates the Hobbesian view and, as I will argue, the dominant distorted concept of justice. It should be clear by now that I do not counter the emphasis on egoism with an equal and opposite emphasis on altruism—on "universal love"—but rather with a call to recognize the natural balance of the two. To further assure the reader that I do recognize egoism and its efficacy, here is a rather blatant case of it.

A female lion will not mate while she is caring for her cubs; this in itself is an instance of the altruistic caring inclinations taking precedence over the selfish procreation propensities. A male lion, however, will kill lion cubs, opening the way for the exercise of his own selfish proclivities to procreate. The lion who kills cubs thereby ensures the continuation of his genes, including those that underlie his propensity to kill cubs. If, of course, lions were monogamous, the killed cubs would probably be the progeny of the killer and this would tend to eliminate the cub-killer genes. But lions are not monogamous; the slaughtered cubs probably are hosts to the genes of some other lion. This instance within the selection process favors the infanticidal and adulterous lion and the retention of enough of his developmental characteristics to provide a net positive effect in the long run.

In our Hobbesian world, examples of selfish and nasty behavior, like that of the male lion, abound. We probably need not spend more time on cases of real egoism, but I would like to comment on *perceived* egoism.

The Hobbesian hold on us is so strong that we tend to see virtually all behavior as selfish. To illustrate my point, we could consider competition over food—an interrelationship that appears to many to be intrinsically nasty. To reveal a case of the biologically driven, non-self-conscious inclination involved, we might look to the wolf—not the nasty *lupus* of Freud's dreams, but the real wolf. Wolves devouring carrion look nasty indeed, and perhaps this perception of nastiness led to Freud's misunderstanding of their true psyche. The pack leader (usually but not always a male) will bare his teeth and snarl if another member appears to encroach on his morsel. No altruism or even cooperation here, it would seem. But beneath this appearance of selfishness is a reality including much genetically programmed openness.

Fangs and snarls notwithstanding, the leader rarely harms others in the pack. The leader's inclination to eat without obstruction and the pack's inclination to accept this when the signal is given are consequences of the developmental value to the wolf community of having a strong, well-fed leader for their cooperative activities. Wolves' manner of hunting is obviously cooperative, but, this apparent show of nastiness is also part of a cooperative approach to eating that maintains the strength of the community. That same leader, after satisfying his appetite, will, when cavorting with the pack, often lie on his back to reveal his soft, vulnerable underbelly to the rest: a characteristic primitive sign of openness.

Homo homini lupus means to Freud that *men*, like mythical Hobbesian wolves, are nasty and brutish to one another; for one who understands wolves, like Estés, it would mean that humans, like real wolves, are naturally competitive and cooperative, aggressive and nurturing, sometimes selfish and solitary but more often communal and open.

Anthropomorphism

Let us now address further the problem of anthropomorphic interpretations of the kinds of behavior just discussed. Our natural tendency to view bats—especially vampire bats—as nasty little creatures might have been modified by the above account of their sacrificial behavior; bats appear to be rather nice in this light.[48] Similarly, our impression of the nasty wolf might give way to an image of a kinder, gentler, more cooperative beast, if we really get to know wolves. On the other hand, knowing that the male lion eats baby lions so that he can indulge himself in the pleasures of procreation would turn most of us against "the king of beasts." Such positive and negative feelings toward animal behavior are quite common and, I suppose, natural, but are really inappropriate. Assuming that the examples of altruism and egoism above all arise from the biological dimension of the animals, and not from self-consciousness, then human values should not be attached to them. We can neither commend the bat for sacrifice nor blame the lion for infanticide, for neither knows or has control over what it is doing. The only appropriate evaluation is based on the criterion of development; does the behavior contribute to the development of this organism within this environment and the consequent continuation of its genes? Whether altruistic or selfish, if it makes such a contribution it is good and to that extent will be selected, but if it impedes that development it is bad and will probably be rejected. In this context, that is all that *good* and *bad* can mean. Within the process of evolution, there would be many instances of altruistic behavior that turned out to be dysfunctional and therefore bad, and also many cases of selfish behavior that strongly support the development of the community and are therefore *good*. But we must keep in mind that *good* or *bad* here mean no more than genetically programmed to be developmental or dysfunctional; there is no moral connotation at all. To say that the lion is hateful and nasty, or that the bat is loving and nice, would be anthropomorphic.

Throughout this exploration we must also keep in mind—and I would put emphasis on this—that even when applied to the behavior of humans acting responsibly, *altruistic* is not distinguished from *selfish* as *good* is from *bad*. The Hobbesian *man* is selfish and nasty, but selfishness is not necessarily—indeed, not usually—nasty. To repeat the basic definitions: if the behavior increases the probability of the survival of the behaving organism itself, we call the behavior *selfish*; if it increases the probability of survival of another organism, we call it *altruistic*. Both kinds of behavior are necessary for the development process. Both, therefore, are good for evolution. What is bad from this developmental perspective is an imbalance in which one of these becomes dominant to the extent of being dysfunctional. The common use of *selfish* as a pejorative term contains this notion of imbalance; by "selfish person" we do not refer to someone who eats and keeps warm and avoids danger—all selfish acts—but rather to someone whose behavior includes virtually nothing but selfish acts—one who is not at all open to the needs of others.

A Relational Perspective

Frans de Waal's intensive and extensive research in primatology leads him to reject the primacy commonly given to individual aggressive and competitive behavior. It was in the mid-1960s that Konrad Lorenz's work on aggression stimulated considerable debate on this topic as well as several popularizations of the subject that reinforced the Hobbesian view of *man* as naturally solitary and nasty.[49] De Waal began his studies of aggression among primates within the context of this debate and before long was to arrive at an interpretation of aggressive behavior that I think has profound significance. He saw less aggression than the Hobbesian myth would predict, but he did observe aggression. What emerged from his careful observations was an interpretation of the fact of aggression that counters the dominant Western model.

The common view, says de Waal, "stressed the individual, not the social context. To me, the individuals became more and more of an abstraction; it was their relationships that caught my attention."[50] Note that his concern is with the *stress* on the individual—the belief that aggression is a behavior only of isolated individuals attempting to overpower one another. He came to see aggressive behavior, "as one of a multitude of tools available to shape a relationship"(186). He sees aggression itself within the context of "individuals drawn together by attachment and a sense of belonging to the same group" which he calls the *relational model* (173).

Individuals and individuality exist, and so does aggression but, and this is the critical point, individuals and their behaviors exist within a social, a relational context, and to the extent that relations are useful for the survival of the members of the community, the genetic arrangements that induce them survive. Aggression does not destroy relationships; it is one of the behaviors that maintain relationships.

To continue de Waal's interpretation, conflicts between individuals can lead to tolerance, avoidance or aggression. If aggression is the solution and the relationship is a mutually advantageous one, reconciliation will follow. Solitude would appear to be avoided by primates and other animals, and solitary behavior itself needs to be understood within the context of relations. Social relationships of value to the development of the members of the community are the results of cycles of conflict and reconciliation (174, 175).

This is obviously not a romantic fantasy of loving creatures always getting along in an idyllic setting—the opposite of Hobbes's state of nature. To say that primate and other animal communities are social does not follow from a belief in universal love, but from a study of the evolutionary process. The social dimension of behavior, like the selfish dimension, is simply a survival strategy that continues if it works. This is, however, a view in which the so-called "nasty" exist along with the "nice" and the "gentle," all within a social, relational context, not within a collection of isolated individuals. "All individuals are imbedded in the same social fabric, and must prefer their respective positions to the alternatives of a solitary life or the joining of another group" (103).

Continuity and Transcendence

The combination of continuity and transcendence in our evolution causes major problems in talking about this process, as we have seen above and as I will review here. The problem is that the words that we use to capture the continuity of the process conceal its transcendence. There is continuity from animal life to our own in a broad range of inclinations, behaviors, and characteristics, and we reflect this in terms such as *selfish*, *altruistic*, *aggressive*, *cooperative*, and *social*. Such words do capture the fact of continuity in each case. What they fail to capture, however, is the transformation effected by self-consciousness in many cases.

For the non-self-conscious animal, all behaviors are genetically programmed reactions to environmental stimuli and they are consequences of natural and sexual selection. Whether or not there is an overall plan for the universe, evolution can be understood and explained without assuming purpose; it is not a teleological process. Animals do not have eyes for the purpose of seeing; they see because they have eyes. They do not make sacrifices for the purpose of helping others; they help others because they behave in particular genetically induced and naturally selected ways.

But self-consciousness changes all that. There is still continuity, but a new dimension has been added to many inclinations and the consequent behaviors. The self-conscious agent can reflect on the inclination, on the behavior, on its consequences on the self and on others, and can, to some extent, modify the behavior. To the extent that the agent can modify her behavior, she is responsible for it. And to the extent that she sees the consequences of behavior—understands what it is for, what its purpose is—and modifies it in the light of this understanding, the behavior is a consequence of both the genetically induced inclination and her own intended purpose. For the self-conscious agent, development is explained by both consequences and objectives.

Figure 2 represents *one* process with two *interacting* dimensions. The emergence of self-consciousness and the human dimension is not a point in time but a long part of the process. The intention of the image is simply to emphasize these *two* dimensions of the *one* process of our evolution.

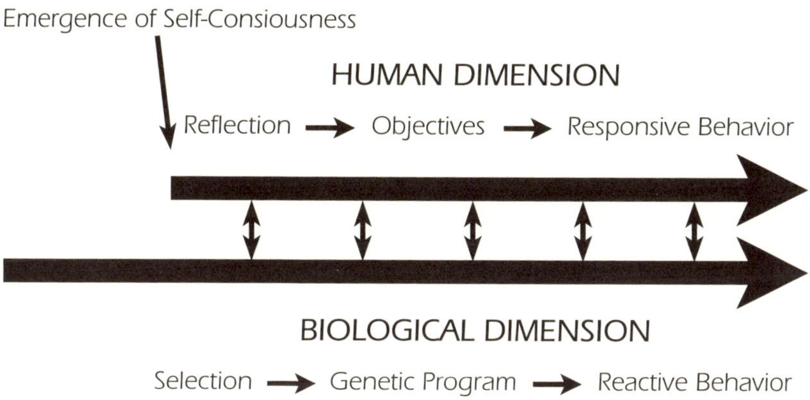

Figure 2.

Both the continuity and transcendence of this new *human* dimension must be kept in mind when discussing our origins as human. Virtually all the terms that represent the continuities of the process from which we emerged are analogical; they have a common meaning throughout but also take on a new meaning after self-consciousness. A non-self-conscious behavior is a reaction to stimuli that is a consequence of a genetic program that has been selected. A behavior influenced by self-consciousness is a consequence of a genetic program induced by natural selection *and* reflection. A non-self-conscious animal *reacts* selfishly or altruistically; a self-conscious human *responds* selfishly or altruistically. Reciprocity and kin are *factors of selection* in the biological dimension, but they are *objectives* in the human dimension.

To ignore the analogy is a problem in both directions. The reductionist sees the self-conscious behavior as simply a more complex version of its non-self-conscious progenitor; the "higher" is explained completely in terms of the "lower." But sometimes the opposite occurs. As I have suggested above, Dawkins does appear to explain the gene in terms of human propensities and behaviors; the "lower" is explained in terms of the "higher." Dawkins indeed goes beyond the limits of analogy. *Selfish human* to *selfish animal* is a useful analogical use of *selfish* because it does capture an actual continuity of process and hence meaning, but from there to *selfish gene* is an analogical leap so great as to render the term meaningless.

Two Basic Hypotheses

Reflecting on all the above, we see before us two hypotheses emerging, upon which our argument will rest.

The first hypothesis is *Evolution is a process of interrelations, and not of autonomy and isolation. Altruistic behavior is, like selfish behavior, a natural and essential part of the process.*[51]

We see among animal communities, including primates, a range of inclinations and consequent behaviors, from selfish to altruistic, from competitive to cooperative, from aggressive to caring—from relatively isolated to open. They must all be seen, however, within the context of the interrelated, organic whole—within a *relational model,* as de Waal puts it. Aggression is a functional part of interrelation. Isolation, never absolute, can be understood only within a relational model. There are no individuals-in-isolation, but only individuals-in-community. The model is, obviously, a biological, organic one, and not the Hobbesian mechanical model drawn from classical physics.

The second hypothesis, introduced above and to be developed further as the exploration continues, is *The evolutionary process is self-contained and continuous. Nevertheless, there is within it, and effected by the energies of the process itself, transformation or transcendence.*

I have proposed that the origin of life was a transformation of the physical process from which life emerged. The most recent transformation, and the one that is the focus our attention here, emerges from the origins of self-consciousness. We, *Homo sapiens,* are a major part of that transformation. We have inherited selfish and altruistic developmental inclinations from our non-self-conscious ancestors, but because we are self-conscious, we have transformed them.

Because of its central importance in this exploration, we will, in the next chapter on the evolution of self-consciousness, focus on the transcendental emergence of the human dimension from the biological.

Chapter 3
The Evolution of Self-Consciousness

Human beings are so remarkable, and so unprecedented . . . that only introspection will suffice to tell us who we are. And such self-examination has to start with our remarkable consciousness, from which all else flows.[1]

[T]here is one uncontrovertible thing we can say about the uniqueness of our own consciousness. This is that, while every other organism we know about lives in the world as presented to them by Nature, human beings live in a world that they consciously symbolize and re-create in their own minds.[2]

With Ian Tattersall, I see human transcendence arising from our new kind of consciousness, itself emerging from the evolution of our social ancestors. My central hypothesis is that morality is the capturing and articulation of developmental inclinations by this new consciousness, and so, as Tattersall proposes, we will begin our exploration of the transcendent human dimension by examining this "remarkable consciousness, from which all else flows."

Defining *Self-Consciousness*

Because of its great importance to my exploration I will invest some time and effort in defining this new consciousness, which I call *self-consciousness.*

I define *self-consciousness* as consciousness of (or awareness of, or reflection on) the self-as-self and of all that the self is conscious of: things, symbols, ideas and concepts, feelings, beliefs, and other selves *as other.* It is often referred to simply as consciousness, however, I want to make very clear the distinction between, on the one hand, simple awareness of inner states (e.g., hunger, fear, satisfaction) and of the environment (e.g., food, heat, predator, potential mate), inducing genetically controlled reactions, and, on the other hand, the capacity to reflect on and contemplate all these objects of awareness, the self, and the other, inducing a response. It is this capacity to reflect, contemplate, understand, reason, intuit, and evaluate that engenders transcendent human behavior.

In the *OED*, which reflects both common and more technical usage, *consciousness* is either clearly a synonym for *self-consciousness* or defined as *self-consciousness*. The *OED* also notes, however, several uses in which *consciousness* is synonymous with simple awareness. A lengthy tour of the *OED* shows that it supports both my use of *self-conscious* and my concern about ambiguity. It is especially important to remove any ambiguity in the use of *consciousness* and *self-consciousness* (or *awareness* and *self-awareness*) in a study that encompasses a range of cognitive activities from the simplest awareness of environment, shared by plants and animals, to the reflection, contemplation, understanding, intuition, and evaluation of which we are capable.

I use *awareness* and *consciousness* as synonyms that refer to simple, nonreflective reception of information from the environment or from within an organism, and *self-consciousness (self-awareness)* to refer to the knowledge of, or reflection on, any of the objects of consciousness, including the self.

The Emergence and Evolution of Self-Consciousness

Now we will explore the emergence and evolution of self-consciousness. We will look at those strands of the continuous evolutionary process within which self-consciousness emerged. It is now clear that there are many such strands; our species has no monopoly on self-consciousness. Its existence is quite obvious in several other species, including other primates, and there may be glimmers of it in some other mammals.[3] Because our objective is to shed light on the origins of justice in human communities, we will dwell on the development of human self-consciousness.

The details of the evolution of the human dimension—of self-consciousness and of the consequent construction of culture on the biological base—are hidden in our past and cannot be known with any certainty. We can, nevertheless, formulate valuable hypotheses about our distant past using a range of scientific discoveries including recent studies of the behavior of contemporary animals, and especially of our close relatives among the primates, whose levels of self-conscious development might be analogous to those of the early hominids.[4]

Although some other animals would appear to be self-conscious, we humans have developed and made use of this capacity to the greatest degree, at least on this planet. Evidence suggests that our ability to reflect, reason, judge and think in symbols did not arise innately but, as Terrence Deacon writes, "develops by internalizing the symbolic process that underlies language. So species that have not acquired the ability to communicate symbolically cannot have acquired the ability to think this way either."[5]

The current debate on whether other animals have true languages and the significance of this for the assessment of their levels and kinds of self-conscious behavior is important in itself but not for our purposes.[6] We do have languages, think symbolically, develop science and art, and have the most developed cultures of any species on earth, by far.[7] The question here is how did this evolve and how is it relevant to the origins of *our* morality and justice?

Our inclinations, behaviors, and characteristics have all been transformed by self-consciousness, and through self-consciousness we construct our selves, our communities, and our cultures as the *human dimension.* I distinguish this, but do not separate it, from the *biological dimension*, controlled by genes and selection without self-consciousness (see Figure 2 above). The human dimension began with the emergence of self-consciousness in our ancestors, probably over a period of time when our ancestors were not yet *Homo sapiens.* This possible incongruity between the biological classification and the human dimension has been noted above and need not concern us.

Self-consciousness profoundly affects all behavior: individual, selfish, competitive, social, altruistic, cooperative. Without self-consciousness, behaviors are consequences of genes and selection; they are not the intentional acts of self-conscious, responsible agents. Before self-consciousness arose, however, there must have been considerable cognitive development to support the complex behaviors that maintain social animal communities. I have referred above to the cognitive requirements of reciprocal altruism. Techniques for maintaining complex hierarchical social systems through conflict resolution, aggression, and reconciliation would also require sophisticated levels of awareness. Among the more cooperative animal species, the awareness of other and of the needs of the other are strong. This awareness, although not necessarily associated with self-awareness, indicates a high degree of cognitive development. Competition among social primates with high levels of awareness would, through natural and sexual selection, induce the continuing evolution of that awareness.[8]

De Waal reviews evidence of caring behavior in several species and outlines the elements of this behavior.[9] Cooperative behavior for hunting or defense is a basis for mutual attachment whereby individuals react to the needs of others. This can be interpreted as the ability to be aroused by the feelings of the other—feelings of hunger, anxiety, cold; de Waal calls this arousal "emotional contagion" (80). In non-self-conscious animals this is no more than a consequence of selection and genetic programs. It might appear to a human observer to be a case of human-type sympathy—a self-conscious commonality of feelings—but would actually be a genetically determined reaction by one animal to a signal transmitted by a non-self-conscious feeling of another, which increases the chances of the survival of their genes. If, however, the animal has some awareness of self *as self*, and therefore of other *as other*, the genetic reaction is transformed. To the extent that it is self-conscious the behavior has a real sympathy dimension; that is, there is a common self-conscious feeling shared by two animals. One knows that the other is anxious, or hungry, or cold, and responds (not reacts) accordingly. This responsive sympathy, in its first manifestations, would be no more than a trace: perhaps 99 percent genetically induced reaction and 1 percent self-conscious response. The self-conscious, reflective dimension would be so small as to have an insignificant influence on the behavior. But it would be there.

What more can be said about this new kind of emerging consciousness that I call *self-consciousness*? Consciousness is a very difficult activity to understand; it is complex, multifaceted, and obscure, and it itself is what we must use to try to understand it. It is possible, nevertheless, to fathom enough of this mysterious subject to help us to see its role in human development within the context of evolution.[10] As Deacon says, "To appreciate why human beings are able to experience conscious states unprecedented in evolution, we do not need to have solved the mystery of consciousness itself" (449).

Self-Consciousness and the Brain

If we are to have some notion of the evolution of consciousness, we must know something about the development of its underlying physiological system. The neural system of an organism can be pictured as complex sets of circuits that receive information from the organism and from its environment and transmit information and reactions to the appropriate parts of the organism and the environment. The very simple neural systems of the simpler organisms have small repertoires of reactions to the information received. They are aware of only the information from the environment needed for their development, and react to it in a fixed way—something like the way an infrared sensor reacts to a change in heat and sets off an alarm. The alarm system is "hard-wired" to do only two things: react to heat and open a switch. As brains evolved they became less rigid; they developed a capacity, putting it simply, to wire themselves for different responses. This flexibility, itself genetically based and a consequence of the process of selection, was of significant developmental advantage, and therefore was selected, and brains evolved as complex structures of both fixed and plastic neural networks.

The human brain is such a structure; it is hard-wired for some things and plastic for others. We are hard-wired for the leg motion of walking, but must develop the right connections for balance; learning to walk is the process of programming our balance system while our *pre*-programmed leg control system operates. Some of the flexibility might involve only a couple of options: "wire" *x* can connect with either *y* or *z*. Other cases of plasticity, found in brains of the higher animals including ourselves, could entail enormous numbers of permutations of many possible connections.

Recent research strongly suggests not only that the brain is plastic, but that its physiological capacity to react to its environment develops over an extended period of time—ten years or more for humans—through its interactions with that environment. We have, then, two kinds of tendencies—or, more precisely, two poles on a spectrum of tendency-types: innate, relatively fixed, *hard-wired* tendencies; and tendencies that arise from those plastic, flexible structures of the brain that are not innate, pre-formed structures at birth but that, through the brain's interaction with the environment, are, according to Steven Quartz and Terrence Sejnowski, *constructed* tendencies.[11] Both are genetically based and have evolved according to the neo-Darwinian process of selection.

In the first case, the tendency is elicited by a structure that is relatively fixed throughout the life of the organism; it is hard-wired by the genetic code. The propensities to duck a blow, or shiver in the cold, or molt periodically are examples of hard-wired tendencies.

Constructed tendencies, on the other hand, do not emerge from a fixed structure laid down at birth. They arise from structures that develop through interaction with the environment. The capacity for such development is itself genetically determined; in other words, the genetic code effects a structure that is not static or fixed but has within itself the capacity to change, and the nature of that change is a consequence of the interactions between the structure and its environment. This plasticity, flexibility, and adaptability have obvious selection advantages, especially in variable environments. They open up possibilities of evolutionary development that would not exist were everything hard-wired. This is especially significant in the development of the human brain. Quartz and Sejnowski write:

> The extent and duration of large-scale brain changes during development has also been underappreciated. Whereas many researchers believe that the major events in brain development end by two years of age, the evidence we have reviewed illustrates these continue well past the first decade of life. . . . Although

we are only beginning to understand how the world and brain interact to build the mind, the story that is unfolding already makes nativist theories appear implausible. What lies ahead promises to be an exciting and far richer account in which the mind emerges from a prolonged interaction with a structured world. (555)

And further:

Exciting new evidence favoring neural constructivism has emerged that challenges the dogma that new neurons are not created in adult brains. . . . It is likely that new neurons are also formed in adult human brains, perhaps even in the cortex. The differentiation of progenitor cells into neurons is therefore not confined to early development. The implications of the new results for lifelong learning are far reaching. (588)

The activities associated with our "human dimension," however (see Figure 2, p. 41), cannot be explained simply in terms of the further evolution of the structure of the brain, even as constructed through interactions with its environment. It would appear that our brain had arrived at approximately its present size and structural complexity *before* we began to develop language, tools, art, science, and morals as we know them today. The potential for all this must have already existed within the size, complexity, and potential for plasticity of the brain of early *Homo sapiens*, perhaps 150,000 years ago, and certainly of our ancestors of 10,000 years ago. Consider, however, the exponential growth of human culture during the last 10,000 years. What, then, is the other factor that explains this growth?

Geoffrey Miller sees three problems in explaining human mental evolution (what I call the *human dimension*):

1. Why do humans have large and complex brains that use much energy when other species survive with small brains?
2. How was an expanding brain selected when its benefits arose long after it stopped expanding?
3. How could selection favor "useless embellishments" such as humor, story-telling, gossip, art, music, self-consciousness, ornate language, imaginative ideologies, religion, and morality."[12]

Miller's point is that these problems cannot be solved by natural selection and that the embellishments have no use in terms of natural selection. I would argue that self-consciousness and morality, as I define them, are hardly "useless embellishments" but rather major contributors to survival that would be naturally selected to the extent that they have a biological base, but apart from that I will not quibble over Miller's statement of the problem.

For these problems that cannot be solved by natural selection, Miller's solution is sexual selection. "Sexual selection," he says "cuts through this Gordian knot" (20). The important point here is that sexual selection, relative to natural selection, becomes a more prominent force in the evolution of the biological foundations for self-conscious/human development. It, however, explains the biological foundations, but not the human dimension, that is, not the transformation of simple consciousness to self-consciousness.

A New Kind of Consciousness

Self-consciousness is not simply more consciousness: the awareness of more objects. That is what more size, complexity, and plasticity would provide, but it does not explain the cultural explosion: language, science, art, technology, morality, law. It is a new *kind* of consciousness, *self*-consciousness, the capacity to reflect on conscious activity and on the *self*, which is the center of that activity.

The simplest organisms are "conscious" of, vaguely aware of, only a very few things. A plant is aware of moisture and radiant energy and reacts accordingly by, for example, turning its leaves to maximize the reception of the sun's energy, but it reacts only when moisture and the sun are there. A dog is aware of many more things and can react to information in many more ways, because, in part, of the plasticity of its brain and its memory. It is conscious of more than is a frog or a petunia. But consciousness of *more* does not seem to explain adequately the development and consequences of self-consciousness.

Self-consciousness is consciousness of what is already an object of consciousness, of those things that are already within the compass of simple awareness, so that a human can know trees, clouds, birds, stones, fear, satisfaction and then say, "I know trees, clouds, birds, stones, fear, satisfaction" and "I know you, I know *other*"; "I know *I*"; "I am conscious of my *self* and of the thoughts and feelings of my self."

We can borrow from Deacon to elaborate this further. All animals, including ourselves, are conscious of the many objects required for nourishment and of other objects that threaten them. They are aware of the relationships between specific sights, sounds, smells, and feels, and nourishment or threat. A rabbit will not run from a carrot and eat a fox. Reflection on our awareness of these objects, however, gives us the capacity to interpret these relationships symbolically: these objects are *food*; those are *threats*. We can then use these symbols to communicate with one another. The developmental advantages of symbols—in cognitive processes and in communication—to the extent that they are genetically based, would effect strong positive selection pressures that would favor the development of the reflection-symbolic interpretation and communication process, a process that, in Deacon's words, "has not just changed the range of possible objects of consciousness, it has also changed the nature of consciousness itself" (450).

Two symbols that underline the radically different nature of self-consciousness are *self* and *other*, distinguishing the *I* as object from all other objects. Reflection on *I-other* and then *I-thou* relationships raises *openness* to a new and transcendent level. The *self*, rather than simply react, can now *respond* to its awareness of *other*, through either openness to *other* or isolation from *other*.

Speculating further on how this new kind of consciousness emerged will help us to understand better the parameters of our human origins. The source of the beginnings of self-consciousness was a well-developed, complex, flexible brain. The capacity of a human to fine-tune herself to best respond to the contingencies of her environment by interacting with that environment would be a tremendous advantage, and the genetic program that effected that capacity would be strongly selected. Under the hypothesis of the continuing structural development of the brain, it would follow that, in a given population at a given time, many capacities would not yet be actualized. Self-consciousness itself could be just waiting for the right conditions—the right interactions with the environment—to emerge.

The conclusions Deacon draws from his own research and that of others in related fields provide us with a picture of an interacting process in which language and brain co-evolve. Within this process, and central to human development, the capacity to interpret relations as symbolic—the capacity to create symbols—is a consequence of self-conscious reflection on these relations. Relations that many animals are aware of, between sights, sounds, and smells on the one hand and foods, predators, and kin on the other, are transformed into symbolic relationships "by reflecting on what is already known" (93). The rabbit is aware of the carrot, but the self-conscious human can go beyond this simple awareness and say "this is a carrot" and then move on to other symbolic relationships: "this is a vegetable," "this is food," "this food is good."

Self-consciousness is not a magic ingredient that appears and immediately produces language, science, art, and the rest of human culture. Although the capacity to reflect is required for symbolic interpretation, it would appear that symbolic interpretation is in turn required for the further evolution of self-consciousness, and this process of the development of the human 'mind' itself co-evolves with the brain. These are interactive and organic, not linear mechanical, processes, and much too complex for us to deal with here. I do, however, want to explore some possibilities regarding the nature of this developmental process.

We can add a useful hypothesis by Daniel Dennett to explain the emergence of self-consciousness.[13] Early hominids, like many other organisms, would communicate with one another in a non-self-conscious way, for example, when in need of help. Add to this the Quartz and Sejnowski hypothesis of constructed tendencies, and these communications could become quite sophisticated and occur in many different circumstances. Dennett proposes that, on some occasions when no other member of the community was present to respond, the communicator heard and then answered his or her own message. This self-help was sometimes developmentally useful, giving a further advantage to the flexible, interacting brain that supported it and making more probable the transmission of the genetic base for this self-constructing brain to subsequent generations.

The recognition of one's own meaningful utterances and of a response to that meaning could have been the first glimmer of self-consciousness—an awareness of the self that could in some way be articulated. The developmental value of this would raise the probabilities of the consequent evolution of this nascent self-awareness into a more profound self-consciousness. Awareness of one's call for help, need for help, consequent assistance, and the relief this would bring would give rise, eventually, to symbols associated with all of these. Symbols emerge and self-consciousness is born. Perhaps we should say that it is *conceived*, for it will develop for eons in an embryonic way, through the coevolutions mentioned above, before emerging as infant but recognizable forms of human self-consciousness.

Deacon discusses the two sides of symbolic interpretations. The individual's symbolic interpretations are unique to each individual. My interpretation of another person, a comment, a work of art, even a scientific treatise is *my* interpretation. I could think that this is a good person or that is a profound statement, but then, on further reflection decide that this person is really a crook and that statement quite superficial. The interpretation of relations as icons or indices, which most animals can make, is not personal in this way; the connection between this smell and that skunk that arises from simple awareness is determined by the physiological factors that compose that process of simple awareness, and not by the *self*. It is the personal character of symbolic interpretation that effects self-determination.

On the other hand, Deacon says, symbols are also a product of society. "Unlike the interpretation of icons and indices (a process which is uniquely personal and insular within each brain), symbolic representations are in part externally interpreted—they are shared"(451). In reflection we talk to ourselves in somewhat the way that we talk to others, so that self-consciousness is an internalized social process (451).

The Significance of All This

The hypothesis that the structural development of the brain continues long after birth and Deacon's refutation of the Cartesian belief in an innate capacity for human cognitive activities, supported by Quartz and Sejnowski, has a significance that should be noted here. Rather than attributing human behavior to a soul or structure that is fixed from the outset, this new view puts great emphasis on the interactions from infancy among humans and with the environment. This dynamic, interactive process is a dominant factor in the formation of cognitive capacity and, indeed, of any behavior related to the activity of the mind. In humans, the genetically determined inherited structure is the source of much more than specific, fixed learning and behavior. Humans are born with a flexible, dynamic brain that develops through *interaction with community* and environment.[14]

The above well-established hypotheses suggest several conclusions that run counter to the dominant paradigm and that are the major elements of my argument:

- The flexibility and highly augmented role of human interaction with the total environment that these strongly supported hypotheses imply counters much of the traditional essentialist mythology about *human nature.* "Life is nasty," "life is solitary," "*man* is a rational planner"—these are empirical propositions that might be the case to some extent in some circumstances. They have no validity or substance as analytical propositions about the fixed essence, the perpetual and static nature, the definition of the human.
- They also refute genetic determinism without rejecting the efficacy of the genetic base. Human behavior has self-conscious, cultural, and biological causes. The biological causes include flexible biological structures that have been constructed by extended interactions between those structures and their environments, including cultures. This flexibility is itself induced by the genetic program but, as should be obvious, human behaviors cannot be traced directly back to the genes. Human behavior arises from complex interactions among self-consciousness, culture, and the biological dimension at the time of the behavior; all three factors themselves are the consequences of these same kinds of interactions during the life of the person behaving, and during the lives of the ancestral individuals and communities. The interactions among the biological base, self-consciousness, and cultures began when self-consciousness emerged, creating immediately a new subject for selection and a phenomenon that cannot be reduced to the biological base.[15]

- Within the present context, these hypotheses underline the necessity of interaction for development, and the *impossibility of isolation.* They suggest also that, although humans should prize the degree of independence and autonomy required for freedom as self-determination, these desiderata must be understood within the context of interdependence and interaction within community, and never as absolutes. As a corollary both to Quartz and Sejnowski's constructivist hypothesis on the continuing development of the brain through interaction with the environment and to the hypothesis on the emergence of self-consciousness supported by Deacon and Dennett, among others, we should repeat with emphasis that community itself is a prerequisite for the development of the human mind's capabilities and of self-consciousness itself, and that the process is an iteration of individual self-conscious development and community development.
- This emphasis on interaction within a relational community supports my claim that reason is not the central or essential form of human cognition. One can reason in virtual isolation. The primary and most developmentally important cognitions would be those which emerged within community interactions: self-conscious feelings, intuitions, profound immediate understandings of the inclinations and needs of self and other, inducing appropriate developmental responses.

Self-Consciousness in Community

Given the hypothesis that the structure of the brain develops through interactions with its environment, it is safe to assume that for our early ancestors much of this interaction would have been with one's own community of early hominids. The organization, flexibility, and adaptability of the brain would be to a great extent a consequence of this interaction in community. The development of language communication within the community would arise from this interaction within the context of openness—of the natural propensity of organisms to be aware of the needs of others and to react in a way that will help to satisfy those needs. As an essential part of a system of mutual support, openness would be positively selected, sexual selection perhaps playing a major role here, and, one might expect, its development would be accelerated by improved communication and especially by the emergence and development of self-consciousness. The brain's capacity to construct itself through interaction with its environment would develop symbiotically with the embryonic self-consciousness. Furthermore, the profundity of the recognition of *other* would evolve symbiotically with the recognition of self.

Earlier I countered Dawkins's notion of the *selfish gene* while emphasizing my otherwise high regard for his work. In a more recent book

Dawkins gives an account of the emergence of human-type life that, I believe, supports my own.[16] He presents a generic picture of evolution, anywhere in the universe, in terms of a series of *Thresholds*. Skipping to those related to the origin of the human, we find Threshold 5, the high-speed information processing or nervous system threshold (156). This is the emergence of the nervous system and brain which provides the capacity to receive and process information rapidly. Threshold 6 he calls the *consciousness threshold* but refers to this also as "conscious awareness" (158), which I would interpret to mean the same as *self-consciousness*. This he associates intimately with the development of language: "Whether or not consciousness requires language, let us anyway recognize the Language Threshold as a major one." He labels this level Threshold 7. He goes on to say: "Language . . . is the networking system by which brains . . . exchange information with sufficient intimacy to allow the development of a cooperative technology" (159).

On our planet we know that our self-consciousness was associated with language and consequently exchanged information with "sufficient intimacy" for "cooperative technology." It would appear that, even though Dawkins gives some extra prominence to egoism with his *selfish gene*, his vision of the origins of our species supports my own. "Exchange information with sufficient *intimacy*" suggests that added to the high speed information processing attained in Threshold 5 is communication within interrelationships characterized by close association and affection. The spontaneous communication we have talked about above takes on a new character through the self-conscious understanding of other as other and the needs of other leading to cooperative techniques for development. Recall that I have defined *cooperation* in terms of a blending of egoism and altruism—of understanding of and concern for both the needs of self and other.

The important point, once again, is that selfishness is not the central and fundamental principle of the process. In Dawkins's words, intimacy and the cooperation it effects are threshold elements of the emergence of the human. There must be, in other words, openness to one another followed by cooperative efforts to satisfy needs. If cooperative techniques are to be effective, life cannot be solitary and nasty.

The Autonomous Ghost in the Rational Machine

Associated with the undue emphasis on autonomy and rationality in the long Western tradition is the explanation of specifically human characteristics in terms of a preformed nonmaterial entity, or some innate capacity, from Plato's forms, the medieval soul, and Descartes's *ghost in the machine*, through Kant's a priori to the present tendency to attribute the learning of language to a child's innate language competence. Noam Chomsky calls the human mind "a biologically given complex system"[17] and, in the company of Descartes, Hume, Russell, and Quine, attempts to elaborate this preformed system whereby we learn.

The need for such a *given* arises from the view of *man* as rational and solitary and of development as linear. If all the great complexity of our world is known through rational processes, through deduction and induction, and communicated through languages with complex formal structures, then the basic forms on which language and reason are built must reside innately in this "biologically given complex system." Deacon, however, claims that the "theory that there are innate rules for grammar commits the fallacy of collapsing this irreducible *social evolutionary* process into a static formal structure" (121). As we have stated above, the physiological development of the human brain, through its interaction with its environment, continues for probably more than a decade after birth. The emergence and development of self-consciousness and the emergence and development of symbolic interpretation and language are interacting processes—codevelopments, we might say—which themselves co-develop with the brain.

Deacon, along with Elissa Newport, puts forward a hypothesis that is elegant, powerful and in line with contemporary evolutionary theory (128). Not only does the mind evolve, he says, but language evolves too. The language that will survive and develop will be the one that can be grasped by the child. The earliest stages of learning involve interactions with immature minds. Successful languages, therefore, are those that can be embraced by minds at an early stage of development. The process begins with insights and intuitions, not deductions and inductions. The capacity to interpret symbolically develops symbiotically with the capacity to reflect, all through interaction with the social and natural environment. The beginnings of this process are not, of course, totally formless and arbitrary; if they were, a trout or a turkey could learn trigonometry. Both the brain of a human infant and the language the infant is born into have the structure required to get the process started. But the structures that support human understanding and communication are plastic, developing, interacting structures, not an a priori, preformed, innate, fixed, insular structure within the human, waiting to receive data from out there.

The message once again is that the traditional and essentialist myths of rationality and autonomy must give way to a recognition of insight and self-conscious feelings interacting within communities as fundamental agents of human development.

Foundations for a Real *State of Nature*

How humanity actually emerged millennia ago will of course never be known in detail. The best scientific theories today, nevertheless, strongly suggest that what happened would have been similar in general outline to the above account: a genetically based but flexible and evolving biological structure elicited developments in communications and conscious behavior that were the beginnings of self-consciousness, and these were selected because they were developmentally useful and developed at perhaps accelerated rates because of the efficacy of sexual selection and the plasticity of the brain and its construction through environmental interaction.

This biological foundation was and still is essential; however, self-consciousness itself frees human development from biological determinism. We are, for example, biologically determined to eat, but the size, complexity, and plasticity of the human brain provides a foundation for an enormous range of activities associated with eating, and it would seem that a specific physiological arrangement is not required for each of these. The brain I have in its present state of development will support unlimited self-conscious decisions and consequent behaviors related to the biological need to eat: prepare a quick snack; cook a gourmet meal; go to a restaurant; gobble down a meal by myself; have a celebratory feast with others; fast; eat/prepare Chinese, Italian, Indian, French, West African, Thai, fusion; and on and on. I can do all these now with the brain I have now because I am self-conscious.

Our hypothesis is that the evolution of self-consciousness involved an interaction among individuals-in-community, based on mutual awareness and support—on cooperation and openness—supported by but not determined by a large, complex, plastic brain, self-consciousness itself interacting with an evolving language. *Interactive, developmental, dynamic, open, cooperative, relational*: these are the adjectives that best describe our real state of nature.

The importance of the implications of this account of the emergence of humanity for what follows cannot be stressed too much. I will be arguing that the gestation period of morality and justice itself began with the conception of self-consciousness, and especially with the birth of *I-Thou.*[18] For the purposes of my dissertation on the origins of justice, this is the foundation for my *state of nature.* The premises on which I will build my theory of justice are the actual conditions and processes of our origins—to the extent, of course, that we can know them. To ensure their clarity, I will summarize these here, emphasizing how they differ from the dominant Western view.

Neither Solitary nor Rational

I have proposed above that the dominant Western model gives primacy to autonomy and rationality as essential characteristics of *man*. I have also said that I see both autonomy and reason, including instrumental reason, as important and necessary human qualities. My concern is the great emphasis placed on these characteristics and the consequent marginalization and exclusion of other essential human qualities. Not all subscribers to this model see life as solitary as Hobbes did, or reason as paramount as did Kant. Nevertheless, the central tendency of the evaluation of human qualities within the dominant paradigm is skewed toward the Hobbesian-Kantian end of the scale. Even if this imbalance is not great, I believe it is sufficient to be developmentally dysfunctional and probably dangerous, and without scientific foundation.

First, with regard to *solitary*: The original humans had evolved in a process based on communication, mutual awareness, and support—on *openness*. This is not to deny that life was often nasty and brutish. As stressed above, selfishness, competition, and aggression evolve along with altruism, cooperation, and nurturing. I am not ignoring the Hobbesian side of humanity. I am stating that an accurate picture of the original condition must include openness and eschew undue emphasis on egoism and isolation. Relative autonomy and self-determination could arise only as consequences of morality and justice and further developments in self-consciousness, and would always be limited by and could be understood only within the realities of the interactions with our total environment, including community and its culture. From the outset, human freedom and autonomy are consequences of interrelations within communities, of cooperationand openness.

Second, with reference to *rational*: If *rational* refers to the capacity to reason, then I reject the claim that the essence of the human is to be rational—that the human (or even *man*) is defined as the *rational animal* who is distinguished from all other animals by reason. I propose that a more fundamental characteristic can be found both to distinguish humans from other organisms and, more importantly, to guide us toward a better understanding of human development. I see the distinctive nature of the human to be primarily associated with self-consciousness, which arises from community interactions and itself is a precondition for reason and for other characteristically human cognitive capacities: sophisticated languages, science, art, morality, institutions, profound relationships. We are, as Deacon says, *the symbolic species.*

The capacities normally defined as reason—to analyze and calculate, to induce and deduce—are of great importance to human development and are part of the *essence* of humanity; they are not, however, the whole essence. Indeed, both in our distant origins and in our human activities today, self-conscious intuitions,[19] feelings, understandings, evaluations, judgments—self-conscious activities that do not involve reasoning processes—appear to me to be much more prevalent than reasoning and, I would propose, include the bases for and support for reasoning itself.

Tattersall says: "The mind . . . is a product of ancient reflexive and emotional components, overlain by a veneer of reason" (234)—a *veneer of reason* over, I would suggest, reflective, self-conscious components, including emotions. The important point is that judgments, including moral judgements, arise from intuitions, feelings, emotions, all of which can be captured by and influenced by self-consciousness, and not only or primarily from reason. This challenge to the centrality of reason in morals is supported by Jonathan Haidt, who says that a social intuitionist model, in which moral judgments are based on intuitions and social and cultural influences rather than on the private reasoning of individuals, is more consistent with recent findings in psychology, anthropology, and primatology.[20] Experiments in cognitive neuroscience, using functional magnetic resonance imaging (fMRI), indicate that "emotional involvement" is greater in moral personal judgments than in moral impersonal and nonmoral judgements, the latter two involving a more reasoned approach.[21] What Greene et al. refer to as emotions in this study would appear to be self-conscious intuitions and feelings, flowing from developmental inclinations.

Altruism and Openness

The concept of *openness*, introduced above, is central to my thesis, and the way I understand it within the biological and human dimensions requires further elaboration. All living organisms are open to their environment in that they constantly receive information and energy from it, and they react to these receptions in ways determined by their genetically induced adaptation. Beyond this reception of information and as a consequence of it, organisms have two basic *attitudes* toward other members of their species: they can be closed to others, or solitary; they can be open to others, or communal. Or, as Buck and Ginsberg put it, they can communicate—send and receive—motivational-emotional states. This "spontaneous communication" (de Waal's "emotional contagion") is, they claim, genetically based and affective.[22]

The vampire bat receives information about the plight of a hungry neighbor and reacts by offering it food. Although the capacity to receive information is probably linked to the reaction to information received, we can distinguish between the two; first there is the awareness of other and other's need through a reception of information, and following is the reaction, which in this case is openness to the other bat and its needs. I call this reaction the *attitude*. The attitude of the animal can be either closed—no reaction to the needs of the other—or open—some reaction to the needs of the other. The basic inclinations associated with closed and open attitudes are egoism and altruism respectively.

Here we are talking about genetically programmed attitudes and inclinations, not rational strategies; just as an animal doesn't consciously decide to be hungry, neither does it plan to be selfish or altruistic. Human behavior, however, has both biological and human dimensions. Because we are self-conscious, we are conditioned but not determined by our genetic programs. The selfish and altruistic inclinations in humans are conditions for our behavior that we could, on reflection, decide to attempt to override. We can choose to focus on the needs of others or ignore them; we can respond positively to our knowledge of the needs of others and consequent inclinations to help, or we can close ourselves off in solitude. But the inclinations are there; we can override them but we cannot eliminate them. The natural inclination to be altruistic, if not blocked, promotes sacrificial, nurturing, and communal behavior, whereas egoistic tendencies, if given free reign, can encourage isolation, competition, and aggression. A biologically based sacrificial behavior might remain totally altruistic when embraced by the human dimension, or this altruistic inclination might be self-consciously modified by egoism. A decision to cooperate would often involve both selfish and altruistic inclinations—an openness to self and to other.

Within the dominant paradigm the emphasis on isolation, competition, and aggression is reinforced by a one-dimensional concept of power that comes, via Hobbes, from classical mechanics. That concept is worth considering.

Power

The actions and interactions of organisms require energy. From the perspective of physics, power is energy or work per unit time. This concept of *power* refers simply to getting something done, but in common discourse and in social science the idea of domination is commonly added to this basic definition; as it was for Hobbes, power = *power-over*. This power of domination, or power-over-other, is the type of power associated with selfish competitive behavior. Energy, however, need not always be working *against* other energy; organisms do not always dominate other organisms. Nature provides myriad examples of energy and organisms working *with* other energy and organisms, and symbols have emerged to express this: *synergy* (from the Greek *working together*) where the result is greater than the sum of the parts, and *symbiosis* (from the Greek *living together*), where organisms of different species benefit from living together.[23]

Altruism and cooperation involve *power-with-other*, not power-over-other—power of partnership rather than power of domination. This power is so common and natural that we hardly notice it. The destructive power-over of a meteor crashing into the earth is obvious, but the enormous energy that produced the flora and fauna that is destroyed by the meteorite—the power-with of life itself—does its work unobtrusively, hidden within the biological processes themselves.

The tendency to associate power with physical activities, whether meteor impacts, bomb explosions, or a punch in the face, but not see power within biological processes seems to be pervasive. I would think that this is the case simply because physical power-over is more obvious than the power-with of living systems.[24] The classical mechanics developed by Galileo and Newton sees the world in terms of point masses moving in space. If they collide, moving masses transfer their energy to one another and a large mass will dominate a smaller one. Hobbes's application of this mechanical power-over of Galileo's physics to human society,[25] was not the first instance of undue emphasis on and gross misapplication of power-over, but it did help to enshrine this distorted one-dimensional view of the world within Western thought.

The continuing domination of the classical mechanics and Cartesian model over Western thought makes it very difficult for even postmodern analysts, such as Michel Foucault, to escape from the Hobbesian one-dimensional view of power. Riane Eisler's rigorous presentation of the two dimensions of power, however, should make it difficult for the masculine mechanist to ignore *power-with.*

Whether power-over or power-with is the active agent of specific non-self-conscious behaviors is, for the most part, a consequence of sexual and/or natural selection. Humans, however, can, to some extent, choose the power that they will use. Because of this the balance effected by natural selection itself could be upset by self-conscious agents.

Hunter-gatherers were among our early ancestors, and hunter-gatherer societies exist today. Agriculture began in the Neolithic period, starting about 10,000 years ago, but because of circumstances many peoples either could not become agricultural, or chose not to. Hunting was a male activity. The gatherers were usually women who supplemented the food that they gathered with small game. Each activity was necessary for the development of this community of omnivores and each was an application of techniques devised by self-consciousness following the natural inclinations to get food. There is some freedom in the development of these techniques, but also strict conditions imposed by biological and physical nature. Hunting is a power-over activity. Although there would probably be cooperation among the hunters, their objective is to dominate, to overpower the hunted. The community is nourished only if the prey is killed. Only one side wins; it is a zero-sum game.

Gathering is not usually a zero-sum game. Taking the fruits of a plant will not harm the plant and probably won't limit its reproductive capacity too much. Indeed, the gatherer will not kill a plant that will be a continuing source of food. In some cases plants might benefit from the culling, or from the broadcasting of seeds. Gathering is a "gentle" power-over, with little or no domination, mixed with some power-with. Agricultural development tends to put greater emphasis on power-with techniques. The soil and the plants that grow in it are not dominated; the agriculturalist works with the soil and the plants, and, with sound ecological management, the result is nourishment for the human community and more productive land. Both sides win; it is a positive-sum game.

The common assumption has been that hunting, the male power-over activity, was the main source of food for the hunter-gatherer community. Now there is good evidence to infer that in most hunter-gatherer societies it is the women who provide most of the food, through gathering and hunting small game[26] and later through agriculture. Power-with is probably a more effective provider than power-over, but this is often not noticed by male researchers.

It should be emphasized that it is the overall process in each case that tends to be power-with or power-over; that is, agriculture is not purely power-with nor is hunting only power-over. Vegetables are killed for human consumption and our hunting ancestors had to follow ecologically sound practices so as to not to kill off the whole herd. Nevertheless, the two approaches have different energy-type central tendencies. The agriculturalist puts emphasis on nurturing the plant and consumes only what is required for sustenance, leaving the rest to seed and feed further crops. The tools and techniques used are not for domination. The hunter's immediate objective, along with the tools and techniques used to meet it, however, is killing.

In one community, the agricultural approach could become the more influential overall approach to community development. This could be a consequence of power-with being the stronger general tendency, or because agriculture has been more successful than hunting, or whatever. In another community, the hunter's power-over approach could become the chosen approach to meeting most objectives. The hunters themselves, having control over techniques and weapons of domination, would probably influence such a general tendency. Early matriarchal communities would have been predominantly power-with societies; Western industrial societies are now, I believe, very much power-over.

Emphasis on either approach for reasons other than the efficacy of each for specific objectives could promote dysfunctional imbalances. A power-over bias would, a priori, seem to be the more dysfunctional of the two simply because of its zero-sum consequences; if effective, there tends to be a loser. In many circumstances the power-with approach might not be as effective, or as immediately effective, as power-over, but at least it tends not to produce losers. And yet, a posteriori, we know that the bias has been for power-over throughout recorded history, power-with being marginalized and, although it must have been always involved even in the "real world," ignored to the extent that it became anonymous. Recently, however, power-with and its efficacy have been gaining recognition, especially among feminist scholars and in remarkable works such as Riane Eisler's *The Chalice and the Blade.*[27] Evidence now suggests that the partnership society might in fact have preceded the dominator society.[28]

The present dominant proclivity toward autonomy and competition encourages the use of power-over and supports the belief that this is the more effective and efficient power. The proclivity seems to arise more from the general assumption that power equals power-over and that competitive approaches are the natural ones than from careful analysis and assessment of actual applications of power. Both power-with and power-over are natural; each can be effective and appropriate for specific objectives. One might expect that if either were to be given an arbitrary, unfounded preference it would be power-with, which reduces negative consequences. Such is, obviously, not the case.

Behavior Within Community: An Overview of the Above

In my exploration of behavior within the evolutionary context I have defined and distinguished several related concepts, which Table 1 attempts to organize and summarize.

I have proposed that all non-self-conscious behavior of animals is a consequence of two basic attitudes toward the other members of that animal's community. Information received by an animal from another member of the community elicits a reaction induced by a genetic program that has evolved through natural selection. For purposes of analysis I break the reaction into three steps: attitude, inclination, and behavior.

First, at the level of basic awareness, the animal is either open or not to information about another and the needs of another. I call this the *attitude*, and it is either *open* or *closed*. If there is an awareness of the other's needs, then there can follow an inclination to behave so as to help satisfy that need, that is, there can be an altruistic inclination inducing a nurturing behavior that can be somewhat sacrificial.

Obviously, if the animal has no capacity for an open attitude in these specific circumstances, then no altruistic inclination will arise. Egoistic inclinations arise from awareness of the animal's own needs and they can effect selfish, competitive and aggressive behaviors to satisfy these needs.

Table 1 outlines these distinctions. They apply to non-self-conscious animals and humans, but in the latter case take on the transcendent human dimension that has been discussed above.

The concepts of morality and justice in this work are informed by and rest on the above distinction between *open/communal* (or, as de Waal puts it, *relational*) and *closed/solitary*, and on the claim that both sets of attitudes, inclinations, and behaviors are natural and necessary components of the evolutionary process and, more specifically, of the human development process. The modern, urban industrial society is characterized by a growing imbalance in favor of the *closed* side: the Hobbesian

TABLE 1

Attitude	Open to other/ communal	Closed to other/ solitary
Inclination	Altruistic	Egoistic
Behavior	Sacrificial/nurturing*	Selfish/aggressive
Associated power	Power-with symbiotic/positive-sum	Power-over domination/zero-sum
Consequences of power	Partnership society†	Dominator society†
Present status	Marginal, peripheral, *other*	Dominant, the perceived "reality"
Central tendencies; these characteristics tend to be more common in:	Women Rural, agrarian, "traditional" societies Writings of: feminists, some development theorists from the South	Men Urban, industrial, "modern" societies Writings of: social science "realists," Western economists, social Darwinists

* Cooperative behavior, also marginalized and losing ground to competition, is not in this abstract table because it is often a blend of altruism and egoism.

† *Partnership* and *dominator* are the terms used by Eisler (1988).

and now dominant side. This is countered—how effectively remains to be seen—by calls for recognition and reinstatement of the *open* side and a return to balance from many quarters. *Openness, connectedness, affiliation,* and *relatedness* are used, for example, in feminist literature with reference to, or to define, the central feminine character, and also in the psychological literature.[29]

The dominant trend is not determined by our biological nature. Self-consciousness can influence attitude, inclination, and behavior, and can choose the more appropriate type of power. The self-conscious individual is, of course, conditioned by her or his culture, and patriarchal cultures show a strong bias toward the *closed* column in the table. It is cultural bias, itself a product of self-consciousness, and not our biological dimension that pushes us toward solitude.

Balance

It is difficult to analyze critically this imbalance and emphasis on the *closed* side without appearing to take a Manichaean approach: openness, altruism is good; isolation, egoism is evil. My ultimate position, which is also the position of many of those who counter the dominant position, is that the problem is not the *closed* side per se but the emphasis on it—its dominance. In other words, the problem is *im*balance and the solution is *balance.*

In the real world there is no line dividing the two sets of characteristics; there is a blend of attitudes, inclinations, behaviors, and powers. The *good,* the *developmental,* is, like the ancient Yin and Yang, a union of the two dimensions. Egoism becomes dysfunctional and dangerous to the extent that it becomes dominant, submerging any concern for the needs of other. An altruist without any concern for self, however, would be ineffective and also dysfunctional.

Cooperative behavior—the behavior that is so important for human development but that seems to be rapidly becoming a vestige—is often a blend of egoism and altruism. Let us pursue this notion further in the company of our vampire bat.

Hunger arises in the context of an awareness of the self and its needs. The inclination for self-protection includes an awareness of other, but other-as-threat to the needs of the self, rather than other-as-other. The vampire bat must have these necessary, good, developmental selfish inclinations if it is to develop. An extreme openness that ignored the self and other-as-threat would herald an early demise. The altruistic bat must be a healthy bat that has taken care of its own needs; hence the altruistic bat must be also a selfish bat. Conversely, given the essential contribution to bat development of the altruistic inclinations, including the one in our example, the selfish bat must be an altruistic bat. Its genetic program will induce it to be closed in some circumstances and open in others. The combination is required and neither is reducible to the other.

Humans can, to some extent and as influenced by their cultures, choose attitudes, inclinations, behaviors, and powers, but if the choices are too biased one way or another, within an individual or a community, the consequences for development could be negative.

Openness and Rationality

In presenting openness as the attitudinal base for the altruistic inclinations of the human, I am associating it with concepts such as the spontaneous communication of Buck and Ginsberg, Batson's empathy, Dovidio's arousal, Jolly's sense of self and others, and de Waal's "emotional contagion" and empathy.[30] These are all affective rather than rational. This is another extremely important point. The dominant Western view emphasizes analytical, calculating reason and thereby reduces human behavior to mechanical self-maximization. An altruistic or cooperative act is often reduced to a selfish one by presenting it as the consequence of a calculation in which the actor concludes that the benefits of helping outweigh the costs of not helping; this simplistic reduction is made to appear scholarly and even scientific in game theory. I obviously do not wish to deny that maximizing behavior based on benefit-cost analysis exists; indeed, I think that it now exists with a vengeance. The point is, once again, that the dominant model with its preoccupation with rationality does not exhaust the intelligibility of human behavior. The more disinterested model for human altruistic behavior might be something like this:

I see a starving child. A genetically based, affective openness to other initiates a feeling of empathy: "I want to help." I can reflect on this self-conscious feeling, and a range of responses can occur:

1. There can be an "impulsive, 'irrational' response"[31] with no cost-benefit calculation; openness immediately induces an altruistic inclination and consequent helping behavior.
2. There can be an impulsive response with an associated calculation, not of the costs and benefits of helping or not helping, but of how best to help; the rational response enters at the behavioral level to help in the choice of behavior.
3. There can be rational cost-benefit calculations, which can suppress the altruistic impulse: the cost is too great to help so I will close myself to the child.

4. There can be rational cost-benefit calculations, which can support my open attitude and altruistic inclination: it is to my benefit to help.
5. There can be rational calculations that indicate that the cost of helping is too great, but this calculation is overwhelmed by the open attitude and altruistic inclination—by the initial impulse.

The first, second, and fifth cases are altruistic; the other two are selfish. The probability of one of these occurring would depend on several factors, including the person's degree of openness, the degree of ensuing empathy, and the propensity to calculate. Openness has a biological base, but, beyond the biological tendency and capacity to communicate, the degree of openness is a function of learning and of culture.[32] The inclination would depend on the communication—who is in need? what is the need?—and on the culturally conditioned interpretation of the communication. The rational overlay, including any calculations, would be determined through some interactive process with the affective elements. The tendency to calculate and the efficacy of the calculation could be associated with levels of openness and inclination.

The importance of these hypotheses lies in their rejection of the notion that the human is simply a nasty, brutish, solitary rational animal who calculates, or that that is all that matters in the *real* world. How often do the words *compassion* or *love* appear in treatises on politics and economics? The dominant feeling seems to be that these are appropriate in domestic affairs and novels but not in the "real world." Western economists refer to nonindustrialized societies of the South as "traditional" societies with "economies of affection," or as the nonmodern societies of the "irrational peasant." Economies of affection will eventually "develop" into modern, rational economies; irrational peasants will become rational when they recognize that the supply curve slopes up, that is, when they understand the "natural laws" of the competitive market-place as they are mapped onto Cartesian coordinates. Gary S. Becker won the Nobel Prize in economics in 1992 "for having extended the domain of microeconomic analysis to a wide range of human behavior and interaction, including nonmarket behavior"; he *defined* rationality in terms of the slope of the supply curve.

It is respectable to say that life is solitary and nasty, but embarrassing to suggest that it is also compassionate and loving. Perhaps this is why we tread softly at first by using terms such as *relatedness*, rather than shocking our readers and jeopardizing our scholarship by claiming that love is a natural force in the world (albeit far from universal, Dr. Dawkins). We reason best in solitude, and being nasty is no impediment to reasoning; but we understand best in community, and being open is an advantage—indeed a prerequisite—to understanding. Reason has become such a fetish, however, that it and anything associated with it, including the brutish, nasty, and solitary, are seen as human characteristics par excellence, while the profound understandings of the six billion humans in millions of communities are virtually ignored. It is this understanding of the vast majority of *real* people in *real* communities that keeps the *real* world going. It is understanding that is immediately affective and intuitive, conditioned by cultures and individual wisdom, sometimes followed by rational calculation, but always self-conscious. It is the real foundation for what is good and what is bad. Reason can help us understand the process of development from many perspectives, as I am trying to do here; it can help us devise better techniques for our development or for our destruction. There is no doubt about the efficacy of reason. What I am calling into doubt is the degree of importance attached to reason, and especially abstract, isolated reason, at the expense of what recent studies would suggest are the more fundamental, more effective and vastly more pervasive powers of the human mind and will.[33] Highly abstract and rational approaches to the understanding of human behavior such as game theory, popular among economists and some other social scientists perhaps because they appear to be scientific to the Cartesian mind, carry the dominant paradigm further from the reality as seen by social psychology and other more fundamental sciences. It would appear that the self-conscious affective side of the human is just as real, just as worthy of the attention of the student of politics and economics, as is the abstract focus on rational behavior.

The Emergence of Purpose

By *teleology* I refer to the understanding of phenomena and activities in terms of their ends or purposes; it is the introduction of goals and objectives to a process that, before self-consciousness, was only a series of consequences. This idea is central to my thesis, but enveloped in ambiguity and difficulty that must be removed.

The first point that must be clear is that, from the evolutionary perspective, self-consciousness is the creator of purpose. The evolutionary process does look like a teleological process, and on occasion even scientists who understand it couch their explanations of it in teleological language. One might say, for example, that "the inclination to eat is for the purpose of survival" or "the eye is for the purpose of seeing" or "the goal of a gene is to survive." Within the perspective of neo-Darwinian theory, however, no recourse to purpose is required to explain such inclinations or phenomena. The inclination to eat exists because it is a consequence of a genetic structure that exists because it contributes to an organism's fitness. The total explanation is in terms of *consequences*, not purposes or ends. We do not have eyes for the purpose of seeing; we see because we have eyes and we have eyes because each evolutionary step in the long and complex process from which eyes developed was selected because of the advantage it provided. Genes survive because they induce behavior that contributes to the fitness of their hosts, and they don't care whether they survive or not.

I have said that purpose has no place within the neo-Darwinian explanation and appears in the process only with the emergence of self-consciousness. Purpose is clearly not needed to understand physical and biological evolution, and its insertion into explanations of this process distorts and obfuscates. Within the present context, therefore, purpose arises only with self-consciousness. As I hope has already been made clear, however, I do not rule out other contexts. This essay looks at justice from within the evolutionary process that begins with energy and culminates, on planet Earth, with human development. It is silent on matters beyond that context—on the question of a cause of the explosion of energy that started the process, or of its ultimate goal. To say that purpose does not appear within the process before self-consciousness, and that, within the process, self-consciousness is the principal cause of purpose, is not to say that there is not some purpose to the whole process. In particular, I see no contradiction at all in the view that there is overall purpose, but that the interactions of physiobiological evolution can be understood without recourse to purpose.

Let us now return to the nature and enormous ramifications of the creation of purpose within our development process. The common factor of all the development inclinations would be seen at an early stage of human development. Eating, fleeing from a predator, keeping warm—these would be associated with survival; perhaps, in the difficult conditions of that era, these positive associations would arise from reflection on their more vivid negative counterparts—starvation, capture, exposure. In any case, along with each inclination would gradually emerge a notion of its link with survival, and then development.

As these inclinations are enhanced and augmented by self-consciousness and by the introduction of new techniques, purpose, objectives, goals would appear for the first time. Better and/or new ways of getting and preparing food would be known to be *for* survival. Techniques to detect and defend against enemies would be known to be *for* survival. The use of animal skins and fire to ward off cold would be known to be *for* survival. Activities, which in the past had been simply determined consequences of evolution, were now also done for a recognized purpose; and the principal, overarching purpose was, and is, survival/development. The recognition of purpose by our early ancestors must have been extremely vague at first, but over millennia reflection on the challenges being faced, on the possible courses of action, on the range of consequences, and on the others involved, gave birth to many intentions, objectives and goals.

Value has been introduced to the process, and is reinforced by *purpose.* I know that food is good and I know that it is good *for my development.* By association I know that gathering, preparing and eating food are all good *for my development.* I know that food is good for my child and that feeding my child is good *for her development.* More specific objectives would, of course, emerge: fire for the purpose of keeping warm; training for the purpose of tool-making; spears for the purpose of hunting; hunting for the purpose of eating. Sadly, as we see all around us, competing, ambiguous, and antidevelopmental objectives would also emerge.

We now have the biological and human foundations required to build hypotheses on the origins of morality.

Chapter 4
The Genesis of Morality

The Birth of Humanity

So far our exploration strongly suggests that our beginnings were often nasty and aggressive, but also nurturing and caring. Life was never solitary; interaction and openness to others and the needs of others were as essential to early human development as were selfish concerns for one's own needs. There were no rational planners or rational maximizers during humanity's infancy. As I have said above, I do not agree with John Rawls that even now, after millennia of development, the lives of individuals or communities are in any significant way the results of rational plans.[1] Certainly it was without professional philosophers and planners that morality emerged, perhaps as early as five million years ago.[2] I don't know how with any degree of certainty; nevertheless, using the hypotheses that flow from the evidence and the explorations above, I do believe that some speculation on this emergence and its conditions can provide some valuable insights.

There is, of course, no single original position or *state of nature*, no point in space and time that can be identified as *the* beginning of self-consciousness, language, science, morals, humanity, although fossil and molecular evidence does point to East Africa as the home of our hominid ancestors. Evolutionary experiments in the interrelated developments of self-consciousness and language communication would have occurred here and there from time to time, with variations in levels of success and failure, over millions of years. To make sense of this process, however, some abstraction from its complexity and interrelatedness is necessary.

What would the original humans, the first self-conscious hominids who were our ancestors, be like? They would have the same basic developmental inclinations as their immediate ancestors, and these would continue to dominate their behavior; the new capacity to reflect was too embryonic to have any noticeable effect. But as this capacity slowly evolved they reflected on more and more of the objects of their awareness, and eventually their basic development inclinations were recognized and reflected on. It is through an exploration of this advent of self-consciousness and especially on these reflections on developmental inclinations that hypotheses on the origin of morality will appear.

I have insisted that, although the evolution of human self-consciousness is an integral part of the process from which the consciousness of other animals emerged, it is not simply a more extensive form of consciousness. Terrence Deacon's study of the evolution of consciousness provides a solid foundation for this claim and, more importantly, for my hypotheses on the evolution of morality. Deacon uses a relatively common model of language in an uncommonly precise and empirically supported way. I will outline his position briefly.

Deacon insists that human language is not merely a more complex version of the communications of other animals. "When we strip away the complexity, only one significant difference between language and nonlanguage communication remains: the common, everyday miracle of word meaning and reference."[3] He refers to this unique human mode of reference as symbolic reference.

A sign, whether a word, a picture, the quack of a duck, or the song of a whale, can be related to an object or referent in three different ways: (1) By seeing a similarity between the sign and the object; this is the iconic interpretation of the relationship between sign and object, making the sign an *icon.* (2) By seeing some contiguity or correlation in space or time between the sign and object; this is the indicative interpretation, making the sign an *index.* (3) By seeing a social convention, tacit agreement or explicit code relating the sign and its object; this is the symbolic interpretation in which the sign becomes a *symbol.*

An animal will interpret a smell as an icon for another animal and can interpret a sound from another animal as a warning—an indication that a predator is near. The warning sound is itself an icon, which, through repeated use as a warning, comes to be interpreted as indicative of warning. Symbols are signs that can be interpreted as icons or indices, but the activity needed to interpret them as symbols requires reflection. Symbolic interpretation involves discovering an implicit pattern in relationships among indices, or among other symbols. This pattern is recognized through reflection on the relationships, and the sign for this association is a symbol. The required reflection on what is already known is self-consciousness.

In the light of Deacon's view of the human as the symbolic species, we will look for the basic symbols of morality within the birth of humanity.

The Origin of Value

A moral value is the goodness, or badness, attributed to a person, behavior, or entity by a moral judgment. Moral value in the present context is not the monetary worth or exchange value but the developmental worth. That which is good supports development; that which is bad impedes development.

In the more complex animals, the satisfaction of a basic developmental inclination appears to be associated with some feeling of satisfaction; after a good feed a dog or cat or lion or chimp appears to "feel good." This might simply be the amelioration of the earlier pangs of hunger or the feeling of satiation that elicits a shut-down of consumption before dangerous levels are reached. In more complex animals there also seems to be some more positive feeling of comfort and contentment—satisfaction as well as satiation. This positive sensation associated with the satisfaction of an inclination, even if it is no more than the amelioration of the negative sensations that trigger the inclination, could be remembered, and this recollection could itself reinforce that inclination and be, consequently, developmentally beneficial.

Whatever this relatively positive sensation is, it is not above the level of index. Just as a signal, in the wild or in the laboratory, regularly associated with the availability of food can become an indicator of a meal, so too this feeling regularly associated with having had a meal could also become such an indicator. The animal's recollection of the difference in feeling before and after eating could reinforce its inclination to eat.

The same kind of feeling of satisfaction could be regularly associated with the satisfaction of other basic developmental inclinations: feelings of warmth, repose, security, sexual satisfaction, and the like. Each of these indices is associated with its correlated object, and the nature and intensity of each will be a function of the inclination and its survival value. The animal will be aware of each of these indices; indeed, it is this awareness that makes them effective reinforcers of the inclination. But none of these is captured by self-consciousness—none is symbolic—at this stage. The association of each index with its reference is independent of each of the others, although, of course, the feelings themselves and their physiological origins would probably be interrelated.

Consider now one of our early ancestors, within whom is developing, at an embryonic level, the capacity to reflect on her own thoughts and feelings. There would have been an emerging recognition of the pattern among these indices and their associations. Some of the feelings associated with eating, finding shelter from the cold or from a predator, having rested, having mated, were recognized as similar; although they refer to different objects, they evoke similar feelings within the individual.

Whatever symbol would have emerged in the mind of our ancestor to associate with these similar relationships would have been the origin of our concept *good.* A full stomach is *good.* Being warm is *good.* Being rested is *good.* The concept *bad* could follow quickly. The pain of an empty stomach is *bad.* Feeling cold is *bad.* Being exhausted is *bad.* Because the references are to the satisfaction of the inclinations of organisms that are in a precultural environment, they are virtually all developmental; that is, they themselves have evolved because they contribute to the biological development of the organism. Even inclinations that we consider to be *bad,* such as infanticidal inclinations that could have been present among our ancestors, are, within the context of evolution, possibly developmental and, if so, could be associated with *good feelings.* We must not let our present ideas of good and bad obscure the essential significance of the claim that developmental inclinations are at the origin of these concepts. At its beginnings, and even though a product of self-consciousness, the content of the concepts of *good* and of *bad* is determined by natural selection. If this sounds like a premise for biological determinism, let me hasten to add that, just as the emergence of life itself immediately began to alter the conditions within which life evolved, so too this emergence of morality in the form of these embryonic concepts of *good* and bad began to dramatically change the environment through the creation of culture. That, however, is a subject that we will turn to a bit later.

How clear these symbols would be at the start and how long it would take to articulate them does not matter at this point. Obviously when I use *full stomach* to capture one of these sensations I do not suggest that *stomach* or even *full* was a clear symbol. The beginnings of humanity were the beginnings of human symbols, and it is difficult for us to grasp the significance of that, although reflecting on the very early development of a child can help. What matters here is that these symbols, these concepts, have been born. There is, in the early human community, a symbol *good* that can be associated with any number of sensations. What is important to emphasize now is that this concept of *good* is the progeny both of basic developmental inclinations and of self-consciousness, self-consciousness being the capacity to reflect on the feelings associated with the satisfaction of these inclinations.

Each of these progenitors is a sine qua non. The symbol *good* is not simply a more complex or developed version of the indices of *good feeling* associated with the satisfaction of inclinations. It is something essentially new that cannot be explained by or reduced to these indices and their associations alone. Self-consciousness, the capacity to reflect, must be an integral part of the explanation. Similarly, *good* is not simply a creation of self-consciousness, or of any cognitive activity alone, including reason. It emerges from both self-consciousness and natural developmental inclinations.

I proposed in Chapter 1 that morals have to do with *values* and *obligations,* with what we believe to be good and bad, and with what we, consequently, believe we ought to do and ought not to do. The emergence of the concepts of *good* and *bad* is the origin of *value.* Before saying more about this we should look at our early ancestors to see if we can find the origin of the other component of morality: *obligation.*

The Origin of Obligation

Animals are aware, inter alia, of food and water. If they are also aware of hunger and thirst, they will consume the food and water. The awareness of hunger is an awareness of unpleasant sensations that trigger a search for and/or consumption of food. This process continues until the animal is satiated, or satisfied. The activities that can be isolated for analytical purposes are the sensation of hunger, the seeking of food, and the consumption of food to the point of satiation and/or satisfaction. The correlation among these activities arose through natural selection. It is obvious that an animal that could not feel hunger, or one that felt hunger but never reacted to it, would be selected out of the process rather quickly.

Along with the awareness of a *good feeling* from which the symbol *good* arises, there was the awareness of the object of the inclination, such as food or shelter. For the "symbolic species," Deacon says that symbols, "don't just represent things in the world, they also represent each other" (99), and their indexing capacity is distributed among references and their relationships (83). Reflection on the strong correlation between the symbols for satisfaction and the symbols for the objects of the inclinations would result in the application of the concept *good,* which arose from reflection on the feelings of satisfaction, to the objects that give satisfaction: *food is good; shelter is good.*

But where does the symbol *inclination* itself come from? It seems to me that *inclination,* at least as I am using the concept, would not have been an object of basic awareness. Animals would be aware of the sensations associated with hunger, thirst, cold, a predator, and the like. Each of these would elicit the appropriate reaction—a search for food, shelter—all of which would require awareness of these objects. The *eliciting* itself, the activation of whatever program within the organism has evolved to satisfy the need, would not itself be an object of cognition.

For the most part an animal is aware of only what it needs to be aware of. A lobster, living in cool water with little temperature change, has no need to be aware of boiling water and so probably feels no pain when thrust into the pot. Most animals do need to be aware of food, shelter, mate, and predator, and so these are objects of their cognitive activity.

To what extent animals are aware of appetites, sensations related to deficits in what is needed to develop, or the sensations of needs satisfied would depend on the advantage that such cognitive activities would give them. But, in any case, it seems that the triggering of the activities required to satisfy needs, which should not be confused with sensations related to deficits such as hunger pains, is probably not an object of awareness. This eliciting of activity to satisfy a development need is the *inclination*; therefore *inclination* is not an object of awareness and therefore not an index. The concept of *inclination* probably did not arise along with the concept of *good*, itself a symbol derived directly from a set of indices.

Nevertheless, *inclination* is now a symbol,[4] so it did obviously arise, and *how* is more important than *when* for our purposes. We will never know what exactly happened in those early millennia of humanity but perhaps it was something like this:

From the indices of the sensations associated with the satisfaction of development needs emerged the symbols/concepts of *good* and *bad*, as proposed above. These symbols were then, through further reflection, distributed to the objects of the inclinations. Then, whether within days, years, or centuries, the unperceived inclination itself emerged through reflection on the correlation between the concepts *good* and *bad* and the inevitable and powerful urges to get what is good and escape from what is bad: the attraction to food, warmth, and mate, and the repulsion from hunger, temperature extremes, and predators. There would be no clear concept of inclination, propensity, tendency, urge. Whereas *good* referred to a set of specific objects such as this piece of meat or that leeward cove—longtime distinct objects of basic awareness—the new symbol might have been only a vague notion arising from reflection on a process that to this day remains obscure. But in some way the developmental inclination itself, the driving force of the whole process, would have been captured by self-consciousness and become a symbol—perhaps as follows.

There would be simple awareness of the indices of elements of the inclination process. Raised to the self-conscious level there would be symbols of the objects of awareness and of the values associated with them. These, in general terms, would be: feeling of need/bad; object of inclination (which will satisfy need)/good; satisfaction of need/good.

There would be many of these mutually reinforcing progressions and further reflection could initiate a primitive idea of negating *bad* and moving toward *good.* I feel hunger pains/hunger pain is bad; I am inclined toward this food/food is good; food satisfies me and ameliorates my hunger pains/satisfaction is good and is the negation of bad.

Obviously, there would be no clear concepts of negation of negation. The point is that the inclination toward food is being pushed to the symbolic level by both positive and negative factors. Eventually, after perhaps long development of the value symbols, the symbol for the value of inclination itself joins self-consciousness: "It is good to get food; I ought to get food."

The *ought* captures the value of the inclination to do or get what is good. This is the association of the *ought* with *value.* But there is nothing whimsical, arbitrary, or subjective about this value judgment. The inclination is a fundamental requirement for survival and development; it *must* be followed if development is to continue. It was being followed, necessarily, before its symbol emerged. The progression from *bad* to *good* is a consequence of a most fundamental law of evolution. It is developmentally good to get food; therefore I must get food. The ultimate importance of the inclination founded on survival itself forces the concept of *obligation* into the *ought,* even if only in a vague and equivocal way. We will clarify the value and obligation dimensions of the *ought* further with the help of Figure 3.

For purposes of analysis, a developmental inclination has two distinct elements. As developmental, its object is something *good* for development; its object has developmental *value.* As a inclination it has the *power* to move the subject toward that object. This is felt and articulated as

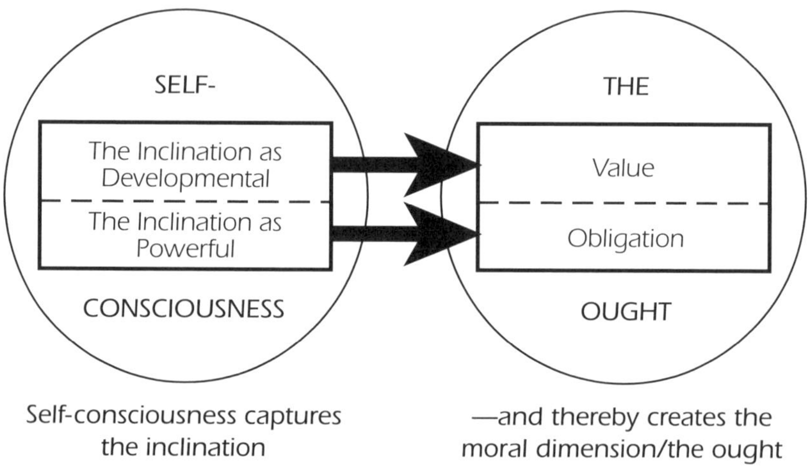

Figure 3.

obligation. When these two elements of the developmental inclination are captured by self-consciousness the *ought* is created. The *ought* is the self-conscious, human articulation of the value and power of developmental inclinations. "I ought to eat" expresses, at its roots, the value of eating and the strong urge to eat; I must eat to develop, and if I do eat I will develop, and that is *good.* The element of *value* is the understanding that this object of a developmental inclination is *good*; this is the normative element, discussed above. The element of obligation—I *must/should* do this—is the self-conscious recognition of the power of the inclination; it is the understanding that, because this is good, I have some obligation to do it—what I would call the *self-conscious moral feeling.*[5]

If the inclination is selfish, then each associated value is *good-for-me,* and the obligation is to oneself. When self-consciousness captures an altruistic inclination, the result is an *open ought*: an *ought* that encompasses a value that is *good-for-other* and a sense of obligation to other. The biological inclination to feed a child becomes "I ought to feed my child," encompassing both "It is good to feed my child" and "I must feed my child."

Before probing further, I should note the obvious fact that the clear and explicit statements representing the elements of morality above are for analytical and illustrative purposes rather than a literal account of the birth of the *ought.* People sometimes make explicit statements like those above, but usually the judgments of value and the feelings of obligation are not articulated, and when morality emerged, since language also was only beginning, explications of the *ought* would be rare indeed.

The basic biological altruistic inclinations are reinforced and expanded in their transcendent variants. As early self-conscious parents began to *know* their children as *other,* the biological drives whereby organisms care for other members of their community would have been gradually enhanced by this self-conscious awareness of obligation to others. The powerful biological bond would be recognized, felt strongly and deeply, reflected upon, profoundly understood.

A human mother knows that she loves her infant as surely, as clearly, and as distinctly as one could know points on a Cartesian reference frame, even though the substance of her understanding is infinitely more profound than the latter. Whereas the genetically programmed inclination to eat lingers on in obvious and active partnership with the transcendent propensities that emerged from it, the human inclination to be open in some cases, such as a mother's love for her child, seems to supersede its genetic forebear. Does any of the biological drive still exist in the strong bond between parent and child today? It seems impossible to know to what extent the biological affinity now operates, but I suspect that the transcendence effected by self-consciousness has transformed it to a much greater extent than it has other affinities. But whether or not the biological drive still plays a part in such transcendent interrelationships, it did inform them at the start and provided their natural foundation.

Parental, familial love might have been the setting in which transcendent openness emerged and developed, but as it developed it would have expanded its range. The human is not restricted by kin or reciprocity as factors of selection. The self-conscious human can choose objects of openness and motivations for openness. These choices can include kin and reciprocity, not as factors of selection but as objectives, and can also encompass many other objects and motives. These choices might be conditioned by the biological dimension and virtually always will be influenced by culture, but their range is global and their motives include the whole selfish-altruistic spectrum.

The important consideration here is that development inclinations in humans transcend their biological forebears in the range of their objects and meaning of developmental, and in their motives.

The Empirical Dimension of the *Ought*

Having put forward this hypothesis on the origin of the *ought* we should now expand our compass to include the other necessary dimension in the human development process—the empirical. Morality emerged as the capturing of our developmental inclinations by self-consciousness. But this process was, like all such evolutionary processes, not isolated. Emerging symbiotically with it was the enhancement and expansion of techniques for development elicited also by self-consciousness. This requires the empirical dimension: knowing what *is*. The *is* and *ought* dimensions of the process are integrated and iterative, but, as argued above, they are distinct, and for purposes of analysis we can view them as two dimensions of the process.

I have proposed that the origin of morality is to be found in the set of inclinations that increase the probability of development. I *believe* that I ought to eat and I ought to feed my child because I *know* that eating is required for development. If I didn't know this my eating would be determined by the biological inclination alone and there would be no symbols for reflections on the objects of *ought*. Why do I believe that I ought to eat? Because I know that I need food to develop and I believe that I ought to develop. The hypothesis "if I have no food I will not develop" is easily tested empirically, leading to the empirically based conclusion "I need food to develop." These empirical propositions in themselves do not flow immediately from the inclination to eat. They arise from cognition: from an understanding of the relevant concepts, from the creation of hypotheses, and from empirical hypothesis testing, whether in an informal or formal scientific mode. The moral dimension, however, does arise directly from the inclination; the proposition "I ought to eat" is a self-conscious articulation of the inclination itself.

The moral and the empirical are very different, and yet neither would exist without the other. The substance of the normative comes from the empirical. Why "I ought to eat" rather than "I ought to whistle all Wagner's operas backward"? Because I want to develop and I know that the former is necessary for my development while the latter probably is not. What it is that I ought to do relative to any chosen goal or objective is an empirical question. The belief itself that I ought to do anything is not empirical—not in any way testable; it is for this reason that I use *believe* rather than *know*. The *ought* comes from the inclination but its object is empirically determined; the *ought*, having its origin in inclination rather than cognition, cannot be reduced to the *is*;[6] nevertheless, there is no *ought* without a knowledge of what is. Conversely, however, an empirical investigation, from the simplest observation to the most complex scientific study, would not be initiated without an *ought*. Whether an explicit statement—"we ought to study this"—or an implicit feeling that it would be good to know something, every empirical exploration must be initiated and directed by a normative judgment and a feeling of obligation. There is no knowledge of what is without first an *ought*. And this whole iterative process is within the context of and guided by the perceptions of development of individuals-in-community.

Morality Is Born

The central lesson here, if the above exploration is at all valid, is that concepts of *value* and *obligation*, that is, the essential elements of *morality*, emerged with humanity itself, from within the evolutionary process. Self-consciousness brought them into existence through reflection on natural developmental inclinations. The original form—and I emphasize *original*, because self-consciousness and then cultures would soon begin to modify it—was determined by natural developmental inclinations. Self-conscious feelings, not reason, rational calculation, or deduction, brought them into existence.

The early value symbols could have been quite clear and distinct; however, the foundations for the concept of obligation would have been then, as they are to this day, vague and ambiguous. But the power and importance of the reality underlying all these embryonic symbols came from eons of evolution. These self-conscious feelings were not subjective or arbitrary or capricious, and clearly they were not the product of the rationalizations of philosophers. They were necessary agents in the emergence of humanity, informing the special character of that emergence, and continuing, along with human culture, to enable human development. Humanity was born, and morality, as an essential agent of human development, was born along with it.

The Social Dimension of Morality

If self-consciousness arose as hypothesized above, that is, through the internalization of social communication within a relational community, then some of the earliest reflections were probably on the self as related to but distinct from other. I have insisted that natural altruistic developmental inclinations are integral components of evolution. Furthermore, if self-consciousness and its symbols are derived from society, then, according to Deacon, "Consciousness of self in this way implicitly includes consciousness of other selves" (452). The awareness of the needs of others and the propensities to behave so as to help satisfy these needs would also be objects of reflection.

De Waal's research leads him to conclude that some of our contemporary primate cousins recognize self and other as distinct and have "cognitive empathy," that is, know what other, as a distinct other, feels. "Perhaps some species evolved social organizations in which it became particularly advantageous to appreciate how companions were doing—not just at an emotional level, but also by imagining their situation. Sharper awareness of the other entailed increased self-awareness."[7]

Although they can appear anywhere, an obvious place to find altruistic inclinations is in the relationship of parent and child. The animal mother's, and often father's, blind, genetically driven urge to nourish, to shelter, to protect offspring, even when this threatens the well-being of the parent, is common to most of the larger and/or more complex species. We, and perhaps some other primates, feel satisfaction in helping one another, and these good feelings might have also been the indices reflected upon to associate altruism with *good.* A most obvious case of this is the mother's feeling of pleasure associated with nursing; this *good* feeling, because of its intensity, could have been a starting point for the reflections of the donor.

This feeling should, however, not be confused with the inclination to help another. Any good feeling that happened to develop in association with an altruistic act would reinforce the inclination but would not *be* the inclination. Nor would this be the starting point of the altruistic behavior. The progression of the altruistic behavior would be the same as the progression for the other inclinations, except that it is initiated by the *other*—by the recipient—and, consequently, the intensity of the signal that would trigger the process would usually be weaker than a signal emanating from within. As I did in the cases of the basic selfish inclinations, I will focus here on the signals that probably were the most intense, guessing that they would have been the ones first interpreted through reflection as symbols. Consider now these two cases from the perspective of intensity:

- Selfish inclination: mother needs nourishment; mother feels hunger; mother seeks nourishment; mother eats; mother feels satisfied.
- Altruistic inclination: child needs nourishment; mother is aware that child needs nourishment; mother feeds child; child feels satisfied; mother is aware of child's satisfaction; mother feels satisfied.

The signals that produce the awareness of the need of other in the altruistic case are less clear and obvious than the signals of the need of the self in the selfish case. My awareness of my hunger pains or feeling of fear are greater than my awareness of your hunger or fear. This difference is no doubt a disadvantage that altruism has had to overcome, and it could be a reason for the apparent preeminence of selfishness. Nevertheless, we know that the human capacity to be open to the needs of others can be great indeed, and, as de Waal has found, there could be a natural awareness of both the needs and satisfaction of needs in others. Within the primordial human community, this awareness of the situation of others would have been reflected upon, and perhaps related to the corresponding feelings of the self and to the altruistic inclinations and, in time, was articulated. Along with the ideas *I, food is good* (value for me), *I need food, I ought to eat to satisfy my need* (obligation for me) would develop the ideas *you, food is good for you* (value for you), *you need food, you ought to eat* (your obligation to yourself) and then, reflecting on whatever experience is associated with empathy and the propensity to be altruistic, *I ought to help you to eat* (my obligation to you).

Both the selfish behavior and the sacrificial behavior of the vampire bat are genetically determined. In the human, however, self-determination develops along with self-consciousness. If a bat is hungry and encounters appropriate food, it will be driven by its genetic program to eat. A hungry human, having the same need for nourishment and biological urge to eat as the bat, is capable of choosing not to eat even if confronted by the most delectable dish. Similarly, a human can choose not to comply with the propensity to help another in any particular instance. Self-consciousness gives us the capacity to override our natural inclinations, to control our natural tendencies, often to a very considerable extent. We do still *react* to environmental conditions according to a genetic code, but we also *respond* by controlling the extent to which, and the way in which, our biologically determined inclination conditions our behavior. The biological inclination is still determined by biological structures constructed by genetically programmed interactions with the environment, but the inclination itself is no longer the sole determinant of behavior; the *self* becomes a major determinant, hence, we have self-determination or freedom.

A human can move a given behavior along the selfish-altruistic spectrum. For example, eating, normally a purely selfish act, could be for a mother nursing an infant also an altruistic act. She might choose to eat food she detests because she believes it to be good for her child. Similarly, an apparently altruistic act could be actually very selfish if the only motivation is to gain personal benefit from it. In other words, self-consciousness creates the capacity to transform the attitudes and inclinations of behaviors from open/altruistic to closed/selfish, and vice versa, or, as would more usually be the case, to add selfish or altruistic overtones to the genetically conditioned characters of behavior. This might suggest that, because of self-consciousness, human behavior would tend to be a blend of open and closed inclinations and attitudes. The cooperation Dawkins speaks of would be an early and essential instance of such blending.

A mother's biological urges to care for herself as well as her progeny and others in the primordial community were still strong and remain so to this day; the essence of freedom is not simply to choose to resist these natural propensities, but more importantly to know that such a choice is possible. The self, even when accepting a powerful urge, is free in that acceptance.[8] The heightened awareness of the caring relationship would itself reinforce the biological tendency; the profound *I-Thou* bond created by self-consciousness could increase the possibility of overriding selfish inclinations and intensifying altruistic tendencies. In a community in which an awareness of the needs of other had evolved through natural selection, the self-conscious dimension could reinforce that biological process. If a non-self-conscious altruistic behavior increases the survival chances of the genes that induce that behavior, then more of those genes and more of that behavior will survive. Self-consciousness could further increase those chances of survival, thereby having an impact on the biological process. Indeed, because culture and our physiological base are so interrelated, our constructed culture has a continuing impact, sometimes positive and sometimes negative, on our evolution by sexual and/or natural selection.

Self-conscious control would also increase the probability of altruistic behavior being extended to a broader community: to those without close genetic ties, to humans in any part of our planet, and, a growing tendency today, to other species. Kin and reciprocity were probably major factors in the evolution of altruism, but the altruistic inclination itself is not limited by such factors, and self-consciousness and culture effect an expansion of the objects of our natural altruistic tendency. If altruism toward distant others became so pervasive that the local community began to suffer, then natural selection could emerge as a natural check and balance.

A Note on the Biological Dimension

We began this discussion of the birth of morality in the context of self-interest: what is good or bad for the self and obligations toward the self. This is the context in which morality probably emerged. Then we explored the altruistic side of morality: what is good or bad for others and obligations to others. I have attempted to present the biological foundations for all of this, but perhaps a more explicit comment on the biological dimension of morality, and especially of value and obligation as they relate to others, would be in order.

The question is what biological change, in terms of the neo-Darwinian synthesis, is required for the evolution of morality, and how can it be explained?

The biological base for all our self-conscious activities including morality is our large, complex, plastic brain. Our brain is about three times as large as the brain of the chimpanzee, and perhaps also about three times as large as the brain of the common ancestor we share with the African apes, who lived about five million years ago. Most of the growth in our brain occurred between that time and 100,000 years ago. Because contemporary apes and some other mammals seem to have a rudimentary self-consciousness, I have assumed that our ancestors became self-conscious early in that five-million-year period, but at least some time during that period of brain growth. It would seem however, that self-consciousness remained in a rudimentary state throughout the long period of brain growth. Evidence of development benefits flowing from self-consciousness appears well after our brain stopped growing. Geoffrey Miller says:

> Technological innovation was at a standstill during most of our brain evolution. Only long after our brains stopped expanding did any tradition of cumulative technological progress develop, or any global colonization beyond the middle latitudes, or any population growth beyond a few million individuals. Arguably, one could not ask for a worse correlation between growth in a biological organ and evidence of its supposed survival benefits.[9]

Evidence suggests little technological change during much of the Palaeolithic period. Simple stone tools from the Lower Palaeolithic, as early as 2,500,000 years ago, have been found, indicating some level of self-conscious development at that time. The hand axe appeared about 700,000 years ago. The Upper Palaeolithic, from about 40,000 years ago, provides evidence of communities with greater complexity, more specialization, a broader range of tools, and art work, which varied by region. Cro-Magnon, very much like us modern humans, lived at this time. During the Neolithic period, starting about 10,000 years ago, the human dimension—technology, agriculture, domestication of animals, art, religion and other cultural developments—began to accelerate at a greater rate.

It is reasonable, in light of the evidence, to hypothesize that there were glimmers of value symbols and perhaps even of obligation during the Lower Palaeolithic, but that an articulated morality, that is, moral symbols entering into language and discourse, would not have appeared until the Upper Palaeolithic or Neolithic periods. Miller claims that sexual selection is required to explain this acceleration of human evolution after the growth period of the human brain. He writes:

> I shall argue that some of our most valued moral virtues had no survival benefits, but they did have strong courtship benefits. . . . A sexual selection perspective allows us to explain sympathy, agreeableness, moral leadership, sexual fidelity, good parenting, charitable generosity, sportsmanship, and our ambitions to provide for the common good. (293)

I accept Miller's argument, but I think there are other explanations as well. I think that qualities such as sympathy—knowing other and the needs of other—and good parenting could also be explained by natural selection. But another explanation, complementing rather than contradicting sexual and natural selection, is also possible.

Let us suppose that the human brain—the brain that supports self-consciousness—developed to approximately its present size, complexity, and structure before the human dimension, including morality, moved beyond its rudimentary state. It could be hypothesized that the brain at that stage of development was capable of supporting self-conscious development up to its present level. This is especially the case given the plasticity of the human brain. Little or no biological development, and, consequently, no explanation in terms of selection, would be required. I will use once again the example of the human dimension of eating to illustrate.

The strategic behaviors of non-self-conscious animals for getting nourishment evolved through selection, perhaps mainly natural selection. Depending on the plasticity of the brain, most if not all new behaviors would be related to a physiological development of the brain or other part of the animal and would be subject to selection. Consider, however, the human dimension of eating. New and varied strategies for producing, getting, preparing, and eating food could all be supported by a Neolithic or even an Upper Palaeolithic brain. If a biological change in the structure of the brain is needed for new behaviors, they could be supported by the continuing development of our plastic brain interacting with its environment for years after birth. But in many if not most cases no change would be required. Given the brain that I have and my capacity to learn and reflect, I can grow a broad range of vegetables in my garden and know how to plant and harvest several grains and grasses. I can get food from my garden, from any number of supermarkets and farmers' markets, and from restaurants. I can cook a wide variety of meals, serve them in different ways, and associate them with various celebrations. I can enhance my food production and preparation by reading, taking courses, or getting information from relatives and friends. Because I am self-conscious, I can do any of these things without genetically induced changes to the structure of my brain. Taking into account their more limited resources, our early self-conscious ancestors could also have expanded their alimentary repertoire without further evolution of the brain.

The same should be the case for moral behavior. Once the brain had developed sufficient plasticity to support self-consciousness at a level that created a broad range of symbols and an effective language, without further change it could sustain moral development perhaps indefinitely. Once a human is able to understand value and obligation toward self and other, there should be no biological limit to the application of that understanding to new and changing circumstances.

Quartz and Sejnowski's neural constructivism, discussed above, supports this view. Unlike the popular position that the development of the brain after birth is simply an increase in innate, specialized circuits, neural constructivism presents evidence to support the hypothesis that evolution not only produces specialized structures for cognitive activity but, more important, effects flexibility that allows the brain to adapt its structure and function through interactions with its environment for many years after birth. If this is the case, then it could be argued that once the human brain had reached a certain level of development, including flexibility, some 100,000 years ago, the development of the brain of each individual after birth, through interaction with the environment, provides the biological foundation for human behavior, including morality.

Evolution does not produce a specialized cortical structure with a part for learning value, another for obligation, another for moral leadership, and so on. These are learned within the context of the given environment, including the culture, and if neural development is required to support this learning, it takes place also through interaction with that environment. There is a genetic base for all this, but that base itself has induced the evolution of a brain that can reflect and whose structure adjusts to a given environment within each individual, so that the consequent judgments and behaviors respond to the particular culture and escape from the determination of that genetic base. We can now return to our focus on the human dimension itself.

On Love

In a social, relational community, interrelations are myriad and vital. In our ancestors' primordial community, as genetically determined interrelations became the object of consciousness, determinism was gradually transferred to the self. Among the many interrelations that self-consciousness would capture were instances of "cognitive empathy" and sympathy,[10] of openness. Their openness to one another and the needs of one another was an intermingling of understanding and willing, more profound than any rational calculation and more constant and intense than any self-centered drive. This free openness to other is best referred to as *love.* It is clearly not a sexual or sensual attraction, for these are founded on egoism: on a drive associated with instant gratification. Although they often mingle at the level of behavior, love as self-conscious openness and love as sexual attraction are radically different in that the former arises from altruism and the latter from egoism; both, of course, contribute to human development.

Self-consciousness creates the choice to modify our inclinations, but as it intensifies our interrelations, it also introduces a new determinism—the determinism of freedom itself. The truest, most intensely self-conscious love—a total mutual openness between free humans—would comprise one choice only. The human mother freely cares for her child in that she can override the biological determinism of the natural inclination to provide care. In most cases, however, we know that her self-conscious choice will be only to care for her child; that choice will not be determined by her genetic program but it will be determined by her self. Other human relationships based on love are likewise self-determined.

My definition of *love* needs to be clarified and perhaps defended. The question is: is this a useful definition? Does it capture this vital and profound interaction of the real world in a way that helps us to understand and communicate?

Love is commonly used to refer to the feelings, the emotions, that are associated with a whole range of attractions, and especially the feelings arising from sensual and sexual attraction. Because feelings are discounted and marginalized, love as a feeling tends to be diminished. As I have insisted before, however, there is nothing more profound, more important, and more certain than a self-conscious feeling of openness toward another human. To say this does not imply a totally new meaning of the word. *Love* is often used as a symbol for the disinterested and profound altruistic, benevolent, potentially sacrificial attitude and inclination of one person for another, as when people speak of the love of a mother for her child, or the love of God for Her creatures. This meaning is very different from love as related to the selfish pleasures of sex or other instant gratifications.

What basic reality would I attach the term *love* to? What does "I love you" mean? Using the concepts developed above, "I love you" means: I know you as other, as good in yourself and not only as good-for-me; I know your real needs; I want to help you to satisfy these needs, even if it requires sacrifice on my part; I want to give myself to you; accordingly, I behave in a nurturing and sacrificial way toward you. In other words, *love* is an open attitude, an altruistic inclination, and a caring, nurturing behavior—each of these elements being self-conscious—of one human to another.

The feelings of pleasure associated with love do, of course, exist. Pleasure can enhance and even reinforce love and as a reinforcer would have played a necessary role in the evolution of love. Referring to these associated feelings of pleasure *as love*, however, obscures the reality beneath them. Within the present model, these feelings/emotions are clearly not the cause or source of love. Love arises from the attitude of openness and its associated altruistic inclinations, captured by self-consciousness. The foundations for the attitude and inclination are genetic. Self-consciousness is the source of their transcendent human dimension—of true human love.

I use *feeling* to refer to an immediate and usually strong awareness of an object or of a state of one's own being. I have objected above to the rationalist tendency to marginalize *feeling* and insisted that self-conscious feeling is a profound, pervasive, and ultimately necessary form of human cognition. My concern with the common emphasis on *feeling* in definitions of *love* is that it directs attention to feelings that love elicits, but that are themselves not foundations. The attitude of openness is a cognitive foundation for love and as such could itself be an immediate self-conscious understanding of the object of love and hence, because not the product of deduction or induction, could be called a *feeling*. But this feeling is a deep, reflective, and responsive awareness of the beloved as good and deserving of love, and not a superficial, reactive awareness of the pleasure that a loving relationship induces.

Feelings can encourage or discourage behavior. Good feelings, like those associated with love, would reinforce the attitude and inclination simply because humans like good feelings. In the example used above, nursing provides physical pleasure, which reinforces the mother's altruistic inclination to nurse, but the pleasure is not the source of the inclination and is distinct from it. Furthermore, in virtually all cases, the human mother who knows her child and his or her needs does not require such reinforcement. A new human relationship, however, might rely heavily on feelings of pleasure to get it going. The love that develops might be pushed forward by feelings of pleasure, but it arises from the cognitive attitude of openness and the altruistic inclination. The feeling of pleasure can be a very important catalyst, but it is no more than a catalyst.

Nurturing behaviors arise from natural inclinations, but not necessarily only from altruistic inclinations. Many warm-blooded animals huddle together to conserve and share body heat, though in most cases not because of altruism induced by cognitive empathy. There are, nevertheless, behaviors that relate to the needs of others and have no apparent egoistic foundation; the sacrificial behavior of the vampire bat is an example from the non-self-conscious realm. The human parent is aware of the needs of the child and wants to help to satisfy these needs, and this self-conscious inclination overrides any pleasure or pain associated with the helping behavior.

There is no self-interest or benefit-cost analysis at the heart of these acts. There is an immediate and profound understanding of the needs of this child, of what must be done to satisfy these needs, and of the intense desire to do it. There is, in other words, the natural openness, but now raised to a transcendent level by self-consciousness. At some point in the development of reflection, the recognition arose that the inclination to help the child is altruistic—that the child is of no use to the parent and is probably a threat. The inclination is to help the child, not because it is good for the parent to do so, but because the child is good in her or himself. Our primordial human would not have articulated this clearly and I have no idea how it would at first have been understood, but there is no doubt that the altruistic inclination was captured by self-consciousness during the process of its development.

The pure altruistic act has been held up as a moral ideal. This is the act for another without any consideration of the benefits to the self, without any ulterior motives. It is an act that flows from an understanding of *other* as good in his or her self, rather than as good for me.

It follows from the above that the understanding of other as good in her or himself is as natural as is the perception of other as a means to my ends. If both human selfishness and human altruism are transcendent versions of genetically based tendencies, then neither is naturally preeminent and any imbalance in their respective incidence might suggest a bias that is a human construction. The *realist* could be correct in describing his/her part of the world as dominated by self-interest, but wrong in assuming that this is a natural condition. If, indeed, rational self-interest is the dominant force in modern industrial society, then rather than accept this as natural and inevitable and seek its explanation in contrived states of nature, we should look for the real source and consequences of its dominant position. If the real source is found in cultures, and if these cultures deviate significantly from a natural balance, then the consequences could be serious.

Why Is Love Important?

Why is this dissertation on love important to the present argument? Because it presents this openness to others as natural, fundamental, and necessary for human development. It is natural because it is born of natural developmental inclinations captured by self-consciousness—itself a product of evolution. It is fundamental because it is a development of the genetically induced basic awareness of other and consequent inclinations, and these activities lie at the base of the evolutionary process. This is not a subjective, superficial, whimsical, arbitrary feeling or emotion. It is necessary because it is a development of one of the two sets of communication and inclination that drive the process itself. When it comes time to discuss our "state of nature", love will have to take its place alongside the selfish side of the human—the "nasty" and the "brutish," rather than be marginalized as just a romantic feeling subject to whimsy and belonging by the hearth.

This discussion of love is especially important to our exploration because it moves this component of human life from a peripheral, ephemeral and ideal place to the real, effective, and permanent center of human development.

Chapter 5
Culture
Our Transcendent Environment

Culture has been discussed above in several contexts and its importance within our human beginnings and development has been emphasized. Here we will focus on the meaning, origins, and development of culture itself.

I have defined *culture* as the total human environment constructed by self-conscious humans. Using their capacity to reflect, humans create symbols, languages, morality, techniques, art, science, institutions, infrastructures—in a word, *cultures.* Cultures, in turn, become ever more significant and powerful conditions for further human development, both at individual and community levels.

Culture as Transcendent

Throughout this exploration I talk about transcendence. For the human individual, self-consciousness is a transcendent consciousness. For the community, culture is a transcendent environment, constructed by self-conscious individuals-in-community. At the outset I defined my use of transcendence and stressed that, as I use it, it has no preternatural or supernatural connotation. Now is a good time to return to it for further elaboration of self-consciousness and culture as integral but transcendent parts of the natural process of human development. To clarify my view of this process and to emphasize that it is both natural and transcendent, I will draw an analogy between culture and the origin of life.

Transcendence is a natural part of the evolutionary process. Like Theodosius Dobzhansky I use the term to refer to a transformation within the process in which radical change occurs leading to a new kind of development, so new and different that it cannot be explained simply in terms of the process from which it emerged. Reductionist explanations are precluded.

An analogy can be seen between the emergence and evolution of life and the emergence and evolution of humanity. Reflection on this analogy can help us grasp the transformation that begot the human community and understand it as a transcendent continuation of the evolutionary process.

Life is a continuation of the development of the complexity of matter/energy. Once it has emerged, however, it introduces a new kind of development to the process—evolution by natural selection—that greatly expands the potential of the process. There is continuity with the past but also a transformation. Evolution by natural selection is a new kind of interactivity between organisms and their environments that cannot be explained simply in terms of greater complexification. In a similar way, self-consciousness is a continuation of the development of consciousness, but, like the emergence of life, it transformed the very process that gave it birth.

Self-consciousness perhaps changed little and did little for centuries or millennia. The evidence from the Lower Palaeolithic period (about 2,500,000 to 200,000 years ago) suggests that there was minimal progress in tool-making during this relatively long period. Culture was born but remained virtually static for about two million years. Then, in the Upper Palaeolithic (from 200,000 years ago) and on into the Neolithic (starting 10,000 years ago), the development of self-consciousness and culture began to accelerate. The variety of tools increased, art and religion emerged, as did dramatic new techniques such as agriculture, and regional variations in tools and art imply that different cultures were developing.

The Inheritance of Acquired Characteristics

Like life itself, self-consciousness introduced inheritable change, but of an even more effective sort. The progeny of an organism inherit the genetic changes of their parents; they do not inherit physiological characteristics acquired by their parents during their lifetimes. Self-consciousness, through the symbiosis of the relational community, developed symbols and languages by which what was known and believed could be communicated, and through learning the cognitive and moral characteristics acquired by each generation were passed on to the next. This accelerated the development of construction by human self-consciousness: the knowledge, the beliefs, the techniques, the productions from all of these: science, art, morals, institutions, goods, and services—in a word: *culture.*

Biological evolution is a slow process. Genetic changes in a organism happen randomly throughout its life—a shot of radiation here, a chemical reaction there, a free radical at the right place at the right time—and those that are included at the time of procreation will be inherited and will induce some physiological change in the offspring. Natural and sexual selection will then do their job. Chance genetic changes are followed by the usually slow process of selection or, as is more often the case, rejection.

By comparison, cultural evolution is fast; Figure 1 above suggests exponential growth, and the evidence would seem to support that. One generation of humans begins where the previous left off, more or less, whereas each new generation of most living organisms start from scratch. Unless there has been a mutation of the "nest-building gene" in a parent, a bird will build virtually the same nest as the parents, and so will its offspring, and so on. When we humans learn, however, the acquired knowledge and beliefs of previous generations are included. Einstein did not have to begin where Newton did; his contribution to culture was based on the cumulative science up to his time, including Galileo, Newton, Michelson, Morley, Lorentz, Maxwell, Planck, and countless others. Einstein acquired their characteristics (at least those that he found useful or interesting) and then went on from there. They, of course, had done likewise.

The scientists noted above plus many others made up Einstein's theoretical physics culture—the scientific environment in which he developed as a scientist. He had many other interests and so had many other environments within which to develop. He drew on these cultural environments, and he contributed to the continuing construction of culture.

I am not sure why I chose Einstein as an example here. He is a worthy one and well known, and I have heard the "Einstein sitting on Newton's shoulders" analogy several times, but I do not want to suggest at all that "great men" are the main contributors to culture. Most of our cultures, and probably the parts that really matter, were constructed by the billions of women and men whom history texts ignore. The environment that sustains our physiological life, including the oxidizing atmosphere, was produced by billions and billions of organisms, during four billion years, from the simplest ancient bacterium to our present flora and fauna. The cultural environment that sustains our cognitive and moral life was and is being produced by billions of humans for the past hundreds of thousands of years. Because of its exponential growth rate, of course, much of our interaction is with recent cultural constructions, but just as primordial cells within us and around us still have efficacy, so too the full sweep of culture over space and time can interact with us.

Culture, Cooperation, and Communication

Life evolved through the efficacy of cooperative interactions. Symbiosis produced the large, complex, internally differentiated cells that gave the process a major push forward. As Richard Fortey says, "The world is full of symbiosis."[1] De Waal's relational model applies throughout the process. Or, in Tattersall's words, "functional complexes cannot and do not exist in isolation."[2] To what extent is this true of culture?

The factors that induced the emergence of culture and then its accelerated development are the factors found throughout the evolution of life. Alison Jolly identifies these as follows:

"The attributes of living organisms, as they dawned within the primeval slurry, are cooperation, communication, and differentiation of the parts, a boundary between self and not-self, and self-maintenance and reproduction."[3] These primordial factors, raised to a self-conscious level, are what enables the development of individuals, communities, and cultures. Cooperation and communication are essential for the development and sharing of ideas and techniques, within a community and from generation to generation. Differentiation of the parts of a community, in response to the needs of the community, gives rise to effective and efficient divisions of labor. The "boundary" must be understood within the context of a relational community; it allows individual differences and initiatives to work cooperatively for the good of community. And, of course, individual survival and development and the reproduction of the community are the sine qua non of development.

These factors in the development of all living things are by definition developmental. If humans had raised these to a self-conscious level without reducing their developmental efficacy, then our world would be a very much better place. Early cultural change must have been biologically developmental because it would have been linked closely to the biological evolution from which it emerged. But self-conscious agents are not determined by biological foundations, and human freedom has allowed some developmentally negative factors to creep into communities and cultures. Jolly proposes "four huge new factors": material greed; the storage or transfer of surplus production; social status, which allows some individuals to command the labor of others and appropriate their surplus; and the power of ideas (402).

Most would accept that material greed is both increasing and dysfunctional. The amassing of wealth and social status, as Jolly presents them, are related as factors of *power-over*: the power of domination discussed above. The power of the patriarchy and of capital are seen by many to be good and natural, but as they appear in virtually all human cultures, they are human constructions and probably to a great extent antidevelopmental. The power of ideas, I would say, encompasses the whole construction of cultures, and can, of course, be used for good or evil. Jolly is concerned about our species' *hubris*: inordinate pride in our capacity to control/dominate nature (404). Ultimately, the control of nature cannot go beyond limits that nature itself fixes. If we do not understand this, then we could do ourselves serious damage.

Biological evolution has a Hobbesian side; even the loveable bonobos can be nasty at times. But, as de Waal has discovered, aggression in ape communities is usually followed by reconciliation and is part of the development of relational communities. We humans have not used the immense developmental advantage that self-consciousness gives us to improve on the conflict resolution found in other species and, probably, in our primordial ancestors. There are conflicts between cultures and within them, and these have been causes of violence, regression, and war. Some conflicts today appear to be irreconcilable. The power of ideas in the garb of ideology—sets of strongly held beliefs that have little or no empirical or moral foundation but that strongly control behavior—is a major culprit here. Ideology divides and in many instances kills. The torture and murder of innocents has been and still is justified by ideologies, and often by ideologies that center on a divinity. Religion that is informed by a bond between a loving God and Her creation, and bonds among Her creatures,[4] and that eschews doctrine and dogma which divides and enables domination—virtually always patriarchal domination—could be a positive moral developmental force in a community. It is not easy to find such a religion within any culture.

The conflict of ideas need not be dysfunctional. This and competition are significant factors in cultural development. Dialectical development is most obvious in the development of ideas and techniques, but also in art and institutional and moral development. Rather than juxtapose competition and cooperation as if they were two sides of a coin, I would prefer to see them both within the context of an interrelated organic and often symbiotic system. Here I would draw again on de Waal's relational model and his discovery that, in primate communities, even aggression can play a role in maintaining and developing community relationships.

One major difference between biological evolution and culture is this: Within biological evolution, natural selection maintains checks and balances on the system. For example, aggressive behavior is kept in check and made developmental by the cycle of *relationship-aggression-reconciliation-relationship* recognized by de Waal.[5] This cycle flows from behaviors that have been selected because they induce fitness. Cultural development is not determined by selection. Checks and balances can arise within cultures to ameliorate dysfunctional development, but the question is how is *dysfunctional* defined? It is not defined by the biological dimension but by each community, and it is possible that one community would accept behavior and consequent development that other communities would consider most dysfunctional. Nazism is one obvious example. In such cases other communities can intervene and indeed have intervened. Beyond this, as I have proposed above, *nature* itself, even if not through the strict process of natural selection, sets ultimate parameters beyond which a community's behavior cannot go without doing itself serious damage. Ecological limits are an obvious example.

Culture is, then, the cumulative creation of self-conscious individuals-in-community. It is at base the creation of communities acting cooperatively and symbiotically, although conflict is always present within the relational context. Culture is the continuously constructed environment within which humans live, and as such it conditions all behavior and its own continuing construction. Communities have their own cultures, but communities interact and influence one another, the mutual influence increasing with increasing communication. The direction that a culture takes is conditioned by its definition of development (implicit or explicit). This can be constrained by checks and balances from within the community, from other communities, and, ultimately, directly by *nature. Natural* constraints or parameters are analogous to natural selection; the differences are that they are one set of constraints among others, the others arising from within cultures, and they themselves can be influenced and pushed outward, to some extent, by self-conscious communities.

Culture and Values

I have proposed above that *good* would initially be associated with the immediate feeling of satisfaction and then with that which satisfies development needs. Eventually development itself would be recognized as the common factor; it would be seen as itself good and as the basis for all other value judgments. A symbol encompassing all that is required for development would probably have emerged at a time by which there was significant cultural development. The objects of the basic biological inclinations, food, shelter, and so on, would be joined by other objects constructed by self-conscious agents—cultural values—and would share with them the symbol *good.*

To the extent that cultural values were closely associated with objects of biological inclination, those inclinations would elicit responses to them. A Seder, for example, is a cultural creation with historical and religious roots, but, as a nutritious meal in a social setting it also satisfies basic biological inclinations. Many other cultural values, however, would offer little or no satisfaction of this type, and some, such as fasting, would conflict with basic inclinations. Education, propaganda, and coercion would be employed to establish these nondevelopmental and/or dysfunctional cultural values, as well as the related and constructed definition of development.

The impact of culture on value is very difficult to deal with. On the one hand, I claim that there is continuity between the biological and transcendental processes. Concepts of *good* and *bad*—of value—arise from the biological, and then these symbols encompass the transcendent dimension of human development. Furthermore, the biological dimension is ever-present and influential, and sets parameters for cultural development. On the other hand, although the cultural dimension never completely escapes from the biological, it is truly transcendental. It is conditioned by, but not determined by the biological; it influences and modifies the biological; it pushes outward the biological parameters that constrain it. Its values range from re-creations and modifications of the biological to those that are radically different and sometimes opposed, and the methods of institutionalizing them include association with biological inclinations, training, education, propaganda and various forms of coercion.

Our exploration has led us to the hypothesis that the origins of the two elements of morality—obligation and value—are the capturing and articulation by self-consciousness of developmental inclinations, their objects and their satisfaction. Developmental inclinations are, of course, toward development needs. Our biologically based needs continue, however, the emergence of self-consciousness creates new human needs—transcendent needs—which we will consider now.

The Emergence of Transcendent Needs

I have proposed that morality emerged through the capacity of the first humans to reflect on needs and on inclinations to satisfy those needs. Humans at first would have the same basic physiological requirements as their non-self-conscious ancestors. It is a fact, however, that we humans now have a range of needs that goes beyond those related to physiological development. Precisely when and how these needs arose in the course of human development no one can say, but we know that they have emerged. Because they are to a great extent influenced by cultures they vary from culture to culture and time to time. There are strong central tendencies among them, however, and they can be identified by reflecting on the central characteristics of human development.

As soon as it emerged, self-consciousness gave rise to a new dimension of development that, like physiological development, has specific requirements. The capacity of the individual to reflect, understand, reason, evaluate, and judge, to relate to others and to culture, to develop in ways that are naturally sound and socially and culturally acceptable—these aspects of human development thrive only to the extent that the individual has training and education, free mobility and association with others, and free expression, is recognized, respected, and responded to by others, lives in a healthy and pleasing environment, and has some say in the development of her or his community.

Transcendent needs arose from both our selfish inclinations and our propensity to openness. The distinction between self and other would have been grasped; other would be known *as other.* In many cases, *other* would be seen as a requirement for the satisfaction of the needs of *I*, as a means to selfish ends. But openness, as an altruistic, self-sacrificing tendency, would elicit a recognition of other as good and as an end rather than a means. What we might now call the highest human needs flow from this. The recognition of other as other would lead to the feeling of a need for our interrelations with other as other, that is, a need for love, for community, for communication, all because these relationships are good in themselves, as ends and as means to self-development.

Other transcendent needs appear to arise from both selfish and altruistic inclinations. From the need for community arises the need for free association and mobility, and free expression. Empirical evidence abounds supporting the claim that humans cannot develop as humans without association with other humans;[6] for this, mobility within one's community is required. Language and communication develop, and, in communicating with others, it is also clear that one must be able to express oneself freely.

As self-conscious communication evolves, the value of truth, of honest and sincere verbal and other symbolic interrelations, is recognized; truth becomes a need. Form beyond the purely functional is recognized, appreciated and enjoyed, and beauty becomes a need.

The quintessentially human concept of purpose emerges and with it reflections on individual objectives and goals. From this arises the need to have some control over one's own destiny and the need to work to secure what is required to meet one's objectives.

These transcendent needs place emphasis on the individual's need for self-determination within a community context. There is much empirical evidence that biological needs are real needs for physiological development. What kind of evidence would tend to confirm similar claims about these transcendent needs? Is there evidence of an inclination to *self*-actualization through *social* activity. We could go further and seek evidence of an inclination to work, that is, to produce what is required to meet objectives and goals, and not simply "to be employed"; the desire to be in control of one's production process; the desire to identify with one's product. If we have such needs, would their frustration impede human development itself?

I believe that every real need, including the transcendent needs, can be confirmed empirically. I am not able to provide sufficient evidence to confirm the reality of all transcendent needs, but I will, by way of example and illustration, touch briefly on some evidence from psychology to support the hypothesis that the broad and central need for self-actualization in a social context is a real need; that is, its frustration impedes human development.

Throughout the past century there has been a tendency in Western psychology to explain human behavior in terms of stimuli and responses, needs and drives—of organisms reacting to and driven to master their environment. More recently, however, individuals' beliefs, expectations, preferences, and decisions have played a more prominent role is theories of behavior.[7] As Martin Seligman says, "Personal control has become scientifically respectable."[8]

The stimulus/response approach reduces human behavior to a rather mechanistic biological level and is not unlike the Hobbesian view of individuals as isolated point masses physically interacting in space. The new emphasis on personal control, on concepts such as locus of control and self-efficacy, shifts the focus away from mechanical drives and toward cognition and reflection on inclinations by a self-conscious individual. It also focuses on the power of the agent to respond,[9] rather than on the reactions of somewhat inert things. This shift in emphasis is, I would suggest, a move away from the Hobbesian model and toward a vision of the person that is more compatible with ours. The personal control theories attach much greater importance to self-efficacy: to the power of the active and self-conscious agent. Furthermore, in this set of models greater significance is attached to the interactions among individuals and with environments and these interactions are more organic, less mechanistic, than in the stimulus/response theories. The object of their study is more the individual-in-community than the individual-in-isolation, and *power-with* as well as *power-over*.

Noting that these trends in Western psychology are toward greater compatibility with the present view of humanity and away from the dominant Western approach[10] might be a first step in suggesting the possibility that our hypotheses have some merit and that looking at more evidence could be worthwhile. Within the context of personal control theories there is some relevant evidence.

People do seem to feel better when they are, or believe they are, in control of their activity. Empirical research has associated the feeling of not being in control with motivational and cognitive deficits, low self-esteem, and affective deficits such as anxiety and depression.[11] An important aspect of these findings is the interrelationship among control and the various deficits, especially motivation and self-esteem. Self-esteem is not a need but a feeling that arises in someone who controls her or his own activities and that, in turn, may contribute to that control.

Although much of the empirical work in these studies has focused on control of specific tasks or situations, there is some indication of similar associations between lack of control and these deficits in larger, institutional contexts.[12] Seligman claims that the large increase in unipolar depression in the United States reported in several major studies is largely the result of "the waxing of the individual and the waning of the commons."[13] He links his own conclusions on the correlation between depression and lack of control with the maximizing, inward-looking "California self," isolated and without the support of a true community. "So individualism without commitment to the commons produces depression and meaninglessness on a massive scale" he says (94). The solution does not appear to come easily to Seligman, however, because he sees the problem within the Western individualism/communalism dichotomy in which control should be associated with the autonomous individual. He calls for "a balance between individualism, with its perilous freedoms, and commitment to the common good" (95).

This would appear to be the kind of balance that this exploration sees as developmental. I would suggest that the depression and meaninglessness arise from an autonomous, isolated individualism that frustrates the development of the individual-in-community. The health and self-actualization of the individual depends on her or his development within a relational community. That isolation destroys the human spirit has been well documented, from Itard's Wild Boy of Aveyron to the present.[14]

The above, clearly, is not intended to be a complete listing and confirmation of needs arising from self-consciousness. I simply want to make two points: first, the emergence of self-consciousness gave rise to new kinds of needs and new dimensions of old needs, both of which in turn created conditions for a new kind of development; second, the claim that these are real developmental needs can be empirically confirmed.

These new needs reflected the social nature of their origins and integrated this with the radically new development requirements of self-conscious, purposive humans, who could reflect on and wanted control over their destinies. All this happened over very long periods of time, in many and diverse communities, with success and failure, progress and regress, sudden breakthroughs and critical setbacks, but, obviously, it did happen.

Biological and Transcendent Needs

We should now distinguish further between biological and transcendental needs. To help clarify this holistic and integrated picture of the human we will focus our analysis, as I have done before, on the biological and transcendent dimensions of one very basic and common need: the need for food. The basis for my need for food is obviously biological. In spite of our transcendence, this need in itself cannot be removed or fundamentally changed. This biological need remains essentially the same, but, at the same time, is integrated with the transcendent dimension in many ways.

Like nonreflecting animals, I am aware of hunger pains, but, unlike them, I can reflect on them and know that, indeed, say that, "I am hungry." I also know what will satisfy my hunger, what is pleasing to my taste and what isn't, what contributes to health and what would promote disease, what is readily available to eat and what is scarce. I can ponder what to have for my next meal, how to prepare it, with whom to share it. I can recall the flavors and aromas of some past meal and I can know the pain of starvation, immediately or, for most of us in Canada, vicariously. I can know about restaurants that prepare delicious meals and I can know about famine.

The original biological need for food now sits essentially unchanged at the base of an interrelated set of transcendent needs and wants that arise from the above reflections. I can articulate the biological need: I *need* protein, carbohydrates, vitamins, fluids, anti-oxidants; I *want* fish, potatoes, broccoli, and green tea. The articulation of this need already associates it with the transcendent level, where it can be integrated further with several transcendent needs. For example: I need nourishment and, with it, a bit of propriety and decorum; I want poached salmon, boiled new potatoes, and broccoli with cheese sauce, all served on plates, with knives and forks and the standard Western conventions. Or, I need nourishment and I need association with other humans; I want to eat salmon, potatoes, and broccoli with my family. Or, I need food and I need to be creative; I want to prepare a gourmet meal of salmon with fine herbs and all the trimmings. Or, I need food and I need to have some control over my destiny; I want to have a say in our government's agricultural and fisheries policies.

Although these needs/wants transcend the biological, they are based on biological needs in whole or in part. None of the above examples would exist without the biological need, but they cannot be reduced to the biological need; even though this example is of a most basic biological need, the transcendent dimension is clear. A pack of hyenas devouring carrion and a group of friends sharing epicurean delights are satisfying that same basic need for nourishment, but the transcendent dimension that has emerged from this need's integration with self-consciousness and its creativity cannot itself be reduced to that need.

There are, of course, also transcendent needs/wants that are less dependent on or less closely linked to biological needs—some that are, perhaps, not linked at all. Self-determination and self-actualization needs, flowing from purpose and discussed above, would appear to transcend the biological dimension completely. I heard Midori, the outstanding violinist, say during a television interview that she needed music just as she needed food and water. "Without my violin I just wouldn't be me," she insisted. This is a clear case of a transcendent self-actualization need for transcendent survival and development. Midori (she uses only one name) needs food and water to survive and develop physiologically. But Midori is not just a physiological being. She, within the context, the opportunities, and the constraints of her culture and her physiology, has created a Midori who, inter alia, is a superb violinist. The total Midori needs a violin to survive and develop as Midori, just as much as she needs water and food. She was not speaking metaphorically when she expressed her need for music.

Human Needs and Value

We now can return to the central question of value and the status of value or normative judgments within the present context of the evolution of needs, again using the same very basic need as an illustrative example.

The biological appetite that drives me to satisfy my need for food is essentially the same as that found in all animals and, indeed, in plants. I, however, know that I have this appetite, and I know why I have it: I know that I must have nourishment to develop. I share with other organisms other basic propensities for what is needed for biological development. I know these propensities, and I know that they are propensities for what I require if I am to develop as a human. I also know that without satisfying these needs, and therefore without the appetites that drive me to satisfy them, I could not develop. I can articulate this knowledge in empirical propositions: for biological development I need *x* protein, *y* carbohydrates, *z* fluids.

But I can also articulate the need in a nonempirical way. I have proposed above that the first humans would have used their newborn self-consciousness to reflect on needs, on inclinations to satisfy those needs, and on feelings of satisfaction, and develop ideas of *good*—of *value*. They would eventually be able to think and say that it is good to have food. The proposition "I need food if I am to develop" is clearly empirical;

the link between food and development can be demonstrated by empirical tests. There is no test, however, to confirm the proposition "It is good to have food." This proposition is normative. It expresses a value judgement, a belief that it is good that I eat. It arises from the empirical fact that food is necessary, but is itself not a statement of that fact, but instead is about a value judgment, a belief. Being a belief, however, makes it neither gratuitous nor arbitrary. As I have proposed above, *value* emerged from the reflections on the objects and satisfaction of basic needs in the earliest human communities. As such, beliefs about what is good or bad are as necessary for development as empirical knowledge and are even more fundamental.

Those normative beliefs that are physiologically developmental are all related to the inclinations for physiological requirements for development. They severally and together imply that development is good. This more fundamental belief that *development is good* is not often articulated, but is the foundation for the rest.

As soon as self-consciousness appeared, culture was born, and with culture the transcendent needs discussed above. Just as the physiological needs are associated with values and value judgments, so too are transcendent needs, but the association is very different. Physiological needs are determined by the evolutionary process, whereas transcendent needs are constructed by humans (although often conditioned by the process). During the early years, perhaps millennia, of our ancestors' development, most needs and values would have been physiological and simple cultural variations on the physiological. The cultural variations could include methods of food preparation, ways of keeping warm, approaches to security, and the like. These would vary from community to community; distinctive cultures would have arisen at an early stage of human evolution, as indicated by regional variations in art and techniques.

Gradually some of the transcendent needs discussed above would appear. They could be initiated broadly by the community, by groups within the community, or by influential individuals. They could be closely or more distantly related to physiological needs. Some might have little impact on development and would be better called *wants*. Some new needs/wants determined by culture could be dysfunctional when measured against physiological requirements. In virtually all cases, once a value, whether physiological, cultural, or a mix of these, has established itself within a community, it will be taught to its progeny.

The development goal and objectives of a community are defined by its set of physiological and cultural values. That which satisfies basic physiological needs will always be valued in a developing community, but the variations on these plus the transcendent needs/wants will make the community distinctive. Variations that break the parameters set by the physiological base, however, will impede development.

The Construction of Culture

Morality is born into a community that already has direction— not a mechanical, fixed and determined direction, but a broad set of tendencies that statistically center on development within the existing environment. What is *good* and what is *bad* is not arbitrary. The relativity of values is circumscribed by the ambient circumstances. And given the fundamental inclinations upon which morality is based, *good* from the outset includes both *good-for-me* and *good-for-other.* This, I must repeat, is of critical import to my hypotheses. I believe that the common Western belief that only *good-for-me* is the natural condition has led to vast confusion and much of the obfuscation of morality discussed just above because of the futile search for other than natural foundations for *good-for-you.* Rawls reflects this quandary so clearly in the following: "The difference between the sense of justice and the love of mankind is that the latter is supererogatory, going beyond the moral requirements and not invoking the exemptions which the principles of natural duty and obligation allow."[15]

Rawls, following the mainstream Western tradition, removes love of humankind from his rational principles of justice, from moral requirements, from the *natural.* He sees natural principles as products of the rational maximizer, whereas I would say that the rational maximizer is but a small part of nature and hardly a producer of its significant principles. I would also say that the love of humankind does not go beyond moral requirements but is one of their real foundations, as well as being the human foundation of obligation. Rawls's discussion of undefined feelings and sentiments in an attempt to rescue his position is an inevitable consequence of his faulty and unnatural "original position."

The primordial human community would have begun to construct its culture—its moral systems, its institutions, its science, its techniques, its art—on the empirical and moral foundations it was also beginning to build. At first, behavior was still dominated by the biological base, for the construction of culture was just beginning and the humans' newfound understanding of their world had not yet made its impact. It is within this context of biological domination that culture and its moral dimension, including moral systems related to rights and duties, of justice, first emerged. This biological base already includes, entrenched within its "natural principles," the inclinations that will become moral goods associated with and defined by human development, and thereby encompassing from the outset both the good for the development of the self and the good for the development of the other.

The elements of the primeval systems—the raw materials from which justice evolved—would have been the first ideas about *what is*, evaluations of *what is good*, and moral judgments on *what ought to be*. These empirical and normative elements would have been only recently formed and so would exhibit the tentative, hesitant, and experimental character of infancy. We must keep in mind, however, that they would have rested on very solid foundations indeed: on millennia of development constantly checked by natural and sexual selection. Although lacking in form—the transcendent form gradually created by self-consciousness—they had a surfeit of substance, accumulated from their long evolutionary journey.

As noted above, this imbalance of nature over nurture, of the entrenched and powerful physiological drives over the initial embryonic traces of culture, would have maintained a level of biological determinism over the infant human community that would have been little different from the era before self-consciousness. But once self-consciousness had entered the process, no matter how unpretentiously, its development and its effects were extraordinary. As suggested in Figure 1 (p. 19), the growth of these effects—the expansion of the constructed culture—was, and still is, exponential, shifting the control of the process, also at an exponential rate, from the biological base to the self and to culture. At the beginning of the exponential curve, however, neither the greatness of human culture nor its distortions and degradations were present to compete with the biological base for command.

In exploring these beginnings, the complexity, variation, and profundity of the developmental and dysfunctional dimensions of millennia of cultural construction can be ignored; we can focus on what the riches of the evolutionary process would have brought to bear on its remarkable new creations: self-consciousness and culture.

With no Hobbes, no "realists," no economists, no dominating masculine ideologies or institutions, the altruistic inclinations still had pride of place alongside the egoistic ones. These inclinations had not yet suffered from the dysfunctional aspects of cultural construction; they would necessarily be, except for any mutational deviations not yet selected out, developmental. In other words, the transcendental manifestations of the basic developmental inclinations emerge in a virtually pure developmental form. As these inclinations began to be enhanced by their union with self-consciousness, however, they also ran the constant and growing risk of being distorted by that same union. Self-consciousness and self-determination enable individuals and communities to deviate from the natural developmental parameters. Murder is an obvious example of an individual deviation. The emphasis on and glorification of competition, and the consequent marginalization of cooperation, is an example at the community level.

Cultures surround us now but were not a part of the original condition. We must not commit the anachronistic sin of projecting contemporary culture, or any culture, onto our image of our beginnings, onto our *state of nature*. Our beginnings are the beginnings of culture.

Culture as Developmental

I have proposed that *developmental* is the criterion for value: for *good* and *bad*. This is nonproblematic within the context of biological evolution; *good* means no more than that which increases the probability of survival/development. At the cultural level, however, it is not so simple. *Good*, I would suggest, still means developmental. But the meaning of *developmental* itself varies from culture to culture, over space and time. It is defined by the goals and objectives of cultures.

Does it follow that human values are totally subjective and relative? I would say not. The variation in cultures and their values is both considerable and significant; however, in spite of the freedom found in self-conscious construction, the biological base both influences and limits these constructions. In general terms and in the long run, cultural values must encourage behavior that is life enhancing, or, at least, not life threatening, if the community is to develop. Unfortunately, cultures can be dysfunctional but not dysfunctional enough to trigger biological constraints, at least in the short run.

Values can have direct biological bases, or can arise from sources within a culture such as religion, myth, tradition, folklore, and the like, or can be the progeny of both of these. In many cases cultural values are compatible with and probably were informed by biological requirements. The sanctity of life and the need to support and enhance life are common values in all cultures, although the associated goals, means, and expressions vary greatly. To illustrate this we will reflect on the cultural values promoted by some religions.

The ten commandments, well known in the Western world, include a number of admonitions that are developmentally sound even from the biological perspective. "Thou shalt not kill" is an obvious example of an expression of a value that has biological foundations and is consequently objective and absolute. The Christian New Testament command "Thou shalt love thy neighbor as thyself" is an order to be open to others and their needs and thereby enhance their lives as you would enhance your own life: a positive command that reflects the selfish-altruistic balance in the biological dimension. The developmental community should accept this also as an absolute. In the Decalogue are other commandments that support development: "Thou shalt not steal"; "Thou shalt not bear false witness"(lie). Some others are not developmental for the whole community, for example: "Thou shalt not covet" followed by a list of a man's possessions: house, wife, servant, handmaid, ox, ass, or anything that is *his*. Here three groups of humans—wives, servants, and handmaids—appear to be objects owned by a man, rather than persons, and not even worthy of having the command directed at them. If we strip the command of its patriarchal, power-over-other character and its rejection of natural *I-Thou* relationships, then we are left at least with some good advice: don't spend time eagerly longing for things clearly beyond your reach or to which you have no claim.

The Buddha's decalogue has governed behavior in similar fashion for ages in the East:

> 1. Kill not, but have regard for life. 2. Steal not, neither do ye rob; but help everybody to be master of the fruits of his labor. 3. Abstain from impurity, and lead a life of chastity. 4. Lie not, but be truthful. Speak the truth with discretion, fearlessly and in a loving heart. 5. Invent not evil reports, neither do ye repeat them. Carp not, but look for the good sides of your fellow-beings, so that ye may with sincerity defend them against their enemies. 6. Swear not, but speak decently and with dignity. 7. Waste not the time with gossip, but speak to the purpose or keep silence. 8. Covet not, nor envy, but rejoice at the fortunes of other people. 9. Cleanse your heart of malice and cherish no hatred, not even against your enemies; but embrace all living beings with kindness. 10. Free your mind of ignorance and be anxious to learn the truth.[16]

The commandments of the Decalogue from *Exodus* are negative: "Thou shalt not . . ." The Buddha's decalogue joins each negative command with a positive admonition: "Kill not, but have regard for life." Overall this decalogue is developmental for a whole community and across cultures; the values it promotes are virtually all objective and absolute. Direct, positive developmental commands such as these are fairly common across cultures.

The importance of community is an obvious and central doctrine of the Judeo-Christian tradition. The Buddha proclaims the same message in the East:

> Having pointed out to the five bhikkhus the truth, the Buddha said: "A man that stands alone, having decided to obey the truth, may be weak and slip back into his old ways. Therefore, stand ye together, assist one another, and strengthen one another's efforts. Be like unto brothers; one in love, one in holiness, and one in your zeal for the truth."

Supporting my emphasis on the importance of balance, Confucius sees the balance of egoism and altruism to be natural: "Be true to your nature and treat others as you treat yourself." Living according to nature—the Principle of Heaven or Nature (*T'ien-li*)—the human becomes a person of virtue (of *jen*), conscientious (*chung*) and altruistic (*shu*), balancing and harmonizing the self and the community.[17]

The Qur'an commands openness beyond kin: "Show kindness unto parents, unto near kindred and orphans and the needy, and unto your neighbour who is your kin and your neighbour who is not your kin." (Chapter II)

Many within the dominant Western paradigm, believing that only the egoistic side is natural, emphasize the need for altruism to be commanded: "We are commanded to love our neighbor because our 'natural' attitude toward the 'other' is one of either indifference or hostility."[18]

Perhaps one of the more significant deviations from our evolutionary foundations in the morality of many cultures and especially major religions is the preoccupation with the isolated act. The notion of a sin as a specific act is a powerful moral influence. Murder, rape, and theft are, of course, specific acts that are antidevelopmental and morally bad. Development as a process, however, points to the significance of the behavioral trend in the moral judgment of human development. We might say that a person is good to the extent that her or his responsible behavior tends, over time, to be developmental, for self and community. If a community is to be viable, the central tendency of the behavioral trends of its members must meet the basic requirements of biological, social, and psychological development, as the evidence presented above indicates, as well as the particular developmental norms of the culture.

A healthy community can withstand occasional aberrant behavior, but it is obvious that major deviations from developmental behavior by a few, or minor deviations by many, or combinations of these will threaten development. Checks and balances control dangerous excesses. Flagrant threats to development that virtually all abhor, such as murder, are forcefully checked in all communities, although in many societies some members, and especially women, are injured and killed in the name of cultural, and usually patriarchal, principles.

The responses to more subtle threats to development may arise as a gradual shift in cultural values. Cultures promote smoking as enjoyable, manly, sexy, a symbol of autonomy, especially for children and women. Nature counters with cancer and cardiovascular diseases. Humans respond by devaluing smoking. Western cultures promote sun-tanned skin as healthy and beautiful. Nature counters by darkening some skin further with melanoma. Culture responds, not so much by devaluing tans, but by valuing potions that block ultraviolet radiation.

This is not to suggest that the biological controls are perfect or even always adequate. Cultures promoted big cars with big engines as symbols of manliness and power. Nature countered with an impressive array of environmental threats. Cultures responded for a while by devaluing the big car and engine. Now corporate culture responds with even larger SUVs with even larger engines, and sells them, with great success, as values associated with the very nature they harm. Whether or not the high value placed on this and a huge range of conspicuous consumption by the wealthy elites of the planet will be controlled in time to prevent irreparable ecological, or even psychological and social damage is an open question. The point is that the fundamental inclinations for biological development set limits on the values and consequent behavioral trends that human communities construct, and when these limits are broken, nature exacts a price. If the cultural response is not adequate, then the price nature exacts will rise. Humans construct their many and varied cultures, but not arbitrarily, or capriciously, or with impunity. Serial killers, rapists, despots, and megalomaniacs set on conquest do arise, but as aberrations. If their inclinations represented the trend line in a community and the central tendency of its behavior, its extinction would quickly follow. Many behaviors threaten the social, psychological, and environmental health of communities, and the biological base reacts by actualizing those threats.

What we might call the *truly human* values, that is, those highly valued behaviors that are signal creations of our self-consciousness—love of other as other with no selfish motive, honesty, love of beauty and the capacity to create beauty, profound understanding, highly tuned rationality—transcend our biological foundations to the greatest degree, but the association with those foundations is not severed. In fact, it is when one sees the biological connection that the true transcendence becomes most clear. This is especially the case with regard to love. As noted above, there is a strong tendency to associate love with sexual attraction and often reduce it to egoism; however, if we understand love in the context of biological evolution we see that the reduction of human love to the sexual is not at all appropriate.

If we recall the altruistic behavior of the vampire bat we see a case of open, sacrificial behavior that is not at all associated with sex. Love, I have proposed, is the transcendent form of this fundamental openness that determines much animal behavior. Sexual attraction, on the other hand, appeals to egoism—to the desire for self-gratification. The basic sexual determinants can be raised to a self-conscious level by humans, thereby becoming human responses as well as biological reactions, but this transcendent egoism in itself is not based on the same kind of inclination as is altruistic love. This, of course, in no way reduces the importance of sexual attraction, nor does it refute the obvious fact that in human relations, egoistic sexual attraction and altruistic love often become intimately intertwined. But it does follow that love cannot be reduced to sexual attraction, nor is it associated with it in any necessary or fundamental way. This is a clear indication of how the evolutionary view refutes the common reductionism, materialism and pessimism that is promoted by the dominant Western culture.

Cultural Aberration

Now let us look at a cultural aberration that stands out as an extreme deviation from anything that could be called developmental from either a biological or cultural perspective, and that is abhorred by virtually everyone who is not in its grip. It is a culture that, ironically, claims to be a natural emanation of evolution, but which grossly misinterprets neo-Darwinian theory. I refer to Nazism or National Socialism, the latter term used commonly by contemporary Nazis. I include this reference to it because it is an extraordinary example of the power of a lazy and mediocre human to create an ideology promoting extremely dysfunctional behavior within a community that threatened development in many communities. Its very existence is a refutation of the biological determinism upon which it bases its grotesque dogma.

Nazis claim that the "Aryan race" are superior to all others and that they have the right to defend their race against threats from others. Whatever they say about their defense, the Second World War and related events show clearly what they mean. They claim that the superiority of the "Aryan race" and their right to "defend" it are based on the laws of nature.

The belief in "White" racial superiority has no scientific justification. Difference among peoples can be accounted for by cultural development, and it should be noted that "Whites" have destroyed or seriously damaged many nonwhite cultures, in Asia, throughout the Americas, and in Africa through the slave trade and colonization, for example. The biological dimension of our species, and especially the neural structure that supports self-conscious cognitive and affective behavior, has not changed significantly during the period of greatest cultural development, as has been noted above. Differences among individuals and peoples are a matter of opportunity that enables the actualization of capacity, rather than the capacity itself.

The level of ignorance and deceitfulness of the Nazis is clear in their use of the word *Aryan*. The Aryans were a people who settled in Iran and northern India in prehistoric times. More recently the term was used as a synonym for *Indo-European*. It now refers only to Indo-European languages. During the nineteenth century the idea of an "Aryan race" was promoted. Aryans were credited with all of human progress, and some Germanic peoples considered themselves to be the purest Aryans.

This chimera had been rejected by anthropologists in the early twentieth century, but was used by Hitler and the Nazis to justify the extermination of Jews and other "non-Aryans." The following quotation from Geoffrey Miller provides a pointed refutation to this kind of racism which pretends to be scientific:

> It should go without saying, but I'll say it anyway: all of the significant evolution in our species occurred in populations with brown and black skins living in Africa. At the beginning of hominid evolution five million years ago, our ape-like ancestors had dark skin just like chimpanzees and gorillas. When modern *Homo sapiens* evolved a hundred thousand years ago, we still had dark skins. When brain sizes tripled, they tripled in Africans. When sexual choice shaped human nature, it shaped Africans. When language, music and art evolved, they evolved in Africans. Lighter skins evolved in some European and Asian populations long after the human mind evolved its present capacities.
>
> The skin color of our ancestors does not have much scientific importance. But it does have a political importance given the persistence of anti-black racism. I think that a powerful antidote to such racism is the realization that the human mind is a product of black African females favoring intelligence, kindness, creativity, and articulate language in black African males, and vice versa. Afrocentrism is an appropriate attitude to take when we are talking about human evolution.[19]

We all come from Africa; our ancestors were black. Whiteness is of little biological importance, but, according to Miller, *kindness* was. Kindness means nothing to the Nazis and one wonders what meaning *white* has for them. They killed 5,700,000 Jews who were as white as they are. Variations in "race" are insignificant when compared to variations in culture, and the confirmation of that comes from the extreme deviation of the Nazi culture from the norm.

Nazis justify their aggression and violence also in terms of "the law of nature" and specifically, the "struggle for survival." They interpret struggle in a literal sense and as *the* way of nature. I have discussed this above, noting that Darwin himself used the term in a metaphorical way, and throughout this exploration have shown that cooperation and openness to others are as essential to the evolutionary process as are competition and isolating oneself, or one's community, from others. The Nazi misinterpretation of struggle and the consequent understanding of evolution as essentially a nasty process is all too common and is, indeed, the view within the dominant Western paradigm. The Nazis carried this to ideological extremes, justifying huge and horrible atrocities, and I would not want to associate these evils with the Hobbesian myth in general. Nevertheless, I suggest that this is further evidence that the view of life as *naturally* and *essentially* nasty and isolated, and as an aggressive, competitive struggle for self-maximization, does justify that very dysfunctional behavior, and often glorifies it. This view only rarely induces extremes like Nazism, but it does, I believe, excuse and encourage constant and ubiquitous violence, abuse, and oppression.

Too many people still associate Nazism with the theory of evolution, ignoring the blatant misrepresentation of that theory by the Nazis. This abuse of science and history to support a dysfunctional ideology and give it genocidal power is an indication of how far a culture can deviate from a developmentally sound path. The power that Hitler and his ideology had over so many Germans is shown vividly in the remarkable documentary *Triumph of the Will* directed by Leni Riefenstahl in 1935. The power of culture, the power of ideology, and the power of one human are all demonstrated by the tragic events during Nazi rule.

Another important lesson to be learned from Nazism is that the human dimension cannot be understood through a reduction to its biological base. This cultural aberration could perhaps be reduced to a fictitious Hobbesian state of nature, but not to the real and balanced origins of humanity. Such aberrations are, ironically and sadly, the products of cultural construction.

What lessons do we learn from these kinds of events? We see the power of self-consciousness in generating ideas and ideologies and in shaping cultures. This power, when dysfunctional and antidevelopmental, and reaching the might of Nazism, or Europe during colonization, or the Stalinist era, is not restrained by the biological dimension—at least not in the short term. To have this power we might assume that self-consciousness, language, and communication must be well developed. There are no Hitlers among the bonobos and there probably wasn't anything like him and his ideology until the patriarchy became established (to be discussed later). The early development of humanity and of cultural construction, including morality and justice, was probably within a more balanced context—not simply a struggle or a state of war. The relational, social nature of our non-human ancestors, which we inherited as part of our biological dimension, would have held the power of self-consciousness in check, promoting the construction of developmental cultures. Otherwise, we would not be here today to ponder all this.[20]

The biological dimension is still present and always will be, but there is no guarantee that, except in the long term, it will provide the checks and balances needed to thwart dysfunctional trends. We, as agents of nature, will have to do that ourselves, and, if we are to do it developmentally, we will have to understand the origins from which we have evolved.

Chapter 6
The Origins of Rights

The preceding chapters have laid the foundations for our exploration of the origins of justice. The essential elements of justice are human rights and obligations, and this chapter deals with those elements. Chapter 7 will consider the origins of justice itself.

I have noted above that Rawls and Nozick did not present their *states of nature* as actual conditions in some distant past, but as fictitious foundations for their theories of justice. The problem I see with these foundations, as with other Hobbesian-type states of nature and the related dominant Western view of *man* (from Aristotle, Descartes, Kant, Mill, to Rawls and Nozick), is that they are gross misrepresentations of the natural and original human condition, although less of a misrepresentation of the contemporary Western human condition as it has been modified by culture. In the following attempt to discover the origins of justice and its elements I will avoid views of *human* that are informed by the biases and idiosyncrasies of cultures and, in particular, the distortions of the dominant Western view. To do this I will continue to concentrate on our beginnings, and explore rights, obligations, and justice as they must have emerged from our biological base, without being influenced by cultures. Indeed, I see the beginnings of justice as an integral and central part of the dawning of culture.

We will make use of hypothetical scenarios, but these are not figments of my imagination. They are hypotheses that can be and to some extent have been tested and that relate to real original conditions at real places in real time. Further testing would, consequently, get us closer and closer to the real origins of justice.

What we are exploring here, as we have above, is the transition from a prehuman condition in which behavior was driven by biological forces, to the beginnings of the human condition in which humans were self-consciously starting to use symbols, develop language, reflect on their condition, and construct cultures. Evolution did not follow a simple, linear path, and so there would have been many neonate human experiments over time and space, many failing and some succeeding in various ways. We will have to perform the usual abstractions to make some sense of this complexity and hypothesize about successful transitions from which we evolved.

The range of human characteristics and ensuing behaviors has been proposed in the preceding chapters. Because of the importance of these to our search for the foundations of justice, I will review the salient points.

The quintessential human quality is self-consciousness. The origin of humanity is the emergence of self-consciousness: the immediate awareness of the self and its activities and of its thoughts and feelings. Humans, like other animals, know, but humans also know that they know.

The first humans had, obviously, the characteristics required for the development that had brought them to that stage of the evolutionary process. They had the genetically programmed inclinations that would cause them to do what was needed for their procreation—inclinations directed toward the satisfaction of the needs of the self and inclinations directed toward the satisfaction of the needs of others in the community. Life in this prehuman state was nasty but, obviously, life was not *simply* nasty in any objective sense. It could not have been, given the fact that this community had in fact evolved to this point; if only nasty and selfish as popularly portrayed, life would indeed be short—too short for procreation. It was, as a positive requirement for development, competitive and egocentric, but the necessary and powerful inclination to be open to others and to their needs made this life also nurturing and caring. The balanced combination of egoistic and altruistic propensities, developed over ages of evolutionary experiment, must have been rich indeed to have brought life to this level of sophisticated complexity, flexibility, and capacity for further development.

Most important, this life was never solitary. In both its nasty and nurturing characters it was always an interaction among individuals-in-community. The isolated life was and is a fiction devoid of meaning. Developing communities were relational and social.

A Positive Starting Point

From the above it follows that our starting point is not the negative view of humanity of Hobbes, or the many variations on his theme that inform the dominant Western vision. The emphasis is not on *man* as fallen. It forcefully rejects extreme but not uncommon positions like, in Verdi's *Otello*, Iago's "I am wicked because I am a man and I feel the primeval slime in me." Our essence is not wickedness because the "primeval slime" was in reality rich in immense potential for life and development. I prefer Alison Jolly's description: "The attributes of live organisms, as they dawned within the primeval slurry, are cooperation, communication, and differentiation of the parts, a boundary between the self and not-self, and self-maintenance and reproduction."[1]

The evidence as I see it suggests a *state of nature* in which life was *abundant* in the requirements for *development* including the *concern for self* and the *competitiveness* needed for development and was tempered and balanced by the *openness to others and their needs* required by individuals who were seldom isolated but were *individuals-in-community*. This is a much more positive view of the state of nature than the Hobbesian or Freudian view, or than dominant Western views in general. Furthermore, this positive view is of a nonconstructed human community—of humanity as it arose from its natural sources rather than from a preexisting culture. Some who share a more optimistic picture than Iago or Hobbes or Freud attribute our more positive human qualities to more recent human development, moral and/or religious, seeing nothing positive in our origins.

Those in the Western rationalist tradition, who have not recognized nature's own potential for positive development, have proposed reason, in one way or another, as the source of "goodness" and morality itself. For Aristotle, "none of the moral virtues arises in us by nature;"[2] moral virtue comes of habit and "legislators make the citizens good by forming habits in them," through the rational process of making constitutions and laws. The masses, by nature, respond only to fear, and so, if they are to become virtuous, the noble and rational states*man* must create the system of laws and sanctions that will appeal to their fear of punishment.[3]

Hobbes, two millennia later, presented in even more pessimistic tones the same basic image: "For the Lawes of Nature of themselves, without the terrour of some Power, to cause them to be observed, are contrary to our naturall Passions."[4] Through *reason man* discovers the two basic laws of nature from which the sovereign power originates and rescues humanity "from that miserable condition of Warre" (223).

In this tradition, represented here by Aristotle and Hobbes, our natural inclinations are so sordid that we must be rescued by reason through its creation of law. Kant pressed the point even further by insisting that duty must totally eschew natural inclinations and be found in pure reason.

The present hypotheses, as I have noted more than once, do not deny the sordid side of human nature, nor do they ignore the necessary role of reason in human development. The difference between them and this major Western view, as reflected by three of its most significant spokesmen, is, quite literally, radical. My hypotheses present the *primordial* humans as cooperative and altruistic as well as competitive and egoistic. Furthermore, competition and egoism arise from basic inclinations that are developmental, without having yet been associated with the factors that make life nasty and brutish, which are to a great extent human constructions that disrupt natural balances.

The capacity for good and for right is within the primeval slime; to be *base* is not to be *sordid*. The base of human development was animal development, which, because biologically successful, contained within itself the potential for the prodigious evolution that followed. There is no need, therefore, to seek out a source, an origin, an ultimate explanation for right and obligation beyond the natural process itself. The development of the elements and systems of justice are natural and required supports that order, sustain, and enhance human development. Reason becomes a necessary agent in this development, but it is not its source. The roots of our development were already growing and healthy within the "slime."[5]

The Western negative assumptions about human origins make law and state themselves negative: negations of negation at best. They are seen primarily as controls on our nasty, brutish natural inclinations—on our natural wickedness. These controls must themselves be kept in check and that, for many, is the function of rights.[6] State and its laws protect us from one another; rights protect us from the state.

If, on the other hand, natural inclinations, both altruistic and egoistic, are primarily positive, as they must be for development to have taken place, then law and state will arise, not simply as controls over the nasty side, but more as enhancers of the continuing development process. The claim that law, the statesman, the sovereign, pure reason, or some mixture of these was necessary to salvage our species from vice, from a state of war, from immoral inclinations, and to create whatever virtue and peace we do enjoy, raises a most difficult question: how did our species not only survive the state of war, but develop through it to such an extent that reason, laws, and states were possible? The very fact of this development refutes most unequivocally the negative image of our origins that dominates Western thought, and in so doing it removes the need for anachronistic, mythical, and unfounded explanations of those origins.

Because I believe it to be of considerable importance, this shift in emphasis away from the dominant, inaugural role of the rational maximizer needs to be considered carefully. Indeed, in setting this hypothesis up as one contrary to the Western view in its contemporary form, as represented by Rawls et al., this might be its most important single feature.

I have proposed that self-consciousness is primarily the capacity to reflect on the self and its affective, cognitive, and other activities, on others, on interrelations, on needs, inclinations, and the satisfaction of needs. From this capacity emerge all the characteristically human cognitive activities, including reasoning, which is given precedence in Western society, and the more immediate and profound understanding that is often discounted as *intuition* and disparaged as *feeling*. It is from this immediate and profound understanding of developmental inclinations that, I claim, morality and then rights, obligations, justice, law, and state flow. Morals, rights, duties, and the self-conscious order that would have been the birth of law all developed concurrently, interactively, organically, and symbiotically with all of the other embryonic effects of self-consciousness, including the development of our capacity to calculate and our propensity to maximize.

There could not have been a time when humans were humans but morality, rights, and duties did not exist. There could not have been, in the beginning, a selective evolution of only the selfish inclinations and only the rational techniques of self-consciousness that then, within the state of war such asymmetry would surely produce, constructed the Leviathan and saved the day. Morality, science, technology, understanding, feeling; concern for self, concern for others; developmental inclinations and dysfunctional inclinations—all these are elements of one integrated process, and all of them were constituent parts of that process from its conception.

If all this is the case, what might we expect to emerge from a human community during the early stages (measured in millennia) of its transition and transcendence from the prehuman? Reflection is widespread throughout this early community, language is developing, morality is established. Symbols are vague, but the growing repertoire of empirical and moral concepts is an evolutionary advantage. There are trends and central tendencies that are influencing development, perhaps as follows.

The Emergence of Human Rights and Obligations

At this time in our ancestors' early evolution, both the empirical and the moral dimensions of infant humanity are developing. Individuals are understanding and sometimes articulating their basic needs and their propensities to satisfy them. "This is food." "I need food." These empirical reflections are new in their form but not in their content. The certainty that this is food and that it is needed rests on eons of evolution;

the inclination is established and precise even though its articulation is new and imprecise. The science that will, through experiment and reason, connect nutrition to life in great detail is still distant, but the understanding of the need, its urgency, its import, its value, is immediate and profound.

Associated with this understanding of needs and of what will satisfy them is the self-conscious and intuitive awareness of the inclinations themselves, their objects and their satisfaction that I have claimed to be the origin of morality. From these moral feelings would arise the self-conscious feeling of claim. For purposes of analysis, we could divide the claim into these components:

- "I need this": the empirical understanding;
- "it is good that I have this": the moral judgment;
- "I ought to have this": the embryonic, obscure notion that "I have a right to this."

To each of these propositions the phrase "for my development" can be added.

We must keep in mind that these propositions are intended to be representations of what was going on in the minds of some hominids who had just recently become self-conscious. They represent what probably were obscure reflections on obscure feelings, ideas in the earliest stages of their formation, thoughts perhaps similar to those of a contemporary very young human child. The underlying basic tendencies, however, would be unambiguous and forceful, produced by generations of natural and sexual selection, for example, the tendency to be aware of nourishing food and the inclination to eat that food, reinforced by feelings of pleasure and/or pain reduction, often associated with an awareness of others in the community who act as providers and protectors. These are the solid foundations on which self-consciousness gradually creates its symbols and its transcendent dimension.

In the text above I do not refer to the common urge to guard what is needed for development from predators. This would seem to be, prima facie, the basis for the claim to what is required, and it is the Hobbesian foundation for the state. I would suggest, however, that it is only one component of the foundation for claims. I believe, in a more positive vein, that the statement "I ought to do/have this" is a further articulation of the inclination to do what is needed for development—further to the emergence of the notion of *good* itself—and that the tendency to protect these needs is integral to that fundamental inclination. In other words, the "I ought to . . .," the claim to do or have what is good, emerges from the positive developmental inclinations themselves, perhaps promoted to some extent by the propensity to guard what is claimed.

This claim lies at the heart of the difference between this hypothesis and the dominant Western view. To associate *claim* and consequently *right* with the propensity to protect oneself and one's possessions from others would be to enter the world vision of Hobbes and Freud: *Homo homini lupus*, the natural condition is war; therefore we need rights and/or a state to protect us from others.[7] Within the present picture of the natural condition, however, the inclinations are the foundation for claims, and because the inclinations are developmental, the claims are developmental rather than protectionist. Furthermore, because the inclinations encompass the needs of both self and others, the ensuing claims would not have emerged to protect self from others, but as new, self-conscious ways to enhance the satisfaction of needs of individuals-in-community.

Obligation as a Foundation for Rights

It seems to me that the notion of *claim* could not have arisen from the awareness of development inclinations without a concomitant understanding of a response to the claim. I might add that, even if claims did arise in isolated individuals, neither they nor the individual making them would survive without adequate responses. The natural condition is not a state of war. A community of nasty and isolated individuals is an evolutionary oxymoron; it is, indeed, inconceivable that such a community could have evolved to a stage at which these nasty individuals would convene to rationally contrive a system of rights and laws to extricate themselves from conditions of war. Centuries before any such rational constructions, the idea of claims would have necessarily been built on the understanding of the nurturing and caring responses from the community: its openness.

Claims arise from the developmental inclinations, but only in the context of an awareness that some others in the community will positively respond to one's need. Just claims, human rights, emerge from the natural conditions of a relational community that include the propensity of its members to respond positively to the claims of others for their development needs.

The developmental inclinations from which these claims emerged had evolved to that point because the required responses to them were forthcoming. This precursor to duty/obligation was a natural and necessary component of the context into which self-conscious claims were born. Some basic inclinations could be satisfied without immediate support from the community, but the needs of most baby mammals and birds are provided by parents or others. In many cases adult vertebrates too get food or security with immediate community support, and/or satisfy needs because of previous "training" by the community. Self-consciousness would have captured this whole interactive context: inclination and its required community response would become a claim, or a right.

It must be made clear that *right* in this search for origins means *human right* or *natural right. Legal right,* often called *positive right,* is a further development within legal systems, arising as a human construction within cultures perhaps many thousands of years after the origins of natural rights that we are discussing here. Legal rights will be discussed in Chapter 8.

As suggested above, not all reactions to inclinations are immediate. Young progeny can be fed, sheltered, and protected directly, but they can also be trained to satisfy these needs by themselves. Whatever independent capacity the animal has would probably have been a consequence of community support at some point in its development. Could any developmental inclination that makes a contribution to fitness have evolved without the appropriate reactions of the community? Inclinations exist because there are such supportive reactions; it follows that rights exist because there is human community response from a feeling of duty or obligation (which I use as synonyms).

In other words, rights as claims to what is required for development had to emerge along with obligations. Obligations, indeed, could be considered a prerequisite for rights. This is the case both in understanding and in practice. The first self-conscious understanding of rights would not be a reflection by an isolated individual in a state of war about a claim unfulfilled. It would be the reflection of an individual-in-community about claims fulfilled. It would most probably begin with the child's understanding of needs satisfied by mother, and then by other members of the community. This would be related to an awareness of her/his own openness to others and their needs, and a growing associated knowledge of her/his responsibilities within the community.

The mechanical myth that rights emerge from egoism and then rational egoists calculate a way to deal with them through states and laws that impose duties is highly improbable from an evolutionary perspective. The real world is not linear; it is a complex of organic interactions. Unfortunately, we cannot capture its full complexity, dynamism, and interrelatedness in our still feeble attempts to understand it, but we need not abstract to the extent that the clear and distinct conceptual model that is constructed has little bearing on reality. We can, with some difficulty, see the factors in this process developing simultaneously, interactively, organically—not in a simple and logical linear progression. The central interacting factors would appear to be:

1. the basic awareness of what is required for one's own development;
2. the basic inclination to do/have what is required for one's own development;
3. the basic openness to others and to their needs;
4. the basic openness of others to one's own self and needs;
5. the activities/behaviors for the satisfaction of needs, consequent on 1 to 4;
6. the self-conscious capturing—the immediate understanding—of 1 to 5.

By *basic* I continue to refer to the natural situation before self-consciousness. Factor 1 is the foundation for human empirical (scientific) investigations of development needs. Factors 2, 3, 4, and 5 are the substantive foundations for morality; they provide the initial substance. Factor 6 gives morals its emerging transcendent form and articulation. Reflection (factor 6) on 3 and 4 would reinforce them; the knowledge of one's own openness to others would enhance the understanding of the openness of others to the self and vice versa.

The words *rights* and *obligations* are abstract terms relating to a concurrent, interrelated awareness of both inclinations to development needs and their satisfaction within community, all captured by self-consciousness. Rights and obligations, therefore, are not separate *things* that we *have.* They are two aspects of one integrated developmental process. This contradicts Hobbes's position: "Law and Right differ as much as Obligation and Liberty, which in one and the same matter are inconsistent." Here Hobbes takes right/liberty as an absolute of an isolated individual, and obligation as a limiting control that precludes the absolute. I understand obligation primarily as the sine qua non of rights, and secondarily as one of their limiting factors. To clarify this understanding of rights and duties, we must analyze the *ought* somewhat further.

From the above it follows that the proposition "I have a right to food" is an abbreviated statement capturing these propositions: (1) I need food to develop; (2) to develop is good and food is good; (3) I ought to have food. As proposed above, inclinations for development requirements and their satisfaction form the foundation of normative/moral judgments. The animal develops because of many basic developmental inclinations. The human, through self-consciousness, comes to feel that each of these is good and would eventually feel strongly that development itself is good—a symbolic leap that only self-consciousness could make. "It is good to have food" / "I ought to have food" is encompassed and reinforced by "it is good to develop" / "I ought to develop."

"I need food to develop" is an empirical proposition; it can be, has been, tested. "It is good to develop" is not empirical; there is no test for its validity. It cannot be reduced to the empirical propositions "I like to develop" or even "I am inclined to develop." It is not a statement *about* the existence of the inclination; it is the inclination itself stated symbolically by a self-conscious being. Morals is not *about* inclinations; it is inclinations self-consciously recognized and articulated.

"I *ought* to develop" and "I *ought* to have food" state that not only is it good that I develop/have food, but developing/having food is associated with some sort of obligation or duty. *Ought* is from the Middle English *oughten,* meaning *to be obliged to,* in turn from the Old English *âhte,* which is the past tense of *âgan, to possess. Ought* also used to be the past participle of the verb *to owe.* The *OED*'s first nonobsolete meaning for *ought* is

> **5.** The general verb to express duty or obligation of any kind; strictly used of moral obligation, but also with various weaker shades of meaning, expressing what is befitting, proper, correct, advisable, or naturally expected. (The only current use in standard Eng.)

I have proposed above that the evolution of morals and of rights and duties is not a linear process but, rather, an organic one involving interactions among individuals-in-community. I believe that this is reflected in the apparent ambiguities in the use of *ought* (compounded by its sometime synonym *should*). The proposition "I ought to X" can refer to a duty that is mine, for example, "I ought to work harder." It can also refer clearly to an X that is my due, and a related obligation of some other(s), as in "I ought to be able to live in peace and security." This identifies the need and the *goodness* of living in peace and security, and states that others have an duty to ensure this by not violating my person. "I ought to have food" is a statement of the developmental need and *goodness* of having food; it can be interpreted as a reference to my obligation to eat and/or as a claim that food is my due and that, therefore, others are obliged to assist me in getting food or, at least, not hinder me in getting it. In this light, if we look back at the first example—"I ought to work harder"—although it seems to be about my duty to work hard, in that the claim that "hard work is good" is implied, so too is the assertion that others have some obligation to support me in this work, or at least not impede me.

I would suggest that *ought* virtually always refers to:

- a claim by an individual to something that is believed to be good for that person's development and is that person's due: a *right*; and
- an obligation that falls upon both the person making the claim and others within the relevant community: a *duty.*

A right without the corresponding duty cannot be exercised. It is, we might say, the essence of a right, or simply *what* the right is. "I have a right to free association with others in my community" is a statement of the essence, the *whatness* of a specific right, and can be taken as a testable hypothesis. There is strong evidence[8] that lack of association—isolation—impedes human development, and this confirms the hypothesis; this is a good, developmental claim. But, unless there is an appropriate response to this claim, the right remains in the realm of essences. For the right to be exercised, for the person to actually freely associate with others, a community response is required. Even if one is incarcerated and in solitary confinement, she or he can make this claim and justify it as a valid claim even though, given this particular community response, the claimant cannot associate with others. The claim remains a valid developmental claim, but in this instance cannot be exercised.

It does not follow from this that rights are alienable. Awareness of a need and the appropriate community openness are original conditions for a right. The right to food and the right to free association have been recognized and scientifically confirmed as real development needs, and, for millennia and throughout the world, communities have been open to these needs. If some people in one community become closed to these needs, that dysfunctional aberration would not alienate the rights. The free association and mobility of slaves and women have been, and still are, limited in many communities, but these limitations are based on faulty rational arguments that slaves or women are exceptions who do not have the rights of *free men*. These arguments in no way refute the fact that these humans need free association and mobility for their development, and that primordial human communities were open to their needs. The Jews under Nazi rule had the exercise of their rights severely restricted. The millions who were murdered had the exercise of their rights totally eliminated. But throughout, most (sadly not all) of the global community understood that, even though they could not exercise them, these victims did have rights and therefore their violation by the Nazis was evil. The recognition of obligation as a condition for rights is not an arbitrary majority decision that can be rescinded at will, or with a culture-based rational argument. It is a condition that arose because it was necessary for survival and development.

An Illustration

If all this seems somewhat abstruse, perhaps an illustration from a *state of nature* will help.

Visiting our primordial human community we find a newly self-conscious hominid reflecting in a rudimentary way on a piece of fruit—

perhaps an apple. The genetically programmed and unarticulated propensities are all present and working well. This primal human—dare we call him Adam?—has an inclination to eat the apple because food is required for his development, and millennia of natural selection has produced a complex and sophisticated set of appetites to increase the probabilities of this requirement being met. The pre-self-conscious inclinations will include associations stored in his memory banks that relate the eating of the apple to an alleviation of the pains of hunger and, perhaps, to an enjoyment of the taste. Symbols, over time, would appear in Adam's reflecting mind and would be akin to "this reduces pain," "this gives me pleasure," "I like this," "I want this." It might have taken some time for a self-conscious recognition of eating the apple and survival/development to appear. Reflection on the associations between the primal development drive and specific inclinations might arise first in other circumstances where the connection is more immediate and obvious—flight from a hungry carnivore, for instance, in which the life-saving propensity to run fast would be consciously recognized as such; to run fast would be understood in this context, not as pleasurable, but as needed to survive. Once the idea "I need this" had emerged in more immediately life threatening circumstances—and in his world there would be many—it would find easy application to less obvious cases such as apple eating. Adam would understand not only his desire for this good thing, but also his need for it.

Consider now the consequences for Adam of his understanding of reducing hunger pains, increasing pleasure, and needs for survival and development within his environment. He is not isolated. He is surrounded by agents who could interfere with his apple eating. Most threats would come from other species, some from other hominid communities, and some even from the competitive inclinations within his own community. Reflection on these possible and actual impediments to his eating the apple or satisfying any of his development needs the apple represents, would heighten his understanding of his need for the apple and his consequent claim to it. But it would also focus his awareness on those in his community who did not threaten but rather supported his satisfaction of needs. This understanding of the openness of others toward him might begin with one other— more likely than not his mother, sister, aunt—whom we will call Eve. We must look carefully at Eve's role in the evolution of Adam's understanding of his rights.

First, it is inconceivable that this community could have survived, let alone developed to the advanced stage at which self-consciousness and an understanding of rights and duties would arise, if it was primarily selfish and nasty—if openness was not performing its major evolutionary function. But, for purposes of analysis, let us imagine a nasty, Hobbesian collectivity and place Adam in its midst. If all he saw around him were nasty, brutish, selfish hominids, out to grab his apple and impede by force his other development needs the instant his defenses were down, it would be virtually impossible for ideas of "my need," "my due," "my right," to emerge. Any understanding that could arise in such a state of war would be directed toward strategies for immediate defense. Perhaps most important, the primordial understanding of self-worth, self-esteem, self-actualization that would be a basis for making the claim for development needs could not grow in such an environment, just as this understanding could not grow in a child today in similar circumstances. Long before there was any possibility of a rational calculation to solve the state of war in this chimeric collectivity, there would be a social collapse born of frustration and hopelessness in the absence of the openness required for development.

The "realist" might reply at this point that the conditions I say are required are found within the family and are marginal to the broader society. They might now appear marginal in the competitive society whose construction the "realists" accelerate, but they are central to the origins of all that is human. In any case, *family* as we know it did not exist in these primal communities. Intercourse was not associated with birth, and so there would be no concept of father. Support for the young and the frail would probably have been shared throughout the community, especially by the women. Adam would have grown up surrounded by openness, supporting the satisfaction of his needs and protecting him from the nasty and the brutish. His understanding of "I need this apple" and eventually "I ought to have this apple" would receive its substance from this context. In a relational community in which empathy has developed, the *I* would have recognition, esteem, importance, status, and support within the community giving the *I claim* some significance and hope of fulfilment. The idea that this is *my due* cannot arise without this is *your duty*.

It is within these developmental interactions raised to a transcendent level by countless self-conscious Adams and Eves that morality and the moral claims and responses we call rights and duties were born. There were no rational disputations or calculations in attendance; they would be useful aids during the long process of articulation and institutionalization of rights and obligations, but they were not its progenitors.

Inclination as an object of cognition is the *essence* of inclination—a reification abstracted from the life within which it acts. This is the inclination of psychological treatises. But the foundation of morality and human rights is the *existing, interacting* inclination, immediately grasped by self-consciousness as it is interacting, immediately experienced by the self-conscious individual as it urges that individual to behave this way rather than that. To use, or perhaps abuse, Kantian terminology, it is inclination as *noumenon*, not as *phenomenon.* My inclinations are integral parts of me; I understand them in the same way I have an immediate self-conscious awareness of *I* —of my *self.* This is essentially different from my mediated knowledge of that which is not *I*, such as the apple.

Rights Defined

A useful definition of human rights must reflect the origins of rights. Rights emerge when inclinations for what is needed for development are recognized self-consciously in a social context that ensures the probable satisfaction of the inclination, that is, in which others are open to these needs and assist in their satisfaction or, at least, do not impede their satisfaction. The essence of the right is determined by a real developmental need; the exercise of the right is determined by the acceptance of the appropriate obligation within the community. Developmental need and obligation are sine qua nons of legitimate and exercisable rights.

In this light, then we can define human right as *a claim for a developmental need, accepted by and supported by the community.* This explanation and definition is radically different from the traditional Western definitions. To make the contrast explicit, consider the following.

Henry Shue says: "A moral right provides (1) the rational basis for a justified demand (2) that the actual enjoyment of a substance be (3) socially guaranteed against standard threats."[9] True to the dominant paradigm, Shue sees a right as a "rational basis." This clearly conflicts with my definition, nevertheless, let us ask what this rational basis might be. Shue answers:

> I do not know how to characterize in general and in the abstract what counts as a rational basis or an adequate justification. I could say that a demand for social guarantees has been justified when good enough reasons have been given for it, but this simply transfers the focus to what count as good enough reasons. This problem pervades philosophy, and I could not say anything very useful about it without saying a lot. But to have a right is to be in a position to make demands of others, and to be in such a position is, among other things, for one's situation to fall under general principles that are good reasons why one's demands ought to be granted. A person who has a right has especially compelling reasons—especially deep principles—on his or her side. (13)

This problem does indeed pervade philosophy, and I would propose that it does so because of the assumption of a rational foundation. Adam has a right to an apple because it is the object of a developmental inclination. He knows this intuitively, and so does Eve. Because Eve knows this and because she is open to Adam, she accepts whatever obligation toward Adam is appropriate under the circumstances. As part of our analysis of this, we can say that the *reason* that apple is among Adam's rights is that it is good for his development. Adam probably would not have been capable of presenting a rational argument to Eve to compel her to meet his demands. That is not a problem because, as I have proposed, rights do not emerge in a context of demands, compulsion, or "standard threats," in the negative atmosphere of the Western paradigm's state of nature. Adam's community was naturally open to his claim.

The Shue approach is typical of the dominant Western view that I have been countering. The two characteristic elements of this view, which create the problem that pervades philosophy, are (1) individuals are isolated in a selfish, closed society where one must make demands and a nasty society where one must be protected from threats; and (2) the solution to this negative situation is reason. Others are compelled to meet my demands by the power of reason rather than physical strength. Right is the alternative to might. The Hobbesian influence is obvious.

I must say once again that I am very aware of the need for reason and of the nasty side of humans. It is abundantly clear that, as communities developed and became larger and more complex, and human needs, especially transcendent needs, expanded, reason had to be applied to the problems associated with identifying legitimate rights and the fair distribution of the exercise of rights. Furthermore, although rational arguments are not the foundations of rights, a rational argument could be made to convince someone that such-and-such is indeed a right, and this argument might be compelling. It is also clear that the nasty side of society requires that demands have to be made and people have to be protected from threats. This is the function of systems and institutions of justice, of positive rights and law, which will be discussed in the following chapters. But these are further developments required by the selfish, closed side of humanity, by social complexity, and by the fact that even the most open people cannot know the vast and intricate array of development needs in a large and complex society. They are further developments of justice within cultures and play no part in the origin of rights, or in a consequent definition of rights.

What Rights Are Legitimate?

"I need X" is an empirical proposition. "I have a right to X" is a moral proposition. If this is a legitimate right, the need must be developmental. Whether or not a need is developmental (relative to a given culture) is an empirical question. Whether the rights that flow from the development goals and objectives of a particular community are developmental according to a more universal set of goals and objectives is also an empirical question. The "right" to murder Jews was "legitimate" given Nazi goals, but it is universally rejected outside Nazism. "Rights" legitimized by the culture of apartheid and the Stalinist regime are other examples of rights whose legitimacy is rejected outside those cultures. I am not aware of these cases being defended by recourse to cultural relativism.

In most cases the test for legitimacy is simple and the results obvious and virtually universally accepted. The right to life and the rights to life's requirements—food, shelter, security, and so forth—are legitimate because all these are required for development. The legitimacy of many rights to transcendent needs are also easily verified empirically. The right to association, mobility, self-determination, and freedom of expression are all clearly necessary for good human development.

I would propose the following as candidates for a list of fundamental requirements for human development and, therefore, a set of legitimate rights: food, shelter, nonthreatening physical environment, security, health, knowledge, work, freedom of conscience, freedom of expression, freedom of association, self-determination. Although interrelated to some extent, none of these can be reduced to another and each is a foundation for a whole range of requirements. Each can be shown empirically to be necessary for human development whereas specific requirements derived from these foundations usually cannot be. For example, it cannot be denied that I need food and free association if I am to develop, but it does not follow that I need a meal at a fine restaurant in Paris with the recent winners of the Nobel Prize. A list of fundamental development needs can be understood and accepted, and yet the application of each need to specific individuals and communities can be extremely difficult.

We will look briefly at the above proposed list and compare it with that of the United Nations Covenants on human rights; see Table 2. I do this to show that, although my hypotheses on the origin of rights and consequent definition are radically different from the dominant view of rights, nevertheless the rights that are implied by my hypotheses differ little from those that are widely accepted. (Whether or not this list is complete and/or fully accepted should have no bearing on the acceptance of my hypotheses on origins.)

The few rights included in the UN covenants but not on my list are derived from the fundamental rights and are ways of effecting the exercise of fundamental rights. They are virtually all essential to human development and could be considered to be universal and absolute, as are those on our list. I believe, nevertheless, that there are advantages to separating out those rights that are most indisputably based on universal needs for human development and are not themselves derived from more fundamental rights. They themselves will not vary over time or place; they stand out clearly for emphasis; they constitute a definite minimum in the sense that the list cannot be reduced further, but they are the foundation for human development.

This list of rights is, necessarily, also a list of needs. We have discussed the empirical bases for some development needs, which would also be the bases for the legitimacy of the corresponding rights. Here we will simply run through the list, clarify the meaning and comment on legitimacy.

Food and shelter (including all required protection against climatic conditions) are obvious physiological needs. The need for a nonthreatening physical environment can no longer be taken for granted; what was always implicit must now be made explicit and emphasized more than in the UN Covenants and other lists of rights. Security is protection from all violations of the person and the person's property. Violations of the person include any action that does physical or psychological harm as well as slanderous assaults on the person. Security includes or provides a basis for many civil rights such as equality under the law and due process. Health and knowledge are obvious needs but are often listed as health care and education. These latter are responses to the needs, rather than the needs themselves.

The right to work is a controversial one and not accepted in a positive sense in much of the West. Without work, however, the individual cannot be secure, self-determined, and a free contributor to both self and community development. Freedoms of conscience, expression, and association, the traditional positive civil rights, are requirements for true human development, as opposed to physiological development, and yet the

TABLE 2

Fundamental right	*UN covenant right*	*UN covenant*/ article*
Food	Food	I/11
Shelter	Clothing, housing	I/11
Nonthreatening	Environmental	I/12
environment	hygiene	I/12
Security	Life, liberty, . . .	II/6ff
Health	Health	I/12
Knowledge	Education	I/13
Work	Work	I/6
Freedom of conscience	Freedom of conscience	II/18
Freedom of expression	Freedom of expression	II/19
Freedom of association	Freedom of association	II/22
Self-determination	Self-determination	I, II/1
	Take part in public affairs†	II/25

* I = economic, social, cultural; II = civil, political.

† I assume this under self-determination.

need for them can be confirmed empirically. Self-determination, the need to determine one's own development path and have some control over one's development process includes or provides a basis for political rights and, as noted above, requires the right to work. Within the field of development studies itself there is growing evidence that nonparticipation through work and political involvement is an impediment to development.

Self-actualization—the creation of the self by the self—requires the exercise of all of the above rights but, in particular, the right to self-determination to define the path and the right to work in order to get the resources needed to follow it.

A person has physiological needs for both self-actualization and physiological development; I need food to sustain my body, as does any animal, but also to work with if I choose to be a chef—a decision other animals cannot make. We must distinguish, then, between purely human needs (self-actualization needs) and those aspects of some needs that are physiological. I would suggest that freedom of conscience, freedom of expression, and self-determination are purely human while the rest, in varying degrees, are both human and physiological. This distinction between physiological needs and needs associated with the actualization of the self—the needs of the transcendent part of our development—is of great importance, especially if we are to avoid reductionism.

As already noted, the objective of this chapter is to examine the origins of human rights in general and not to focus on particular rights. For such purposes the definition of fundamental rights is essential; a particular listing of them is not. The above list and brief commentary, however, help to clarify the meaning of human rights as developmental and includes, I believe, the major requirements for human development. What is needed for development is an empirical question; it should be raised frequently and answered in the light of the appropriate and developmental goals and objectives of the community.

The way rights are exercised and the way society will distribute resources for the exercise of rights will vary from society to society. Much of this variation will depend on the availability of resources and much will depend on the culture. I believe, however, that to be developmental a community must accept a set of basic rights based on real needs, similar to those listed above, make the best use of scarce resources to maximize the equitable exercise of these rights, and refrain from violating the rights of any or all of its members on any cultural grounds.

Human Rights as Universal and Inalienable

There are needs for human development, both physiological and transcendent, that are common to all humans. For example, every human needs food and every human needs association with other humans. How these needs are satisfied will vary from culture to culture and from person to person, but the need itself is universal. It follows, then, that there are universal human rights. Are all legitimate rights universal? I can't think of any need for human development that some humans have and others do not, so I would say that all legitimate human rights are universal, but since this is an empirical question, I am not certain, and this has no bearing on my hypotheses on human rights.

Along with universality, a characteristic of human rights that is often debated is inalienability. God-given rights would be inalienable because what God gives only She can take away. State-given rights are alienable because what states give, states can take. Rights in the present context, however, are not *things* that are given and taken. They are claims based on obligation and need. What these claims are depends only on real developmental need—not on the rationalizations or whims of a state (or a professional thinker). These rights are exercised because communities are naturally open. By definition, a legitimate right arises from a real need, and it makes no sense to say that a real need can be alienated. A community can limit the exercise of a right, but, as argued above, this does not alienate the right. Incarceration, for example, limits the rights to association and mobility, but the person in jail still recognizes these needs and the community still is open to them, even while curtailing the application of that openness in this particular case.

A closed community, if there were such a thing, could frustrate the exercise of rights to such an extent that its members would never recognize them, but such a community would be so dysfunctional as to not be viable. The required openness is neither arbitrary nor a decision of some segment of the community such as the state. It is a necessary developmental condition within communities. I would propose that, to the extent that a community is developing, it must be sufficiently open to induce appropriate responses to developmental claims based on developmental needs that exist simply because of the nature of the human. In this respect, then, human rights can be said to be inalienable.

Conclusion

The salient elements of my hypotheses on the origin of rights are

- Rights emerge through reflection on developmental inclinations.
- What a right is—the *essence* of a right—is determined by the need associated with the inclination.
- A right is legitimate if the inclination is developmental (the object is

a real need for human development). Whether or not it is developmental is an empirical question.

- A right can be exercised if there is an appropriate response to the need by others in the community (the community is open to the person and her or his need). Fundamental human rights began to be exercised and continue to be exercised because there was, during our early development, and continues to be the required degree of openness within communities.
- The two sine qua nons of legitimate and exercisable rights are, therefore:

    a reflection on an inclination for a real developmental need, and
    an accepted obligation to respond appropriately to that need in the community.

We have now the raw materials for our *state of nature* or *primordial human community*. We will, therefore, move on, in the next chapter, to search within it for the origins of justice.

Chapter 7
The Origins of Justice

The difference between the sense of justice and the love of mankind is that the latter is supererogatory, going beyond the moral requirements and not invoking the exemptions which the principles of natural duty and obligation allow.[1]

Rawls, following the mainstream Western tradition, does not see love as a principle of justice, as a moral requirement, as *natural.* Love has no place because his principles are rational; they are products of the rational planner. Our hypotheses present emerging humanity as the producer of principles, and love as a major principle of morals and a natural and essential foundation for rights and justice. Love is anything but supererogatory within human evolution.

Both love and obligation are manifestations of the same attitude of openness to other and to the needs of other from which justice emerges. Justice and love are equally natural, arise from the same developmental foundations and neither has a rational base. Law requires sanctions only because "natural duty and obligation" are not always adequate to the task of ensuring the fair distribution of the resources needed for the exercise of rights, especially in large and complex societies.

The previous chapters have put forward hypotheses about the origin of morality and then the origin of human rights. The present chapter takes the next and culminating step in the search for the origin of justice itself.

But what do we mean by "justice itself"?

The just individual recognizes the rights of others and accepts his or her duty to respond to those rights in an appropriate way. When more than one person has a legitimate claim and the resources required to meet those claims are limited, then appropriateness includes the fair distribution of resources to meet the obligation. As a community increases in size and complexity, it needs a means to ensure an impartial fulfilment of this duty. This gives rise to the exercise of authority to ensure a fair distribution of resources needed for the exercise of rights and the protection of rights.

The following exploration of the origins of justice begins with the emergence of the self-conscious feeling of obligation to the rights of others and the consequent response, and then looks at the institutionalization of this within the community.

From the beginning I have emphasized the differences between this exploration and the traditional Western treatises on morality, rights, and justice. I have especially noted that this essay is a search for the origins of justice in our obscure but actual past, rather than in the realm of ideas. In this chapter we will build on our hypotheses on morals and rights within the context of our early ancestors. We will begin by reviewing and elaborating our conceptual framework. In the light of that framework, we will then apply our evolutionary perspective to the early development of morality and rights/obligations in order to discover what the actual principles of justice might be. The first scenario used here will be very general, allowing us to focus attention on the convergence of the basic laws of evolution with the basic characteristics of evolving communities of self-conscious and moral individuals. We will then develop these principles further by adding some specifics. Four different scenarios will be used to test and elaborate the principles and to move the hypothetical context closer to our real beginnings.

A Conceptual Framework

Arising from this exploration is an abstract approximation of real interactive processes, all related to morality and, in this chapter, to justice itself. This is not what I think justice ought to be like; it is what the evidence leads me to think justice actually is.

Our exploration began with morality and discovered the origins of its elements, value and obligation, in the reflections of the first humans on developmental inclinations, themselves products of the evolutionary process. These inclinations for what is needed for human development and the community's response to these needs gave birth to obligations and rights. All this development took place within the transcendental human dimension of self-consciousness and culture, with the biological dimension continuing throughout the process. Development was sustained by social communities with a balance of egoism and altruism, competition and cooperation, solitude and openness.

The moral judgment is made by the individual-in-community; that is, it is a self-conscious response of individual humans interacting with other humans and their environment, including and especially their culture. As I have insisted throughout, there is no isolated or autonomous individual; we continuously interact with our environment, including our community and its culture. Moral judgments are products of these interactions, within individuals. Moral codes are also produced by interaction within a community, but they reside in the community, rather than in the individual.

By *moral code* I mean the articulations of moral judgments that have emerged within a community and that are communicated throughout and shared within that community. If many people in a community have made the judgments that murder is bad and one ought not to kill, then the articulation of the judgment—"Thou shalt not kill"—could become part of that community's moral code. Any systematized attempt to promote all or part of a moral code could be called a *moral system*. The state is now the most ubiquitous moral system, but earlier and simpler communities would have had institutions that carried out analogous functions. Organized and institutionalized religions are moral systems, although that is not all that they are. To the extent that they systematically promote some or all of a moral code, educational systems and social organizations are also, inter alia, moral systems.

If all members of a community made all the appropriate developmental moral judgments and always behaved according to these judgments, then no moral systems, or only noncoercive systems, would be required. If the members of a community all behave in accord with their moral judgments, but need some help in determining which moral judgments are developmental and what is the appropriate response to the many rights of many members, then an explicit moral code and some appropriate persuasive moral systems will be required. If, as is really the case, members of a community do not all share the developmental moral beliefs deemed to be appropriate by a community or do not always behave in accordance to these moral judgments, then a moral system that can command rather than only enlighten and persuade will be needed. This is the legal system—a moral system with the power to command moral behavior. The moral code is the community's articulation of the moral judgments of its members. Commands will be associated with those elements of the code that are deemed to be necessary for the development of the community and its members; these are laws.

But what is a good and legitimate law? We know that what is deemed to be developmental by a community or by those who dominate a community is often not developmental for some or most of that community; there are often discrepancies between perceived and real development as there are often dominant groups or individuals in a community who impose their own perception of *the good*. What then is the *just society*? The just individual, naturally and without coercion, responds appropriately to the rights of others—gives to others their due. If there are many others, fairness requires the appropriate distribution of whatever resources are required to satisfy their just claims. The just society ensures that this is the case. Here some rational calculations might be needed to work out a distribution plan, but these calculations are in no sense the source or origin of justice. The test of justice is the fair distribution of developmental resources for the exercise of the rights of all members of the community. To carry this out effectively the large and complex community will need a system of laws.

The criteria for legitimate laws and legal systems can be deduced from our hypotheses. The moral behavior to be commanded must be developmental, that is, behavior that will not impede and/or will enhance the development of all of the individuals in this community. It must, then, be based on an understanding of the development goals and objectives of this whole community.

To be legitimate a law must command behavior based on a moral judgment that:

- is developmental within the context of the goals and objectives of all, or at least most, of the members of that community;
- does not impede or frustrate the appropriate development of any members of the community;
- receives its power to command from the community, and therefore through a process understood by and accepted by the community;
- is made known, along with associated sanctions, to all members of the community.

To be legitimate, the lawmaker must be an agent of the community and must make legitimate and only legitimate laws, as defined above.

To ensure justice, the legal system must be a system that:

- identifies appropriate developmental moral judgments and, on behalf of the community, gives them the power to command;
- enacts laws to promote the fair distribution of the resources for the exercise of people's rights and, in doing this, ensures that no one is prevented from receiving her or his due in order that some others can receive theirs;
- determines fair and effective sanctions for disobeying the law;
- ensures that the members of the community know each law and corresponding sanction when legislated;
- judges whether behavior is commensurate with these laws, and applies the appropriate sanction;

- effects all activity required for the fair execution of all of these requisites.

Laws, arising from moral codes, are the orders of an accepted authority, designed to guarantee and facilitate the exercise of the rights of all members of the community, appropriately promulgated and with appropriate sanctions. Laws respond to human rights; laws do not create human rights. In responding to human rights, laws often give members of the community claims that will help them to exercise a human right. These are called *positive rights* or *legal rights*. Unlike human rights, they are creations of the law/state and can be modified or rescinded by the state. For example, all societies now give qualified citizens the legal right to drive a car to facilitate the exercise of the right to mobility and association.

The hypothesis that law emerges from developmental needs and an open, caring community is perhaps the only aspect of the above conceptual framework that is not an established part of the Western concept of law, but this is a most significant difference. The emphasis on development and openness within the process will become clearer as we go on. Having provided the relevant definitions, we can now begin to look for the origins of moral codes and moral systems: the origins of justice.

The Original Conditions

The culmination of our exploration of morality was the moral judgment.[2] I have noted above that the moral judgment resides within the individual, whereas the elements of the system that promotes justice are all out there in the community. The character of moral judgments and therefore morality itself in this work arises from the hypothesis of a foundation in altruistic and egoistic inclinations for development, within each individual. Analogously, the character of the justice system in this account will arise from its hypotheses about the nature of community from which it arises. The image of community from which the dominant Western theories/models of justice are founded are all, with some variations, the Hobbesian model. In the community that emerges from the present hypotheses about human nature, all the Hobbesian characteristics are present. They are, however, not the primary or dominant characteristics. Because each member of the community has both natural egoistic and altruistic tendencies, and since human cognition is seen to go well beyond rational activity, we find in the community openness, sacrificial behavior and cooperation, as well as self-conscious affection, feeling, intuition, and understanding—all of which are playing a significant role in the development of the community.

We have now the raw materials for a scenario that represents the original and actual conditions for the birth of justice. We must keep in mind that this *state of nature* is not a point in time, not a static state, but an extended segment of a dynamic process continuing from the conception of humanity. It is virtually impossible to grasp all of the complexity and interactions over the duration of this transitional period, but to have as accurate an understanding as possible, it will be necessary to keep abstraction to a minimum, even at the expense of prolonging and convoluting the exploration. I will avoid, as much as possible, imposing twenty-first-century values, approaches, and social science theories and models onto our early beginnings. Based on what we do know of our distant past, I will try to develop some reasonable hypotheses about what actually happened then. The exploration follows from these assumptions:

- All human capacities, values, principles, institutions, art, science, and moral systems, all of what human individuals-in-community and cultures are today, came from within the process that we are examining; all of the potential for further development was there. This is a truism within an evolutionary perspective, and yet it needs to be stated explicitly and then constantly kept in mind.
- What we know about the early development of humans and about the development of animals and especially our closest genetic relatives, the great apes, can provide some bases for speculation on our beginnings.
- From the fact of our own existence and that of our cultures it necessarily follows that there were early human communities that were successful in those areas of development upon which our development rests. This is also a truism that needs to be stated and reflected on.

Our attention will focus on primal human communities, well into their processes of transition and, therefore, not really *states of nature*. That is, self-consciousness has emerged and established itself throughout these communities and is now a growing factor in their development. The empirical dimension of self-consciousness is progressing, with more individuals able to identify objects and interactions around them, distinguish self from other, know other as other, attach symbols and vocalizations to objects, and refine oral communications. Relations essential to development are starting to be understood and important connections are being made, marking the birth of reason, but rational calculations and systems are still in their infancy.

The moral dimension is also advancing as notions of good and bad and of rights and duties arise from basic inclinations, are associated with objects and interrelations, and enter into the infant language. Because these empirical and normative products of self-consciousness are consequences of its interactions with the world into which it was born, they are all transcendent manifestations of the entrenched development propensities. These manifestations are still tentative and vague; the *self* is, like today's infant, probing, experimenting, failing, trying again, unsure even of *self.* An influential culture has not yet been constructed. Until *self* and then culture are stronger and more secure, the solid, mature, well-tested, basic biological inclinations continue, to a great extent, to control the radically new process and provide the substance for its development.

We are, therefore, searching for the beginnings of just behavior and the principles and institutions of justice in communities that had neither the great benefits of culture nor the costly distortions that are part of all cultural constructions. Having been refined by the precise and disinterested sieve of natural/sexual selection, the factors influencing these beginnings are highly developmental. They include the full required range of inclinations for the development of self and others, and the central tendencies of the egoistic and altruistic inclinations are, necessarily, developmental.

These communities are not "states of war," nor are they populated by rational maximizers. We would probably not apply the adjectives *nice* or *gentle* to these communities, but neither were they *nasty* or *brutish*; the evidence we have presented suggests that they were relatively peaceful. Because they had evolved to this stage, there must have been in each community a balance[3] of nurturing and contention, caring and controlling, openness and detachment, sacrifice and selfishness. This is very important. The characteristics of these original communities are not arbitrary. We have evolved from successful communities, by definition; that proposition is absolutely certain. Those communities must have had what is required for success; that is also absolutely certain. *What* was required for success is not so certain. My answer to this, based on the egoistic-altruistic balance, is, of course, a hypothesis but the evidence indicates that it is a much stronger hypothesis than is the *state of war* or even the rational maximizer model.

Within the present hypothesis, the challenge is to try to understand how the foundational morality, including moral judgments and notions of right and obligation, might have evolved into systems of justice. Beginning at the biological level, two types of activity effect evolution: (1) changes in the organisms themselves, that is, mutations that introduce new propensities and behaviors to be chosen or rejected by the process of sexual and/or natural selection; and (2) changes in the environment that alter selection pressures, which in turn induce new or adjusted behaviors. In the human community, selection, and especially sexual selection, continues to respond to these changes but self-consciousness gradually shifts much of the responses to change to the reflective self and culture. Through technology we now can respond to rapid changes that the relatively very slow process of natural selection could not possibly cope with. Responses to somewhat less rapid changes involve a combination of natural selection and technology.

At the birth of humanity the same factors apply to the source and response to significant structural and behavioral change, but in very different proportions. Without self-consciousness, evolution is effected by non-human processes, and natural/sexual selection is the only agent. One of the early and most efficacious manifestations of self-consciousness, however, was the capacity it gave humans to respond in new ways to their environments and adapt in new ways to change. These adaptations in turn would immediately make self-consciousness itself an agent of change. At first, however, the impact of the products of self-consciousness on the process would have been negligible. The effect of the first chipped stone tools on evolution, for example, would be dwarfed by the continuing consequences of the selection process. Today, however, the impact of human culture on our development, and on the evolution of much of the life of our planet, conceals, modifies, and replaces the forces of biological evolution. Our scenarios must reflect the minimal impact of the human dimension during the early development of humanity, and not today's major cultural influence.

With these considerations in mind we can now apply the hypotheses that our exploration has produced to some scenarios that, based on the evidence, might reflect our actual origins. Within these we will probe the character and behavior of our early ancestors to try to discover how justice might have emerged.

Some Possible Scenarios

> Contrary to the popular view that the hunter-gatherer way of life was impoverished and brutish, Later Stone Age people [25,000 to 30,000 years ago] were highly skilled and had a good deal of leisure and a rich spiritual life, as their cave paintings and rock engravings show.[4]

The *states of nature* from Hobbes to Nozick are based on that "popular view." Our evidence leads us to the contrary view, that real human communities develop because most of the behavior of those within them emerged from a balance of egoistic and altruistic developmental inclinations in a life that was somewhat pleasant, prosperous, and peaceful. We will begin with a very general scenario that focuses on this view. It will be a first approximation within which the elements of justice will be found. We will then vary and refine the model to provide more insight and specificity into the birth of justice.

Consider an early human community in a period of relative abundance. This community did well with its newfound empirical and normative repertoire. Its members knew what was needed for development and had feelings of what is good and bad. They understood what they and others must claim for development, and responded appropriately to such claims. Imagine, however, that an uncommon period of drought set in, making food and water scarce and exerting a new pressure on the basic inclinations for nourishment and their self-conscious affirmations. If the pressure was great, the powerful selfish inclinations of the most powerful members of the community might have produced a nasty and brutish situation—even a state of war. This was always a possibility and, along with the food shortage, could easily have led to the extinction of such a community. Since the community we are looking for was a precursor of our own, however, it by definition avoided extinction. Let us consider, therefore, what might enable this community to survive such a crisis.[5]

In this community there were, before self-consciousness, well-developed cooperative approaches for the care of the young. This is common in many species and can involve male as well as female members. In this community, we will assume that the tendency toward openness to others and to their needs was somewhat more concentrated among the women, but not totally lacking among the men. The division of labor that assigned women to gathering and small game hunting and men to big game hunting had not yet happened, although there was some separation of the sexes promoted by the women as a component of their protective strategies for the children.[6] The women, then, were the first to respond to the growing food crisis. Their basic inclinations indicated that there was a problem, and this was made explicit by their understanding of needs and the satisfaction thereof. Their basic inclinations to respond to the needs of others–their feeling of obligation—had been supported and reinforced by self-consciousness, and so their intensified concern was directed toward both themselves, individually, and others in their community. They responded by using their new understanding and some rudimentary reasoning capacity to develop a strategy for making the best use of the food available and also to protect their stores from the more selfish and aggressive members of the community. This was a successful experiment in the allocation of scarce resources for the general welfare of the community, involving the application of the neophyte self-consciousness, in its empirical and normative dimensions, in conjunction with mature development inclinations.

The advantage provided by the empirical dimension was the understanding of needs, the capacity to devise strategies to satisfy these needs, and the ability to communicate all this. The normative advantages would arise from the intensification of the existing openness by self-consciousness, inducing a feeling of obligation. Because all these capacities deriving from self-consciousness were at a very rudimentary stage and the basic inclinations from which they emerged were already refined for handling crises, the ensuing advantages were marginal. But these marginal advantages were adequate to the task in this case, securing the survival of the community.

Whatever genetic base was involved in the new advantages would be treated positively by natural and sexual selection, but I will not enter into the intricacies of that. I will focus instead on the probably much stronger reinforcement of the self-conscious response to the crisis induced by self-consciousness itself. Members of the community knew that they had survived this difficulty and also understood why they had survived; they were able to associate the methods used and their moral feelings with survival. They understood these methods and feelings, and the associated propensities, as good. Some of those who had not shared in the survival strategy and even opposed it, now began also to see that strategy as good, and this change in perception was reinforced through primitive communication. The process had left an empirical and moral legacy that was to be used, enhanced, and reinforced within the community on subsequent occasions.

The Birth of Justice

We can now reflect further on this general scenario to see if what we now call *justice* can be identified within it. Before the crisis the notion of right/duty had started to develop in the community, but only as a trace and mainly within the more cooperative and caring women's sector. Self-consciousness had been born and was beginning its infancy in relatively abundant times. Basic empirical and normative symbols had appeared throughout the community, and some of these were associated with the interrelations among needs, satisfaction of needs, and need providers, but the *ought* had surfaced primarily in the self-consciousness of the care givers—as a reflection on their openness to the needs of others and the strong inclination to satisfy these needs, even though often difficult to do. Its form was, in the first instances, a self-conscious but vague notion of "my response to your claim to what you need"—the precursor of "my duty and your right." This notion was, however, raised from quiescence by the crisis. The need dimension of rights was accentuated by occurrences of unsatisfied need, especially among the very young. The response/duty side was brought into relief by those claims and by the importance of the self-conscious responses to them during the crisis. As proposed previously, the claims themselves would not have arisen if the claimants were not already aware of the ongoing responses to their needs. If the chicken/egg kind of question demands an answer, it would follow from this case that the right/duty dialectic begins with duty.

Notions of right and duty, now embedded in the community, were, along with the other consequences of the basic developmental inclinations and self-consciousness, clarified, reinforced, and enhanced during the subsequent period of development. Each ensuing crisis added further emphasis to them, accelerating their evolution as developmental concepts and beliefs. They were challenged by those in the community whose development had followed a variant course, as well as by agents outside the community, but they met the challenges to become institutionalized within the community. Without contracts, constitutions, promulgations—without rationales, justifications, conferences—the institution of justice came to be.

The simple statement of the moral principle that captures this just behavior would be that other members of the community ought to do/have what is required for their development. I do not believe that it would be appropriate to say "all members," because at this stage of development the dominant altruistic inclination would probably focus on those already within the customary ambit of care. Now, however, the limitations of the basic inclinations are subject to expansion by self-consciousness. The idea "it is good to help *these* others"—an idea that has gained efficacy in the community—can eventually encompass "*those* others" and, perhaps in time, "all others."

The notion of equality is not part of this statement of the principle because it would not have been part of their understanding of the needs, of the way to satisfy them, or of the operant inclinations. Equality, whether equality under the law, equal opportunity, or any fair measure of equality, is obviously the ideal; there ought to be equality. Here, however, we are not prescribing what ought to be. We are trying to know what actually was. Even today, tens and perhaps hundreds of thousands of years after these origins, humanity has not achieved the ideals of justice and so we should not expect to find them among our early ancestors.

Some simple calculations might have been involved in the survival strategy, but no calculations relating to equality would have been possible or required. The response to needs arose from reflection on inclinations, not reason; justice arose from the self-conscious understanding of the response, not reason. Nor were calculations required to determine what is best for one's own personal advantage;[7] both claims and responses to claims arose from inclinations relating to real needs of the self and others, not from calculations on how individual pleasure can be maximized in competition with other calculations on how to maintain some kind of equality.

As communities became larger and more complex and had greater interaction with other communities, and because there are selfish inclinations, the methods and strategies employed to maintain and enhance the institution of justice, to ensure the fair distribution of resources, came to include, inter alia, many reasons and rational calculations. The *methods and strategies* of the system of justice were arrived at through reason; reason became more and more a significant condition of the development of the system of justice. The salient point is that reason is not the origin of justice; in this hypothesis, justice arises from the self-conscious manifestations of basic development inclinations. No rational calculations or principles of reason, including the statement of the moral principle of just behavior above, are the origins or the foundations of justice. They can be the origins or the principles or the foundations of a specific, constructed approach to justice, or, as are the philosophers' "theories," they could be rational explanations or justifications for this or that method or extent of distribution of resources, but only after justice had emerged.

More Specific Scenarios

This general overview of the origins of justice and the introduction of the principal elements of these origins has called attention to the essential features of justice—those that arise from its foundations and not from various cultural constructions. We move now to more specific accounts of these origins within more specific and varied scenarios that provide a range of possible origins. In order to maximize their reality and strengthen them as hypotheses, they are constructed to reflect more of the anthropological, archaeological, and palaeontological evidence, as well as the observations of primatologists of our closest contemporary relatives, the great apes.

I must emphasize that this is not a zoological, anthropological, archaeological, or palaeontological study; it does not claim to advance these sciences one bit. It simply presents evidence from these sciences in order to produce diverse but realistic pictures of our past for the purposes of understanding justice. I do not and cannot enter into the process of hypothesis-testing within any of these sciences.

Interpreting the Evidence

In Chapter 2 we looked at the work of Richard Dawkins and suggested that, although his understanding of evolution is excellent, a bias distorts his discussion of the gene and, consequently, his general characterization of the evolutionary process. His bias, in my own biased view, reflects the dominant Western masculine paradigm. This same kind of bias has influenced not only the *states of nature* from Hobbes to Nozick but also the sciences that deal with our origins, prehistory, and early history: palaeontology, archaeology, and anthropology. In the early days of these sciences the Western biases were so blatant that racist interpretations followed.[8] John Lubbock, for example, used the primitive archaeology, anthropology, and evolutionary theory of his day to conclude that Europeans were biologically superior to other humans and that those non-Europeans would become extinct through natural selection.[9] This provided a moral justification for colonization and any of its negative consequences.

Today the evidence from our distant past is still meager: stone tools from the Lower Palaeolithic, traces of art in the Middle Palaeolithic, more art, more specialized tools, and other bits of evidence from the Upper Palaeolithic and into the Neolithic. Interpretation and even identification are still very difficult and strongly influenced by assumptions. The Western masculine bias still has much room to proliferate among the huge gaps in the evidence. Although now on the wane, the tendency is still to assume that our progenitors, 10,000 years ago, 100,000 years ago, 1,000,000 years ago, were like us—in particular, that they were rather selfish, nasty folk living in male-dominated societies. The evidence can easily be interpreted to support this assumption. Many Upper Palaeolithic wall paintings, for example, are interpreted to represent man the hunter/warrior and demonstrate that man as hunter/warrior was the center and dominant force of the society.

Questions relating to identification and interpretation, and exposing this bias, however, are now being asked: Do those lines in this cave painting represent spears or the branches of plants? Are these hunted animals or domesticated animals? Are these pictures representative of the whole community, or are they the works of a small cult? Do these pictures depict real life in the community, or myths, or memories, or hallucinations? Are these pictures of males or females, humans or animals? Do these pictures reflect violence or tenderness?[10] The mounting critical analysis today leads to the firm conclusion that the *male hunter/warrior* characterization is not at all obvious and that competing interpretations are possible, including the hypotheses of female-dominated communities and of communities without significant gender domination.[11]

One other bias that arises from the processual view of the past found in many palaeontological and archaeological studies of hominids is the emphasis on process at the expense of the individuals in the process. The great gap in time and the paucity of evidence, of course, make it impossible to observe individuals and their behavior, and this can encourage levels of abstraction and aggregation that produce simple, linear, mechanistic models similar to those of economics. Combined with assumptions of male domination, the role of women can be downplayed or ignored. The activity of the male warrior/hunter is perceived to be central to the process, but the activity of the female, who is the *reproducer* of the community and also a major—in many cases, *the* major—*producer* in the community, is marginalized. There are now some attempts to interpret the evidence in sociopsychological and gender terms, bringing to the fore individual and group behaviors that had been ignored. My own interpretation makes considerable use of such a sociopsychological and gendered approach, especially in its consideration of self-consciousness and consequent activities among males, females, and other sub-groups in a community.

Many of the salient findings that challenge the traditional Western and masculine biases in interpretation have been brought together by authors such as Eisler, Mies, Jolly, and Reed. Studies of some palaeontologists, archaeologists, and anthropologists and their gendered interpretations raise significant questions about the *man the hunter/warrior* model[12] and suggest two other hypotheses about our origins, both outside the Hobbesian myth: a matriarchal society[13] and a balanced partnership community in which neither matriarch nor patriarch is dominant.[14] These two merge into one because matriarchy itself tends to be open and cooperative; matriarchal dominance would actually result in a reduction of dominance. Supporting this is the evidence that leadership rather than dominance was a significant factor in hominid evolution. De Waal writes:

> the dismantling of despotic hierarchies in the course of hominoid evolution brought an emphasis on leadership rather than dominance, and made the privileges of high status contingent upon services to the community (such as effective conflict management). Community concern comes into play here.[15]

In any case, the *state of nature* would not be a *state of war*, as Hobbes put it, nor would competition, aggression, domination, egoism, and rationality be its principal characteristics. These all would be present in, as much evidence suggests, relatively peaceful and cooperative communities.

Our Cousins the Apes

It now appears that we have evolved from a primate that was the common progenitor of us and the African apes, and that this ancestor lived some five million years ago.[16] Some of the supporting evidence for my scenario building comes, therefore, from ongoing studies of these African apes, our closest living relatives.

In the introduction to this work I expressed my awareness of the concerns that many people have about the use of neo-Darwinian theory to help explain human behavior, and I am sure that the introduction of apes into this search for justice will brand it as reductionism and biologism, in spite of my many disclaimers. Nevertheless, I believe what is known of apes to be significant evidence for several compelling reasons. The apes are our closest genetic relatives, some sharing more than 98 percent of our DNA.[17] They would appear to be self-conscious with some rudimentary reasoning power.[18] They can make and use tools; our species has been called *Homo faber* (*man the tool maker*) recognizing that this is an essential human characteristic. Several long-term experiments with apes indicate that they have a capacity for symbolic language requiring the abstraction and comprehension skills similar to those of a two- or three-year-old human. Experiments with mirrors suggest that they have an understanding of self and other.[19] In language experiments, they communicate with humans by using hand signs or specially designed computer keyboards; the fact that they are tending to evolve toward an erect posture, like the human, would suggest the concomitant evolution of vocalization, as the trachea straightens out.

This and other evidence make it highly probable that we and they have descended from the same ancestor. They are the closest animals to us genetically, physiologically, emotionally, and cognitively and may also be very similar to our common ancestor. Since we cannot observe our own origins directly, they can give us many insights into what our real *state of nature* might have been like. In this regard, the extensive observations of ape behavior tend to confirm the recent hypotheses about our origins which are contrary to the traditional, Hobbesian, patriarchal view, as noted above.

We see a range of behaviors among the apes that suggests the possible range of early human behavior. In all cases there are strong bonds between mothers and their progeny. Orangutans are the most solitary; the males are intolerant of one another and there is little bonding within or across sexes. Gorillas, although relatively not social, are polygamous with strong bonds between a male and his mates. Chimpanzees are more social, living in large groups, but males especially are quite aggressive and infanticide is not uncommon among them. Male chimpanzees bond and cooperate for hunting and for protection of their shared territory. Females do not bond strongly with one male or with other females. Bonobos, discovered in 1929, are the most sociable, peaceful, and perhaps intelligent of all the apes.[20] They are much less violent than their close relatives the chimpanzees (they are classified as two species of the same genus), using a wide variety of sexual activity to diffuse tension and anger. Unlike humans, they rarely harm or kill members of their own species, and infanticide has never been observed. And, as de Waal points out,

> Male-biassed evolutionary scenarios—Man the Hunter, Man the Toolmaker and so on—are being challenged by the discovery that females play a central, perhaps even dominant, role in the social life of one of our nearest relatives. In the past few years many strands of knowledge have come together concerning a relatively unknown ape with an unorthodox repertoire of behavior: the bonobo.[21]

This female dominance, however, is a gentle dominance, supporting my earlier claim that when females are dominant, dominance itself diminishes; as de Waal says, it is really leadership or, in Eisler's words, partnership.

It is important to note that this peaceful, sociable, fun-loving species appears to be the closest to humans, not only genetically but in appearance, physiology, and behavior. There is also evidence that humans and the African apes, including chimpanzees and bonobos, have a relatively recent common ancestor, and that, of these three species, the bonobo has changed the least from that common source. About this de Waal says:

> Just imagine that we had never heard of chimpanzees or baboons and had known bonobos first. We would at present most likely believe that early hominids lived in female-centered societies, in which sex served important social functions and in which warfare was rare or absent. In the end, perhaps the most successful reconstruction of our past will be based not on chimpanzees or even on bonobos but on a three-way comparison of chimpanzees, bonobos and humans.[22]

If we place the apes on an axis that measures the characteristics we have been emphasizing, with isolation, egoism, competition, and aggression at one end of the spectrum and openness, altruism, cooperation, and peacefulness at the other, then the bonobo, our closest relative and the species probably most similar to our own progenitor, is the closest to the open end of the spectrum. While this does not prove anything about our own origins, when viewed along with much supporting evidence, it makes it much more reasonable and realistic to say that our real *state of nature* was, relatively, open and peaceful than to imagine that it was "solitary and nasty." Although closer to the opposite end of the spectrum, even the solitary orangutan does not live in a state of war.[23]

The Time Frame

Before creating scenarios about our origins, we should have some idea of when the communities they attempt to represent might have existed. These scenarios are not points in time; the characters, behaviors and events that make them up would have spanned hundreds of thousands of years. The first hominids—*Homo erectus*, the tool-using primate from whom we evolved—probably emerged at the beginning of the Pleistocene or Glacial epoch, about 1,000,000 years ago. The earliest evidence of tool-using hunter/gatherer communities dates from the early Palaeolithic period—about 700,000 years ago. This primordial period of 300,000 years might have seen self-consciousness evolve from embryonic forms similar to those of contemporary apes to levels that support behavior that we can define as human. Most of what is known about the development of these early humans from 700,000 years ago until the Upper Palaeolithic, about 70,000 years ago, is inferred from their tools.

Throughout this long period they remained food hunters and gatherers, their developments influenced by the geological and climatic changes caused by the four glacial stages. During the Upper Palaeolithic period there was an accelerated cultural evolution involving the development of specialized tools produced by polishing and grinding rocks rather than simply chipping, various art forms, and the beginnings of agriculture and the domestication of animals. It is also during this period that other hominids, such as *Homo neanderthalensis*,[24] became extinct, leaving *Homo sapiens*. This laid the foundations for rapid development in the post-glacial Holocene or Recent period, in which the post-glacial climate and forests emerged. It is during this period, the Neolithic, from about 10,000 years ago to the end of prehistory 6,500 years ago, that there is evidence of development of dwellings, complex societies, ceremonies, cooperative hunting, the emergence of property, and some social stratification.

It is reasonable to hypothesize that morality, as discussed in previous chapters, would have emerged along with the early self-conscious hominids, from the early Palaeolithic period, starting perhaps 700,000 years ago. Indeed, the first normative reflections would have arisen with self-consciousness itself, perhaps from 1 to 5 million years ago. Apes and possibly other contemporary animals are probably capable of this, and so we might expect to find embryonic morality among our prehominid ancestors. The gestation period of morality would be very long—

perhaps several million years. The evidence suggests that the changes in tool production until the Upper Pleistocene were slight, indicating that the evolution of the interactions borne of self-consciousness, including forms of cognition and morality, would at first move at biological evolution's own unhurried rate, accelerating very slowly through much of the Pleistocene. Self-consciousness was struggling to get a foothold within the process. The process itself would have struggled to make any headway during the four major advances and retreats of the ice that covered much of the planet. And, in any case, the early stages of any exponential development do not appear to be very different from linear growth. It is toward the end of the period, after the last glaciation and the growth of the forests, that we find evidence of accelerated cultural development, from which we can infer an acceleration of self-conscious capacity and morality.

Simple reflections and the simple tools that nascent self-consciousness created had been an essential part of hominid communities for hundreds of thousands of years and formed the solid foundation for the acceleration in culture beginning in the Upper Palaeolithic. Similarly, the simple moral judgments of countless individuals in the communities of the period would have provided the base for the accelerated moral development that formed an integral part of that culture. Recognizable moral codes and the beginnings of systems of justice would have been part of the more complex social development toward the end of the Palaeolithic and into the Neolithic, during a period from 50,000 to 10,000 years ago. My scenarios will, then, date back 50,000 years or more, cover a time span of tens of thousands of years, and rest on moral foundations that go back a million years, perhaps much longer.

Specific Scenarios

Because we cannot know what actually happened in the communities of our early ancestors I will present a range of possible self-conscious responses and community characteristics, to increase the chances of approximating that reality. Just as there is significant variation in the social life of the different apes, and in different communities within the same species, so too one might expect that there were variations across the early human communities; looking at a range of scenarios is in itself more realistic than focusing on only one.

The first two scenarios are designed to test our hypotheses against a Hobbesian-type state of nature. To account for the fact that the two communities in these scenarios have evolved to the level of the scenario, the interpretation of evolution that we are using requires that, as the scenario begins, they have a balance of altruistic and egoistic developmental inclinations that is at least minimally developmental. They deviate radically from the Hobbesian in this regard.

The second pair of scenarios depict two communities that, the evidence suggests, we might have actually evolved from. They are models based on what is known about our origins plus what is known, in much greater detail, about our two closest living relatives: the chimpanzee and the bonobo.

Each of these scenarios is composed of early humans whose self-consciousness has developed to the extent that most of them make moral judgments, have exercised their rudimentary powers of reasoning, and have developed some symbolic form of communication, and whose relationships are getting more and more complex. Although characteristics of chimpanzees and bonobos influence two scenarios, the early humans in these communities have much more developed self-consciousness and morality than do these extant African apes. In all cases, the levels of *both* open and egoistic behavior must have been sufficient to sustain development up to the time of the scenarios.

The Hobbesian-Type Scenarios

These first two scenarios focus on self-consciousness associated with the minimum balance of developmental inclinations required for evolution to this time. They make no claims about male or female dominance. They concentrate instead on two threatening antidevelopmental behaviors: stealing and killing. It is realistic to suppose that these would have been among the earliest threats to development to be countered with the aid of self-consciousness; this approach allows us to immediately contrast our hypotheses with those from Hobbes to Nozick, within the context of the same threats that preoccupied them.

Scenario 1

Stealing would not in itself be a new behavior. Among this community's non-self-conscious ancestors, egoistic inclinations would have driven some to take food from others, especially in times of great scarcity; this would be countered by egoistically induced retaliation by those being robbed, but also by altruistically induced retaliation by parents or other relatives and friends of those being robbed. Killing within the community—indeed, within the species—would have been rare, even as retaliation for stealing.

Self-consciousness has given those with a propensity to steal techniques to do so more effectively. In some cases these techniques include killing the victim, and at times retaliation also includes killing;

self-consciousness, in these cases, increases the effectiveness and efficiency of antidevelopmental behaviors, and raises their incidence. In a non-self-conscious community, such aberrations would be taken care of by selection, perhaps at the expense of the whole community within which they emerged. Selection, however, works slowly and, in this community, self-consciousness is accelerating these antidevelopmental traits beyond the capacity of natural and even sexual selection to respond effectively. Any effective checks and balances must arise from self-consciousness itself and the morals it has induced, and since this community, by definition, does survive, we can look to what these might have been.

The first reflections on the threats of stealing and killing are induced by threats to the self and to those to whom the self is open; both egoistic and altruistic inclinations are at work. The value judgments "murder is bad" and "stealing is bad" would be made, even if not yet articulated, during this period. The corresponding *ought* statements would follow: "one ought not to kill," "one ought not to steal." These self-conscious moral judgments could occur within the community for some time, made by many of the self-conscious moral agents, before a moral code is conceived.

Among the repertoire of pre-self-conscious developmental inclinations are some cooperative approaches to external threats, primarily defenses against other threatening species. These inclinations would not yet have been applied within the community, and the concept of *threat to community from within* would not yet have been formed. Probably a critical mass of moral judgment, itself requiring a level of self-consciousness within the community, interacting with a minimum level of apparent threat, would have to be reached before a reflective response would be merged with the existing modes of retaliation. But at some point this critical mass within the appropriate conditions was reached. Perhaps the threat and the moral judgments were felt by several people within one closely related group in the community, or perhaps by some of the natural leaders of the community; or perhaps the process was triggered by an actual threat to powerful and relatively articulate members of the community, who could communicate their moral feelings to others who respected them. The result would be a convergence of the following elements:

- the natural inclination to protect against a threat, including the cooperative variant of this inclination;
- the moral judgments relevant to the threat;
- the capacity to apply self-consciousness and, specifically, some reason to all of these;
- the capacity to communicate the consequent moral articulations.

These elements would probably not emerge in quick succession, but eventually an articulation and communication of the moral judgments would mark the beginning of a moral code: a self-conscious agreement within the community that "thou shalt not kill" and "thou shalt not steal." These strong moral feelings, reinforced by awareness that they are shared by others, could later be promulgated to others, including those who pose the threat. Perhaps the initial promulgation would have been associated with retaliation by the creators of the code, or by some of them—an act demonstrating their moral judgment and the sanctions attached to it. This, on the surface, would appear to be the same as previous retaliations, but would be essentially different to the extent that it had a self-conscious component that would give it the character of a primitive but nonetheless real promulgated sanctioned command. Members of the community would reflect on this command, on the authority behind it, and on its sanctions, and would make judgments that would evaluate and perhaps challenge its legitimacy. Surviving such tests would legitimize it, and it would become a law, as I have defined law above: *Laws, arising from moral codes, are the orders of an accepted authority, appropriately promulgated and with appropriate sanctions.* (The general points made here about moral codes and law apply to all four scenarios.)

If it were the case that these first elements of a moral code and these first laws were to protect against the threats of nasty, brutish behaviors, then how does this scenario differ from that of Hobbes, whose Leviathan is a rational response to fear? Well, it differs in a couple of essential ways. It involves a rational application of moral judgments that themselves arise from self-conscious, developmental, and in this case both selfish and cooperative inclinations, and not from reason. Furthermore, because the foundations of moral codes and laws are developmental inclinations, the codes and laws are not limited to those negative orders—"thou shalt not ..."—that protect us from one another. The beginnings of moral systems might often have been commands designed to protect the community from aberrant behavior like killing and stealing, but they are not *born* of fear and egoism, but of positive developmental inclinations from which life-enhancing norms and laws would be just as natural as those that protect life.

Scenario 2

I have mentioned above the capacity of self-consciousness to enhance both developmental and antidevelopmental behavior, and the race that these two tendencies might have had—indeed, have today—to get the upper hand. In this scenario the threats to life and property of scenario 1 are central problems, but the character of the group has evolved away from the minimal developmental balance that brought it to this level. Life has become more truly Hobbesian: nasty, brutish, solitary.

The hunters and defenders have become more *solitary*, and aggressive and even violent tendencies have developed to a greater extent than in scenario 1. The emerging self-consciousness has been applied to the techniques of hunting and war. To the extent that these isolated hunters/warriors do not communicate and cooperate, self-conscious development has been retarded. Nevertheless, because of the similarity between hunting and warfare, self-conscious efforts do improve their techniques; an advance in a technique for hunting, in a weapon or detection strategy, for example, can be applied to war, and vice versa. These economies of scale accelerate the development of techniques that augment the users' capacity to dominate, within otherwise relatively slow cultural development.

Because of their low level of both bonding and inclination to cooperate, these new techniques are primarily associated with domination by individuals. The classical mechanics model derived by Hobbes from his knowledge of Galileo's physics—of point masses moving in space, attempting to overpower one another—can be mapped onto this group. And, as in Hobbes's model, as each individual gains power over others, so does the fear of each other grow, intensifying the inclination to compete and dominate for survival.

While all this is happening in the male sector, what of the women and children? They are occupied with the preeminent tasks of nurturing and being nurtured, of maintaining life in this nasty and difficult context. Hobbes makes no mention of them, nor, for that matter, do any of the professional reasoners along the Hobbes to Nozick line. Whatever the "little lady" might have been doing was of no consequence to the important matters that preoccupied the male hunter/warriors. Had these male rationalists but troubled to make their chimeras look like a real world, they would have seen that while the hunter/warriors were more and more occupied with their technologies of violence, more and more directing violence toward their own species, more and more consumed by fear, more and more competing to deal with the objects of fear, and, because of all this, as Hobbes himself recognized,[25] becoming less and less developmentally productive, the women were struggling to maintain the life of what remnants of community remained. They were the only sources of reproduction and were becoming increasingly the major agents of production.

In this scenario, however, they could not win the struggle. The imbalance came about so quickly and its impact on the women was so destructive that their efforts to control the violence were ineffective against it. Food production diminished; males were so caught up in competition, fear, and violence that even with new hunting techniques production fell. Women had developed new techniques for small animal hunting and food gathering, but their growing preoccupation with protecting themselves and their children from male violence, including an increase in infanticide and cannibalism, reduced their food production also. The violent competition over scarce resources itself made resources more scarce, creating a downward spiral toward extinction.

Those males who still had some open inclinations became objects of suspicion and fear and, being virtually defenseless, were eliminated. When reflection and self-interest did induce a recognition of the crisis, it was too late to rekindle the openness, empathy, and trust required to effect cooperative approaches to solve it. The only developmental moral code to have emerged was among women and adolescents still under their care, but it was marginalized by the males, and the besieged, violated, and overworked women had ever diminishing time and energy to make it effective. Nature eliminated this nasty, brutish experiment.

The More Real and Relational Scenarios

Scenario 3

Although I believe that the bonobo-like progenitor hypothesis that influences scenario 4 is the strongest one, I will respect de Waal's suggestion that the most realistic picture of our actual beginnings might be some synthesis of bonobos, chimpanzees, and humans. All of our scenarios include self-consciousness, moral judgment, and language as essential human characteristics. Scenario 3 synthesizes them with characteristics of perhaps our next closest relative after the bonobo, the chimpanzee. De Waal's picture would lie somewhere between this and scenario 4.

In this case, males are closely bonded and cooperate both in the defense of their community from others nearby and in the hunt for food. Males are more aggressive and violence is more common than in scenario 4, although killing within the community is rare. There is competition for food, and the stronger and more aggressive males usually win. Females are much less aggressive and violent and are more technically advanced—we might say more intelligent—than males. They are open to their offspring and the bond between mother and child, male or female, persists through life; the adult male will return to his mother in times of need or distress. Females do not bond closely with each other or with males.

One might expect self-consciousness to have been applied to the cooperative efforts of the males in both defense and hunting. The consequent enhancement of hunting and fighting techniques, including the development of weapons, would be accelerated by the fact that many of the techniques would be applied to both these closely related activities required for survival and development, as was the case in scenario 2. If this increasing dominance by the males went unchecked within the community, it would threaten the females and children and therefore the survival of the community. Many such communities perhaps did self-destruct because the imbalance grew too quickly to be checked. This community, however, by definition survived and developed, otherwise it would not be our progenitor; appropriate checks and balances must, therefore, have emerged. From where would these checks and balances likely arise?

The males, as in scenario 2, would have been increasingly engaged in applying their still rudimentary self-conscious capacities to the technologies of the hunt and war; some but not enough of them recognized antidevelopmental tendencies and/or articulated these. The females, recognizing the increasing threat of male dominance and of their more efficient use of techniques of violence, began to bond and cooperate among themselves. Some of the males who had recognized the threat to community had this recognition reinforced through communication with females, and supported the female effort and contributed their own well developed cooperative inclinations.

Infanticide was the first problem to be dealt with. Complete support among females and adolescents and growing support from a majority of the males led to prohibitions with sanctions. The moral judgment was strong and its articulation was clear and easy to communicate. The sanctions, supported by a cooperative effort among virtually all females and adolescents and most males, were adequate. The level of infanticide dropped, increasing the development prospects of the community.

This first attempt at reducing violence within the community by law was successful and led quickly (in evolutionary terms) to other laws to ameliorate other problems of violence against females, children, and, eventually, anyone in the community. These were also initiated by women, and the rate of increase in support for them by males continued to be critical, as the checks on violence had to increase faster than the rate of increase of the self-conscious enhanced violence itself. Once again it should be noted that there were no guarantees of success here, as there are none within evolution itself; however, since this community did survive, the developmental forces must have increased faster than the forces of destruction.

Because of the decrease in threats to them and their children, the women were able to concentrate more on child bearing and rearing; it was a long time before they managed to get significant male support here. In this more peaceful community, women were able to apply their self-consciousness, communication skills and enhanced cooperation to agriculture and small game hunting, eventually providing the bulk of nutrition for the whole community. The males could devote more time to hunting and defense techniques, which, because neighboring communities were becoming either more peaceful or self-destructing, and because women were the major food producers, had diminishing developmental value. They, however, recognized the value these activities had in maintaining their own form of dominance in the community and so, justified regularly by self-fulfilled prophecy, continued to follow the same path—indeed, to the present day!

The early laws, some of which would be in the form of taboos, were initiated by women and were negative with sanctions: thou shalt not murder infants; thou shalt not do violence against children, women, and any member of the community. Initially, the moral code contained negative judgments: one ought not murder or be violent against others; but as threats were reduced, many positive ones were added: we ought to cooperate, we ought to care more for children, we ought to be more open to our neighboring communities. Although the developmental balance was sufficient to allow this community to continue to the present, during these early stages it remained precariously closer to the disastrous imbalance of scenario 2 and did not achieve the greater developmental stability and efficiency of scenario 4.

Scenario 4

This community is based on what is probably the strongest single hypothesis about our origins: that we evolved from primates very much like the contemporary bonobo. The common ancestor, if there was one, could have lived several million years ago, but indications that the bonobo has not changed dramatically over such long periods suggests that assigning bonobo-like characteristics to our progenitors is not unrealistic. This, then, is a community of self-conscious hominids, similar to bonobos except more erect, with the capacity to vocalize their emerging language and having a more developed self-consciousness and morality. Like the bonobo, there is strong female bonding and cooperation and a gentle, nonviolent female domination or, as de Waal suggests, leadership. I will refer to this gentle but powerful leadership as *power-with* in contrast to the more usual male domination which I call *power-over*. There is little competition for necessities, little violence, and virtually no killing, and relations with neighboring bonobo-like communities are peaceful. To many readers this might sound too good to be true, but it is based on observed contemporary bonobo reality and recent palaeontological, archaeological, and anthropological evidence, as noted above.

Where might one expect self-consciousness to have asserted itself in this community over the millennia? Here are some possibilities: Openness and cooperation among females is important to development, and so they reflect on these characteristics and understand their developmental qualities; they see them as *good*, feel, self-consciously, that they ought to be developed further, and devise ways of doing this. Reflecting on their own position, in some instances, males begin to feel that female leadership is not good for them; however, given the strong but open form and developmental nature of this leadership, most males accept it as good. The females see the minority male opposition to the status quo to be at least a minor threat and decide on some simple strategies to counter this threat. For the most part the strategy is to ensure that their own control is seen to be developmental and itself not threatening to males. In those extreme cases of male opposition, some sanctions are imposed; because the males are physically stronger than females on average, these sanctions are executed through cooperative female action with some male support.

Sex continues to be used to defuse tensions that could lead to violence. Part of the female strategy to maintain their control makes more self-consciously strategic use of sex for this purpose. Sex, in the pre-self-conscious days, was also used by females to encourage males to share food, and this now leads to the development of rational strategies to use sexual favors for male assistance in child rearing. This would have a significant impact on survival probabilities and so would receive strong support from natural and especially sexual selection to the extent that this capacity to strategize was genetic. But more important, it would be culturally selected if successful, through communication and demonstration effects.

Reflection on the relatively abundant sexual activity also gave rise to some concerns. There is not yet any connection made between intercourse and birth, and nothing to resemble a nuclear family including mother and father; nevertheless, the difficulties and responsibilities of child bearing and rearing are now a central topic of individual reflection and group discussion among females. The persistent sexual overtures of some males, on the rise as self-consciousness enhances sexuality, is seen by many females as an impediment to child bearing and rearing, and they create some laws and make use of existing taboos to put some controls on sexual activity in certain circumstances. We should recall Miller's claims about the efficacy of sexual selection in promoting developmental human qualities such as kindness, sympathy, moral leadership, good parenting, leadership, and generosity.[26] It would seem that a bonobo-type community would especially excel in this regard. If so, the consequent positive developmental changes, interacting with and reinforced by self-consciousness and an open morality, might have led to an upward spiral in human development, as opposed to the downward spiral of the Hobbesian-type scenario 2.

We could go further with this scenario, but this is probably sufficient to highlight some salient points. The first semblance of legislation comes from women, as would be expected given their leadership position and their "role in the hugely important nexus of human social relations."[27] Second, the moral code and ensuing laws are primarily positive rather than negative; they arise from open developmental inclinations much more than from fear and self-interest. The effective judgments are that openness and cooperation are good, and open and cooperative efforts ought to be enhanced; there is less need for *thou shalt not kill* and more for *thou shalt share food and assist in nurture.* Some negative laws with sanctions also emerge: thou shalt not overtly threaten female leadership; thou shalt not interfere with child bearing and rearing. Over the long period of this development there could have been mutual reinforcement between, on the one hand, selection and especially sexual selection and, on the other, the maturing self-consciousness and morality. Most of this developmental synergy would come from the women.

The primitive system or organization within which the code and laws develop—the embryonic *state*—is led by females but, recognizing that cooperation and gentle persuasion, *power-with,* are good and that violence and a *power-over* type domination is bad, the females gradually bring males into this governing body.

Scenario Summation

Nothing is proved here. The scenarios are based on neo-Darwinian theory and solid evidence, but the interpretations of theory and evidence and the ways they are brought together in the scenarios can be challenged. The central point of hypothesis building is to elicit challenges and, through attempts to meet them, move gradually toward confirmation.

Here I want to focus on the main points that emerge from the four scenarios and contrast them to the states of nature of the dominant Western paradigm. The *states of nature* of the dominant Western paradigm look very much like segments of the societies of their authors. The agents are groups of rational calculators, all apparently males and Western, thinking through the solution to a problem, but themselves not caught up in the chaos and turmoil of that problem, or the dangers surrounding it. The problem and its context is always a variation on the Hobbesian theme: it involves threats to life and property in a society of competitive, autonomous, rational maximizers, always selfish and sometimes nasty and on the verge of war.

The political theorists in the dominant paradigm, whether they used a state of nature approach or not, felt no need to concern themselves with the validity and reality of their assumptions about the nature and origin of humanity. The present exploration of the actual origins of justice, however, requires an attempt to approximate the actual conditions in which justice might have emerged. Each scenario attempts to represent a part of a real continuing process.

The scenarios assume that the biological development trends continue and are joined by emerging self-consciousness, which, even though slow to develop, could have enhanced both positive and negative trends and effected a reversal in either. Culture, in its infancy, is being created by these early events and therefore is not a significant influence.

Scenario 2 is a case already too close to extinction to be saved by the powers of self-consciousness, and these powers might indeed accelerate their demise. In the others, and especially scenario 4, self-consciousness and morality have emerged in a more positive developmental milieu and enhanced that positive process. In the struggle between positive and negative self-conscious inclinations and behaviors in scenario 3, the developmental side wins, but perhaps by a small margin.

There is good evidence to support the hypothesis that the real world of our primordial ancestors, where justice must have arisen, was like scenario 4, or something between 3 and 4. Early human society was probably not dominated by males and was surely not dominated by male rational calculators. It is possible that neither males nor females dominated, but that females had significant control over community behavior using, to a great extent, leadership rather than domination: *power-with* rather than *power-over*. The hunter/gatherer division of labor, which would support male domination, probably came long after the origins of justice. It would be naive to suggest that these communities were idyllic, but there is much evidence to support the hypothesis of basically peaceful communities, more preoccupied with beauty and art than weapons and war.[28] There is also much evidence that the maternal influence that informed these relatively cooperative and peaceful societies had been the force that would have saved earlier hominid communities from self-destruction.

In all cases, antidevelopmental inclinations would have to be checked by the appropriate developmental tendencies; otherwise extinction would follow. These checks and balances are critical factors in all four scenarios. In each case there are threats to continued development, and in three cases developmental inclinations control these threats. Because the threats themselves are made more effective by self-consciousness, the developmental responses must have been capable of checking and balancing these exacerbated threats.

Women, who were involved in the critical tasks of reproducing, caring for, and nurturing the community, would probably have had a more highly developed self-consciousness and much greater openness than the men, and this would provide the adequate responses in the three successful scenarios. In the dominant paradigm, the emphasis is on justice as a rational solution for problems among nasty and autonomous individuals, and the agents of justice are men. In the successful scenarios above, the emphasis is on justice as a moral solution to problems in relational and open communities, and women are the primary initiators of justice, although men are not at all excluded.

In each scenario, rational solutions to threats are necessary. But rational solutions are integrated parts of long processes that involve, also necessarily, other elements of the self-conscious repertoire, beginning with the moral judgment and including powerful reflective intuitions and feelings. It is inconceivable that within a situation that threatens survival a rational response would be primary or adequate. It is also inconceivable that the only developmental characteristic available to check extinction would be reason.

The process of developing a system of justice unfolds over tens of thousands of years—hundreds of thousands from the first glimmer of morality. Reason evolves along with the myriad other self-conscious and non-self-conscious, developmental and nondevelopmental factors. We might propose that the rational faculty is in its infancy at the time of the first moral judgments and still a child at the beginning of moral codes and systems of justice. Only an appropriate balance of all of these self-conscious and non-self-conscious agents could spell success.

Rawls, assuming that the *men* who produce justice through reason in an original position would each be unduly influenced by the impact of various solutions on *himself*, sees the need for an imaginary contrivance which he calls "the veil of ignorance."[29] By this he means that those rational calculators who are creating justice would not know what effects the alternatives that they are considering would have on themselves. He says that this veil "is so natural a condition that something like it must have occurred to many" (137), but adds that the only thing like it that he has seen is in an article by an economist. Well, not being an economist, I don't see it as at all natural, and it clearly would not have been used, or even required, in any of the four scenarios. Those who, according to my hypotheses, actually founded a system of justice were concerned about themselves, but also about others and about the community. If they were not, they would have failed.

The scenarios imply that, in any human community, there must be a range of characteristics capable of supporting development. The parameters of this range would include a developmental egoistic-altruistic balance in both biological and transcendental inclinations and a level of cognitive and moral development that would check dysfunctional inclinations and enhance developmental inclinations. These parameters would have encompassed scenarios 1, 3, and 4 above, but excluded the *states of nature* of Hobbes, Nozick, Rawls, and scenario 2. In Hobbes, Rawls, and Nozick there is no mention of anything resembling openness, or of the nonrational cognitive and moral capacities required to solve the problems that this imbalance would induce, and so we can assume that, as in scenario 2, these capacities are not sufficient to ameliorate the *state of war*. Because our progenitors were successful and to the extent that these hypotheses are valid, whatever the specifics of their *states of nature*, they must have evolved within these parameters.

Because humans are self-conscious, within these parameters there is individual freedom to the extent that individuals can influence their moral judgments, can decide to follow these moral judgments or not, and can form judgments into codes and laws. There is individual freedom, but the community as a whole must develop within nature's parameters or face extinction, and in those early stages of human development these parameters would be much less yielding than those today. The moral judgments to support the community's development and the ensuing behavior are not arbitrary but are circumscribed by the biological base. Sexual selection becomes a more potent force here because of self-consciousness. Women's choice of mates could be influenced by their reflective strategies for development and/or to counter threats. They could decide to choose men who are nurturing, cooperative, and peaceful,[30] and to the extent that these qualities have genetic bases, they would increase within the population.

There is, obviously, extremely strong selection pressure on a community to enhance the development of its progeny. A community that did this below a critical level that promotes fitness could become extinct within a few generations. This indicates the primary importance of women in the development process as reproducers[31] and producers, but also the importance of strategies to encourage the cooperation of men in the nurturing of the community.

The openness that support for children and others in need requires in any community is a necessity, not a luxury. Every community would have, necessarily, a minimum level of openness needed for development. In the scenario 4 community, this critical mass of openness is most developed among the women but is also spread to a significant extent throughout the community. In the other scenarios it remains more concentrated, to varying degrees, within the female population. Scenario 4 is, because of its distribution of openness, the most developmentally efficient community and, therefore, the one most likely to develop. In it less time and energy is used by women to protect children and themselves, and more can be devoted to reproduction and production. Men waste less time and energy in unproductive competition and violence, and can themselves make a greater contribution to both production and reproduction. To the extent that a community has scenario 4 type efficiency its chances of survival and development increase; to the extent that it moves toward the other end of this efficiency spectrum its chances of survival decrease. It follows that the chances of a community which developed through the Palaeolithic being like scenario 4, or a mix of 3 and 4, are greater—I would say very much greater—than it being more toward the Hobbesian end of the spectrum.

The next chapter goes somewhat beyond this exploration of the origins of justice to a discussion of the administration of justice and law.

Chapter 8
The Origins of Law

The just community would need laws with attached sanctions to the extent that the openness to and understanding of development needs within the community was not adequate to the task of ensuring the exercise of the rights of all members. The task includes the distribution of the resources required for the exercise of rights and the protection of rights. Laws are needed to compensate for both moral and cognitive weaknesses in virtually all societies. This chapter explores the foundations of these laws within the context of human origins.

Much of the vacuum left by the rejection of divine law and natural law as foundations for human rights and positive law has been filled by positivist theories of rights and law.[1] In general, positivists see law as a coercive order created to protect people from one another, and rights as entitlements granted by law. Morality is not an integral part of this view, and there are no natural or universal bases or criteria for law or rights. This is contrary to the position I have taken in this exploration. I have proposed that morality, human rights/duties, and justice arise from developmental inclinations and have, consequently, a generally positive (not negative) origin and character. Laws, as components of systems of justice, emerged from this positive milieu.

There are some current approaches to law that are not positivist and that are more compatible with my hypotheses. I refer to these as *world order views*; they are reminiscent of the optimistic and holistic character of the earlier natural law theories. They integrate morality, human rights, and law more intimately, and go some way in providing all of them with a universal foundation. This chapter will present law as a natural continuation of the development of morality, rights, and justice in primal human communities, and compare this position with the positivist and world order views on law. The peculiarities of my concept of law arise from its derivation from my hypotheses on human origins and not from these or any other views on law. I have selected some legal theories for purposes of comparison and illustration only. This is not a treatise on Western theories of law.

Like my concept of rights/duties, my concept of law is very different from those of the positivist or realist, but similar in part to the world order views mentioned above.[2] Human rights are the claims of all humans to what they need for development, and to which the open community responds. Law is the social order required for the exercise of human rights. This is the direct opposite of the positivist position that *positive* law is the foundation of *positive* rights—the only rights—and that neither is based on morality.

Natural Law and Positivism

To facilitate analysis and comparison I will start by looking at two major approaches to our understanding of rights and law—natural law theory and legal positivism—through the eyes of some of their major proponents.

The natural law approach is highly integrated and holistic; divine law, natural law, morality, human inclinations, and *positive* law are all intimately interrelated. Natural law itself is the ultimate measure of right and wrong and the universal foundation of law.[3] The positivist approach, in sharp distinction, is segregated and abstract; divine law and morality are separated from *positive* law and natural law does not exist. According to Roscoe Pound, "Analytical jurisprudence broke with philosophy and with ethics completely."[4] The origin and test of law for the positivist lies within the social system and often within the legal system itself. There is no universal foundation.

Positivist approaches to law and rights reflect the vision of Thomas Hobbes, who says that, within the state of nature, "the notions of Right and Wrong, Justice and Injustice have there no place. Where there is no common Power, there is no Law: where no Law, no Injustice."[5] Power creates law and law creates rights. "Laws proper, or properly so called, are commands," states John Austin, and imply sanction, duty, and superiority.[6]

What, in this vision, is a *good* law? For Hobbes there is no test outside the sovereign as long as it does its duty by providing peace and common defense.[7] For Austin "the divine law is the measure or test of positive law" (6). But there is no link through natural law between divine law and *positive* law. What God has revealed we know from that revelation; the rest "we must construe by the principle of utility" (104).

How does Austin's position differ from that of the natural law theorists?

In each case divine law is the test of *positive* law and in each case we are able to measure the latter against the former. For Austin, however, where revelation does not guide us we must estimate the effect of our actions on the goal of happiness or good, whereas in natural law theory we are directed toward our goal, along with all of nature, by natural inclinations. In the words of Thomas Aquinas, "Wherefore according to the order of natural inclinations, is the order of the precepts of natural law."[8] Aquinas, of course, believed that God/divine law is the source of natural law and natural inclinations.

For Aquinas and some other natural law thinkers, God is the unifying agent; natural law and, therefore, natural inclinations are a manifestation of divine law. God is integral to the process and is the factor that integrates divine law, natural law, *positive* law, and morals into one system. Austin refers to God and divine law, but his theory really has little need for a divinity. If one knows nothing through revelation, the principle of utility will suffice. The parallel, but clearly not integral, divine law could be and indeed has been discarded from positivist theory without any impact on its concept of law.

Nor does Austin need the concept of natural law. We determine our actions by the principle of utility; our actions are not determined by natural inclinations. The distinction here is more than subtle. For the positivist, our actions are guided by rational calculations of the predicted consequences of our acts, or from the rules or maxims generalized from repeated experience of consequences.[9] Rational calculation is the source of the rules of human conduct and, hence, of law. Apart from the revealed divine law, which, as noted above, is not an essential part of positivist theory, the source of *positive* law is found within human societies. The vagaries of humanity are, as a consequence, reflected in the variations of the law itself. On the other hand, if natural law, understood as a hierarchy of natural inclinations, is the source of law, then one must look beyond our species for the source and test of law, and there we might expect to find a common and perhaps even universal foundation. In the natural law tradition, this foundation is usually divine law.[10]

The positivist theory can survive—indeed thrive—without the divine; but can natural law exist without divine law? The Western concept of divine law is no longer a dominant idea even in Western thought, let alone throughout the world, and cannot therefore provide a universally accepted foundation for law. Furthermore, for the positivist, the associated teleological concept of natural law has been discredited by the neo-Darwinian theory of evolution; as we have proposed above, there are no purpose, no planned objectives within the evolutionary process until the advent of self-consciousness. The divine and natural bases for law have been severed; the positivist approach now dominates. Is it possible, however, to discover a concept of natural law that is compatible with modern science and that can provide universal and objective foundations for *positive* law? We will see. But before considering our hypotheses as an answer to that question, a second significant difference between positivist and natural law theories should be noted.

Visions of Humanity

The positivist approach shares in a vision of humanity that in its extreme form can be traced to Hobbes. This is the picture of humans as naturally competitive and warring—the picture I have countered throughout this work. It concludes that people need a power to be feared to protect them from one another, and that this power is the sovereign state and its *positive* laws. In contrast to this pessimistic picture of the human condition is the more optimistic view of natural law theorists, and especially their emphasis on human characteristics such as cooperation and altruism. The major basis for this optimism is a belief in the divine, but they see positive characteristics throughout nature. The contrast is seen in Hobbes's contemporary Hugo Grotius, often called the father of international law. For Grotius, the maintenance of social order is the source of law.[11] The human has "an impelling desire for . . . the social life . . . peaceful and organized . . . ; this social trend the Stoics called 'sociableness'" (6). We are not impelled by nature to seek only our own good. The human is distinguished from other animals, but Grotius sees social tendencies in some of them as well and emphasizes the extent of natural altruistic behavior.

By claiming that it rests on natural law, Grotius separates *positive* law from the divine.[12] But, unlike the positivist, Grotius sees the source of law as lying beyond the fears and rational calculations of humanity; it is found in social and altruistic tendencies, common not only to reasoning humans but also to children and animals.

Whereas Austin's legal positivism had no real need for divine law, and positivism evolves to this day without divinity, the natural law of Grotius has not done well without God's support. Hans Kelsen claims that there can be no moral basis for law since "no element common to the contents of the various moral orders is detectable."[13] He argues against the concept of natural law on the ground that it is teleological, confounds the descriptive and normative orders, and thereby conflicts with modern science.[14] "If the natural-law doctrine is consistent, it must assume a religious character" (138).

According to Kelsen, natural law doctrine fails before the tribunal of science, and with it the optimistic vision of humanity and a universal moral foundation for law. The now dominant Western views present laws as the creations of lawmakers, measured only by constitutions, effectiveness, or maxims based on utility calculations, and see rights as creations of laws and consequently, of the state.[15] In schematic form we have:

The Hobbesian sequence would be:

War → fear → reason → alien power-over → law → rights

The contemporary positivist position might be simply:

State (elected or otherwise) → law → rights

The (theocentric) natural law doctrines would be:

(Divine law) → natural law → morality → human rights → positive law

In the positivist tradition human rights arise out of *positive* law and are therefore neither universal nor inalienable. Law itself is relative and arbitrary, its origin and test being within the human community and with no necessary connection to morality. Its basic negative mandate is to protect us and our property from one another; its evolving positive mandate can be explained in terms of the principle of utility. The context of the former is fear; that of the latter is competition and maximization.

Natural law theory, in contrast, is more positive and optimistic. Rights and laws are a part of a universal moral system that has a positive goal and that assumes human cooperation and altruism. This is compatible with the position taken throughout this exploration. I propose that positive law is created by the self-conscious community as a natural outcome of the original morality including human rights/obligations; the development of community is its defining purpose, not command or coercion. The sequence would be:

developmental inclinations → morality (values/obligations) → rights → positive law → exercise of rights → development

I have called the set of propensities for the conditions of an organism's development to maturity its inclination to develop; therefore, by definition, a natural inclination to develop is a basic and necessary condition of the evolutionary process. We have, thereby, returned to a principle of natural law: "Wherefore according to the order of natural inclinations, is the order of the precepts of natural law."[16]

The Origin of Law

Some order required for the satisfaction of development needs will be found in all animal communities. In many this includes hierarchies and behavior analogous to obedience to authority.[17] The need for order, especially in times of scarcity and stress as illustrated in the scenarios in Chapter 7, would have been recognized by our primordial parents, and as the community and its needs became more complex, an articulated order would have developed to ensure a fair distribution of resources to guarantee the exercise of human rights by all members of the community. *Positive* law would be born as a social order required for the satisfaction of development needs, that is, for the exercise of rights. Law was born principally out of concern over the continuing development of individuals in the community and of the community itself, and not out of fear of one another. It was a positive (not *positivist*) response to a community's development needs, not a negative reaction to the hazards of a state of war. Law emerged primarily out of the profound feelings of concern for others, the acute sense of the needs of others, and the strength of the female members of the community, and not from rational men.

These primordial communities were not Hobbesian states of war, nor were they totally at peace. Laws are born within communities with selfish and altruistic characteristics and, as I have suggested, external and internal threats might have been catalysts in this development. Nevertheless, law arising from a state of nature such as scenario 4 in Chapter 8 would be an essentially human, transcendent manifestation of developmental inclinations and therefore a positive emanation from positive and natural foundations.

We must keep in mind that we are not talking about ideal systems of justice created by rational argument. Even our best scenario is a model of a real community, experimenting with new capacities in often hostile environments, fragile and vulnerable in many respects, its developmental qualities perhaps keeping it just a few steps ahead of extinction. Its moral code, its response to rights, and its laws were products of that reality. Like all of the elements of emerging humanity, they were remarkable in their transcendent uniqueness, but they were also in a most imperfect, very flawed embryonic state. Indeed, the systems of justice of today's most developmental societies are some distance from an ideal.

A Positive Concept of *Positive* Law

In the present hypothesis, law is the order required for the exercise of human rights in large and complex communities. It emerges from the cooperative side of the human for a very positive purpose: human development. The egoistic/competitive side of the human requires that sanctions be associated with law if law is to be effective. Like H. L. A. Hart,[18] however, I see no *necessary* connection between law and sanction, although there is an obvious empirical connection.

This concept of law is very different from that of the positivist school and, indeed, much of legal theory. Austin defines laws as commands that imply sanctions and superior-inferior relationships: "A law . . . may be said to be a rule laid down for the guidance of an intelligent being by an intelligent being having power over him."[19] For Kelsen, "The fundamental difference between law and morals is: law is a coercive order, that is, a normative order that attempts to bring about a certain behavior by attaching to the opposite behavior a socially organized coercive act; whereas morals is a social order without such sanctions."[20]

The great emphasis on coercion, command, *power-over*, and sanction in law is probably a product of patriarchy, and negative definitions of law would have arisen from negative views of the human, especially within the positivist school. Hobbes's belief that "every man is Enemy to every man"[21] precludes a practicable law without sanctions; it would be assumed that, without coercion, people would not obey. But in our primordial communities, and especially scenario 4, concern for others and for community would be a greater motive for both legislating and obeying the law than fear and sanctions would be.

The close identification of law with command and coercion gives law a negative and narrow character. In the Hobbesian view, the purpose of law is to protect hostile humans from one another—to isolate the individual and his or her property from others. On the other hand, to see a legal system as the social order required to exercise rights and thereby develop places a positive and broad emphasis on law from the outset. The ideal legal system would be the order required for the exercise of all human rights by all members of the community for the development of the community. Actual legal systems could be judged against this ideal. A specific law would be a prescription needed to enhance the social order with regard to the exercise of a particular right by all or some members of a community; its test would be its contribution to the exercise of that right, and ultimately to development. The issues of execution, sanctions, and other important details would, of course, have to be dealt with, but as essential administrative matters—not as the essence of the law.

The World Order Theories

I would like to turn now to a brief account of some current theorizing in the area of international law—the world order models noted above—that I see as similar to and, perhaps, supportive of the present hypotheses.

Almost forty years ago C. Wilfred Jenks wrote that it was no longer acceptable to claim that international law arose from and regulated the relations among independent states. The basic concept of international law is, he said, interdependence.[22] Jenks's concept of interdependency leads him to the idea that the will of the world community is the basis of obligation and the sociological background of which the law is the expression (90). This is not a community of states but of people.

Furthermore, Jenks insists that his theory of obligation "does not involve the transposition to an international scale of the concept of law as command; it has no Hobbesian or Austinian overtones" (91). For Jenks, the origin of law is positive, universal, and real, not negative, isolated, and hypothetical.

This positive (rather than positivist) approach to rights and law is taken further by McDougal, Lasswell, and Chen:

> The important fact is that the peoples of the world, whatever their differences in cultural traditions and styles of justification, are today increasingly demanding the enhanced protection of all those basic rights . . . by the processes of law in all the different communities of which they are members, including especially the international or world community.[23]

These authors see respect as the core value of human rights. They define respect as "an interrelation among individual human beings in which they reciprocally recognize and honor each other's freedom of choice about participation in the value processes of the world community or any of its component parts" (451).

To satisfy the broad, fundamental and global set of demands that they say exist, McDougal et al. see the need for a law that appears to be much more extensive and much more positive than that of the positivists:

> The culminating achievement for a community that aspires to honor these demands and to secure human rights better may be described as that of a public and civic order in which individuals are subjected to the least possible coercion, from either public or private sources, in the making of their choices about participation in the community's various value processes. (799)

The nature of and the relationships among morality, rights and law are here quite different from the positivist view. Rights arise from value processes and are secured by a social order that includes both public order with severe sanctions and civil order with mild sanctions. Public order goes well beyond the protection of life and property; it regulates "the shaping and sharing of all community values" (800). Civic order provides maximum freedom of choice with minimum coercion (801).

McDougal et al. share my view that, even at the global level, the exercise of rights requires the involvement of individuals, not just states, in the law. Their emphasis, however, is on protection rather than on development. They say, "The individual should be made a full subject of international law, with that access to all arenas, both international and national, which is necessary for him to protect himself" (955).

In the view of McDougal et al., the goal of human rights and, by extension, of law is human dignity.[24] Dignity has become a popular foundation for, or goal of, human rights among those who are not satisfied with the positivist reduction of human rights to positive rights created by positive law.[25] I believe, however, that this concept is too vague and subjective to help us explain these universal claims, and this is one of the reasons I have sought a more objective explanation in the evolutionary process.

Richard Falk continues the theme of interdependency and world order with emphasis on the global problems that threaten our species. In response to them he proposes four normative goals for law: to minimize violence; to maximize welfare; to maximize social justice; to maximize environmental quality.[26] He sees a global populism as the best way to achieve these goals.[27] Like Jenks and McDougal, Falk rejects the state as the sole source of international law and, in fact, sees the need for a world order that transcends present international law and reflects directly the will of individual people rather than the common interest.

As his four goals of law indicate, what is at stake for Falk is the survival and development of humanity more than human dignity. His stated four goals of law include much more than minimum conditions for survival, but also the maximization of all conditions for development. His model arises from extreme negativity—the threats of nuclear war, underdevelopment, and ecological crises—but emerges as positive and broadly developmental. Furthermore, he puts this holistic and dynamic vision into an evolutionary context: "With regard to international law, we can take seriously aspirations for a more decent and humane world, which means that these aspirations are not merely pious, but are grounded in our will to survive and evolve as a species."[28]

Concern for survival and development does not, however, lead Falk to a sustained exploration of evolutionary antecedents of a world order; he in fact identifies one of his rejected options for world order—a concert of great powers—as neo-Darwinian (30), thereby, it would seem, interpreting struggle for survival narrowly and negatively, as did the social Darwinists. I would claim that the present interpretation of neo-Darwinian theory provides an appropriate basis for Falk's view of world order and shows why this exploration of origins does really matter.

Law and Development

In the final analysis, the human rights and laws considered to be important to a community's development will be what that community, or more likely its powerful members, say they are. A tyrant could agree with the present hypotheses and still decide that his or her law would ignore the exercise of rights or, indeed, the very existence of rights. The rights, of course, even though their exercise was impaired by the tyrant, would still exist. My conclusions about rights and law assume that, although human development transcends the neo-Darwinian process, its origins and many of the conditions for its continuation live in that process. The broader evolutionary context of human development cannot be ignored: a context that confers on rights and law a positive developmental character, and that replaces the vague and ambiguous views of rights and law with more solid, comprehensible, and human foundations.

In the present view, human rights are universal and inalienable. They are not narrowly defined in terms of relations between individual and state, or restricted to civil and political rights, but encompass all development needs, including, in the language of the two United Nations Covenants of 1966, economic, social, and cultural rights. Since the purpose of law is to provide the social order required for the exercise of these human rights, it must also encompass all dimensions of human development and meet the universal test of development itself. *Human development is the measure of law.*

I believe that, to the extent that there is development, the real world of communities must be actually behaving according to this model. But, conversely, to the extent that development is retarded or even arrested throughout the world, there are deviations from this ideal. How could we behave, as Falk puts it, as if this normative view really mattered? This question, of course, is too large to be answered here.

The Administration of Justice and the Patriarchy

Morality and legal systems, in spite of their ultimate origins in the open inclinations that drive the biological process, are constructed by our cultures. The expanding freedom from the constraints of physical and biological conditions is, in itself, good. The self-actualization of individuals and communities is a sine qua non of humanity. Cultures contribute to self-actualization, however, they also produce obstacles to individual freedom. The present exploration points to one powerful and ubiquitous obstacle to the self-actualization of many members of many communities: patriarchy.

We understand evolution and human development, not in terms of absolutes but in terms of tendencies. Patriarchy refers to a tendency for males to dominate. This tendency is often very strong but never absolute. Communities are dominated by male elites, and this tendency varies considerably, being strong but weakening somewhat in political societies, close to absolute in some major religions, perhaps moving closest to a partnership balance in some civil societies. Male domination is not a measure of male power or superiority. Hitler was a lazy, weak, and probably rather stupid man. Humanity allows systems and ideologies to take control.

Few deny that we live in a patriarchal world. Most, however, see this as natural and necessary, and some argue that male competitiveness and aggression is the source of human development.[29] But the present exploration and the evidence that supports it suggest that early human development was influenced more by women than by men and that women played a leadership role in community.

According to Riane Eisler, the cultural change from woman-centered communities to patriarchal *power-over* societies began less than seven thousand years ago, through Kurgan invasions across ancient Europe.[30] The Kurgans were called Indo-Europeans or Aryans, idealized by Hitler as the original Europeans, but they were nomads and neither Indian nor European in origin. There were other nomadic invaders as well; "The one thing they all had in common was a dominator model of social organization: a social system in which male dominance, male violence, and a generally hierarchic and authoritarian social structure was the norm" (45).

As Eisler says, these nomadic invasions were not the only cause of the dramatic shift in culture, but she adds that wars and social violence played a central role in the change (47). In any case, it seems that it was well after the birth of humanity, morality, and justice that the patriarchy we know today came to be. The primordial human communities were not states of war; only in later human societies under the domination of patriarchic cultures did the balance shift toward that nasty and closed end of the spectrum, thereby frustrating development potential.

I do not now, however, wish to discuss patriarchy as dysfunctional.[31] What is more immediately relevant to the present context is the apparent dichotomy between the primarily female origins of justice and its predominantly male domination throughout recorded history. If women are the primary creators of justice, why have men become the major administrators of justice?

The controversial but important results of Carol Gilligan's research suggest to me an answer to this question. Gilligan sees two moralities: the morality of women flows from an immediate, compassionate and caring grasp of a situation within a relational context; the morality of men is a rational response to an abstract problem within the context of autonomous, isolated individuals. She calls the former a morality of responsibility and care, the latter a morality of rights.[32] These are presented as the central tendencies of the moralities of males and females based on experiments carried out by Gilligan and others in the United States during the past three decades.

I have argued that justice is the developmental response to human rights and that rights, which are claims to real developmental needs, are exercised because of this response. The response itself arises from openness, from an understanding of the needs of others and the acceptance of an obligation to that need. This is Gilligan's "female morality." Her concept encompasses my ideas of morals, rights, and justice, and although I put more emphasis on the feelings of caring and compassion being self-conscious, our views are virtually the same.

I have also argued that justice emerges primarily among the women in aboriginal communities, and so I agree that morality and justice so described have a strong female association, although I would not label it *female*. Gilligan's conclusions support my hypothesis, particularly as presented in my scenarios, that the kind of justice that would induce development in our early ancestors, based on caring and empathy in a relational community, would be found primarily among the women.

Gilligan's "female morality" is essentially what I consider to be the original and basic morality, for women and men. Her "male morality" could be a tendency for men to be less aware of moral foundations and more likely to focus on peripherals, which are simpler and more obvious objects of awareness, reducing profound morality to something like Nozick's formula (p. 7 above). Whatever the explanation for its appearance, I would not see "male morality" as a second kind of morality. It is, however, what the dominant Western paradigm imagines morality to be.

I have argued throughout against reason being a foundation for morality, rights, or justice and for the idea that justice arises from individuals-in-community and not from isolated, autonomous *man*. I have said, nevertheless, that reason is required to ensure that all members of a community have an opportunity to exercise their rights, and that this is especially the case as communities become larger and more complex. These rational techniques for administering justice have the characteristics of what Gilligan calls "male morality." A system designed to administer justice fairly, or to administer justice for the purposes of powerful elites, as has been more often the case, will arise from a rational plan and will necessarily see individuals as abstract isolated, autonomous units within the calculus. If there is an attempt to guarantee equality under the law, the legislature must, to a great extent, make its determinations for the good of the abstract citizen, without regard to specific relationships or feelings of compassion. The judiciary, dealing with real, individual people, will become engaged in both a rational calculus for the abstract citizen and feelings of compassion for the real, relational individual-in-community.

Women continue to be the relatively silent but powerful originators and foundations of justice, but have become marginalized from its administration. How do we explain this male-female dichotomy and why does Gilligan's "male morality" have characteristics similar to systems of justice? I don't like essentialism, but I don't think it can be totally avoided here. Women were the primary source of justice because they were the primary source of care. That is not to say that men were uncaring; there is abundant evidence of male empathy and caring in many species. The point is that there was a greater tendency for females to be caring than for males. This would be explained by the female role as sole reproducer and major producer of community, including nurturer, protector, and educator.

Men, throughout recorded history, have been the administrators of justice. Why is this? Is it because the male approach to morality is suited to the rational and abstract nature of systems of justice? Or, conversely, was the administration of justice transferred from women to men as a consequence of patriarchic domination, or because women could no longer bear this burden? We might also ask whether "male morality" is a cultural construction induced by male involvement in these systems. And are male philosophers not able to see the real origins of justice because it is obscured by the rationality and abstraction of their own superficial view of morality and its administration?

To return to the problem of essentialism: reproduction of community has been the essential role of women to the present; however, it is now being modified to some extent. In many industrialized societies women's roles as nurturer, protector, educator—the nonbiological reproduction roles in general—are increasingly shared by men. We might foresee a time when the burden of reproduction itself could be removed from women. This indicates that the biological conditions that have maintained the gender status quo are not absolute; self-consciousness and culture are reducing its control and will continue to do so.

As women are freed from their traditional roles, they enter the traditional male world, including the administration of justice. Does this effect a natural synergy between the foundations of justice and its administration? Perhaps. Do men who become more open and involved in caring also inform the administration of justice with the openness of justice itself? Perhaps. Are the central tendencies between male and female morality, as discovered by Gilligan and others, converging?

Perhaps. The gender division determined by the neo-Darwinian process in the communities of our progenitors is, because of the power of self-consciousness and culture, not as essential now. One might hope that the outcome will be communities in which male-female dichotomy will disappear as abstract rationality and the isolated individual is absorbed by the real, relational, and open individual-in-community.

Concluding Comment

I have proposed above that the origins of morality, rights, and law were not Hobbesian, patriarchal communities but rather communities in which women would have taken the lead in creating morality and justice within a context informed by a natural balance of moral and cognitive capacities: an open, relational and relatively peaceful community. Cultural developments over many millennia have led us far from those origins. The characteristics of societies, nevertheless, have rarely gone to Hobbesian extremes, and law has not become simply a coercive order. To use Hart's distinction, people obey the law because they are obliged to, but also, and more fundamentally, because they recognize and respond to their obligations. The patriarchy has not completely frustrated our natural inclinations to openness. Historians and journalists dwell on dominators, wars, violence, and lawlessness, but underlying these events and people of supposed great importance (usually men) are the interactions of countless women, and men, whose developmentally balanced behavior sees to the task of human development, without coercion and mostly without reward.

I have suggested that there are now some challenges to the dominant and dominating system, mainly from civil society, and perhaps we can add that there have been some developmental legislative changes as well. Legislation countering hate and discrimination addresses dysfunctional behaviors promoted by the likes of Nazism and apartheid, as well as more general forms of sexism and racism. Legislation has gone some small way toward ameliorating environmental threats. Welfare legislation does distribute some of the resources needed for the exercise of human rights. There are, however, new laws and deregulations that allow new forms of domination. Many feel that legislation supporting and promoting the free flow of capital (usually referred to simply as "free trade") give greater power-over to capital, threatening workers' rights to security and decent working conditions, women's and children's rights, sovereignty, the environment, cultures, and the possibility of self-actualization through work.

All evolution has been an ebb and flow of developmental conditions, the developmental overcoming the dysfunctional in successful cases.

One might have expected that self-consciousness would have given us the capacity to shift the process more toward the developmental side—to a more constantly balanced and open human evolution. Our cognitive dimension has developed exponentially. Through science and technology we know more and more about what is and how to. But our moral dimension has not kept pace. We do not fully grasp what we ought to do and why we ought to do it. Seeing and reinstating the positive developmental origins of justice would enhance our moral dimension.

Chapter 9
Some Concluding Comments

In their book *The Canadian Way*, Ivan Head and Pierre Trudeau issued the following warning:

> We write these words in 1995, at a time when the concepts of a "planetary environment" and a "global economy" are accepted without challenge. Still to be accepted, however, is a concept inextricably related to the first two, that of a single human society. Unless this universal phenomenon is recognized and embraced, the mortal perils facing the human race and its natural habitat cannot be countered effectively.
>
> Trudeau had drawn from a work by Teilhard de Chardin to make this point to the UN Conference on Human Settlements in 1976: "Love one another, or you will perish.... We have reached a critical path in human evolution in which the only path open to us is to move towards a common passion, a 'conspiracy' of love."
>
> Our future as humans will be influenced immeasurably by our definition of community and our acceptance of the common destiny of our species.[1]

I believe that the evidence the present exploration has led to does suggest strongly that our origins were indeed a "conspiracy of love." It was the breath, the spirit of love that brought together the elements that informed humanity. It was openness, concern for others, that gave life to morality and justice; it was not isolation, aggression, and fear. And, I am bold enough to say, this positive view of our origins could suggest a definition of community and help us to discover our common destiny.

I would not be so bold, however, as to say that I have reached a conclusion. None of the questions raised about the origins of justice can be answered through the application of "sophisticated mathematics," as Rawls put it, or of Nozick's mathematical formula for rational and moral action. The questions raised are for the most part empirical questions, and good answers will come only from good evidence and good interpretations of that evidence. The evidence I have put forward, gleaned from the work of scholars from several disciplines in the natural sciences, is, I believe, good evidence. My interpretation of this evidence is, I believe, good, but, of course, both my selection of evidence and my interpretation are subject to my own bias. In any case, the best one can hope for in an exploration such as this is a set of hypotheses that are strong enough to be worthy of further confirmation, and modification if required.

Here I will summarize my hypotheses, assess the strength of the evidence from which they arise, and reflect on the interpretations of the evidence reached by myself and others. I will end this work by looking briefly at the application of these hypotheses to the present and future of humankind.

Summary

I have challenged the standard and dominant view of justice and its elements. In this view, humans are essentially and naturally selfish and autonomous rational planners and maximizers. Humans are virtually always referred to as *men*, and this is appropriate in that these thinkers ignore the distinctive and robust character of women and their indispensable and dynamic role in human development. From the negative and pessimistic image of *man* comes the vision of a *state of nature* that is, more or less, a *state of war*. Justice arises from human instrumental rationality to protect and isolate *man* and *his* property from other nasty *men*.

In this exploration I have referred to some earlier Western thinkers and have used Rawls and Nozick as examples of recent versions of the same basic vision. The stark contrast between these views of *man* and justice and my hypotheses on human development helps situate and clarify the latter.

My hypotheses are as follows:

1. The communities of our progenitors were essentially social/relational, open, and relatively peaceful, being a balance of egoism and altruism, competition and cooperation, nastiness and nurture. Individuals developed in community, not in isolation. There was a balance of cognition and affection, the fundamental and effective cerebral activities all arising from self-consciousness and including intuition and self-conscious feeling, giving rise to profound understandings without recourse to instrumental reason. Reason would also have developed from self-consciousness during our species' infancy, but would have been one cognitive activity among others, and probably not as important to early development as the others.

2. Symbols of value and obligation arose from the capturing of natural developmental inclinations by self-consciousness. Value and obligation are the principal elements of morality, of human rights and duties, and of justice. Symbols of value emerge from reflections on developmental inclinations and their objects. The feeling of obligation is the self-conscious recognition of inclinations as powerful. Because of the natural balance between egoism and altruism, value includes what is good or bad for self and for others, and obligation to self and to others are both recognized and responded to. The recognition of others and the needs of others I call *openness.*
3. A human right is a claim for something required for development, where development is defined both by biological and transcendental needs and by cultures. The right arises from reflection on the inclination toward what is needed and on the positive response to the claim by others. Both the need and the acceptance by others of an obligation related to that need are sine qua nons of a right. Human rights have, therefore, natural and developmental origins. Because they are essential elements of our evolution as humans—of human nature itself—and not the products of states or laws, they are universal and inalienable.
4. The just individual is a natural outcome of openness at a self-conscious level. Those who recognize others and their needs and respond appropriately to those needs are, by definition, just. As communities grow in size and complexity, however, it will not always be possible for the individual to determine what an appropriate response might be. Furthermore, the mix of egoism and altruism, competition and cooperation, means that some people will decide not to respond appropriately. To solve such problems, systems of justice, including laws, were developed. The function of law is to facilitate the exercise of the rights of all members of the community for development. Systems of justice and laws are required to compensate for deficits in knowledge and/or openness, especially in large and complex communities. Nevertheless, their origins are natural and developmental in that they arise from morality and human rights. The basis and the test of justice and law is human development.

The Evidence

My hypotheses flow from the neo-Darwinian theory of evolution in general and from some interpretations of specific characteristics of evolution.

The evidence for the theory itself is overwhelming. New molecular phylogenic (DNA) evidence further confirms the conclusions reached by many branches of science from Darwin to the present.

The ongoing study of the human genome supports two essential hypotheses in this exploration: (1) there is genetic continuity throughout the living world, and this is best explained by the neo-Darwinian synthesis; (2) we humans have fewer genes in general and fewer uniquely human genes than previously believed, supporting the view that complex and profound human behaviors need explanations that go beyond the genome, and especially to self-consciousness and culture.

Evolution is virtually a fact. I say "virtually" because there is a competing hypothesis that should not be ignored: the creationist hypothesis. Assuming that there is a divine creator, the creationist would have us believe that She created the universe some 6,000 years ago and placed in it all the evidence that points to a continuous evolution starting billions of years ago and evolution leading to humans dating back millions of years, including evidence for the origins of life and humanity within the process. I can't say with absolute, mathematical certainty that She did not do that, but to me it is inconceivable that a wise and good God would be so mischievous as to plant so much deceiving evidence. Furthermore, if there is a Creator, then it seems that Her omnipotence and omniscience would be better demonstrated through the marvels of evolution than by the very human biblical account of six days of hands-on work followed by the need to rest. For all practical purposes, I take evolution to be a fact. Nevertheless, I have said that, although there is no purpose within evolution before self-consciousness emerges, and all the process from fundamental energy to life and on to human life can be explained within that process, this does not preclude the possibility of a Creator. There is no scientific evidence that the universe of hundreds of billions of stars in each of hundreds of billions of galaxies, probably many fostering their own evolutions, is simply an accident; nor is there irrefutable scientific evidence that it isn't.

I cannot be as certain about all the specific characteristics of the process that led to our own species. The hypotheses that altruism is natural and necessary along with egoism, that primate evolution is social/relational, and indeed that all evolution has a communal and cooperative character are, I think, to a great extent confirmed, but some still debate this interpretation. The Hobbesian view of human nature as nasty and solitary has been challenged by the founders of the theory—Darwin, Dobzhansky, Simpson, to name only an obvious few—and by much current research, such as the distinguished work of Frans de Waal and his colleagues. I have discussed the views of Richard Dawkins on the "selfish gene" as an example of an eminent evolutionist who seems to reduce altruism to egoism, and I believe I have presented some serious arguments against his position. My central point is that altruism does exist within the evolutionary process and that, if we distinguish the non-self-conscious altruistic act from the factors for its selection, we see that neither it nor its transcendent descendant can be reduced to egoism.

I have put great emphasis on natural developmental inclinations as both the driving force of evolution and the origin, along with self-consciousness, of morality and all that is moral. These biological inclinations, propensities, or appetites do obviously exist, and given the constant impact of natural and sexual selection, they are virtually always developmental. Although the details elude us, we now have a good idea of how self-consciousness emerged and developed, and morality and other ingredients of our cultures can be explained in a nonreductionist way as self-consciousness capturing and articulating our inclinations, feelings, the objects in our environment, and other humans. New evidence from several sources supports my insistence that morality is not a product of reason.

I have noted more than once the analytical nature of one of my central premises: if a community was, or included, our progenitor, then, by definition, it had the qualities to have developed to that point in time and to continue to develop beyond that time. The empirical question is: what are those qualities? I have answered, based on the evidence I see, that it is the balance of developmental qualities I have listed over and over again throughout this essay.

There is overwhelming evidence that life, throughout its evolution, is never solitary. I have presented strong support for the hypothesis that we evolved and continue to develop as humans through interaction within relational communities—support from biology, primatology, anthropology, cognitive science, and psychology. The unit of analysis for any science of human development must be the *individual-in-community.*

I have not presented rational arguments for ideal systems of justice, but have attempted to present scenarios of actual situations and conditions in order to gain some understanding of our origins. Because these are real and represent the origins of human development, the systems of justice that emerge are anything but ideal or perfect. They are the beginning of a process that is still far from perfection.

Perhaps the least understood of the hypotheses necessary for my argument is that our early ancestors lived in communities that were relatively peaceful and benevolent, and that they were led by women. There is now much evidence for this; however, most of it is open to more than one interpretation. The traditional interpretation of the evidence left by our early ancestors led to the conclusion that their societies were male dominated and somewhat Hobbesian; man the hunter-warrior was in charge. New evidence and new interpretations that avoid male bias (and, of course, run the risk of female bias) provide considerable confirmation of the matriarchal and female-led community hypotheses. This is supported further by studies of our living primate cousins. I accept, in spite of my male bias, that the beginnings and perhaps hundreds of thousands of years of human development was, most probably, in a female-led environment. I do not believe that our ancestors could have survived those difficult times, let alone developed, in a Hobbesian-type patriarchy.

We know that today's world is patriarchal, so the issue of transition is most important. Here the evidence does not provide a clear picture. Nevertheless, although contemporary societies are quite Hobbesian, I am almost convinced that this is neither the natural state nor the original position. We are as we are because of an imbalance induced by several thousands of years of patriarchal cultures. What, we might now ask, does this say about our future?

The Present and Future of Humankind

The forces of domination might now be shifting from state power to economic power.[2] There are still serious conflicts/wars of the traditional kind, but as they are contained within countries or regions, they are not the major mode of domination that they used to be, although they cannot, of course, be ignored. I believe that, among many threats to human development in the world, the emerging ubiquitous mode of domination is *globalization,* a term that its supporters usually say means free trade, but more accurately refers to the free flow of capital across national boundaries. It does not have the bloody appearance of war and, in fact, looks rather benign. But it does dominate. It now has great control over most of humanity, and because it is capital itself that controls, even corporate leaders are subject to the system. Male domination is giving way, perhaps, to the domination of a system with extreme "masculine" characteristics: competitive, rational, abstract, aggressive, uncaring.

If the results of globalization are aggregated and it is abstracted from the people and communities it affects, then it appears to have developmental value. It does increase employment and wealth. The dangers of this domination are seen, however, at real and disaggregated points of impact. Increased wealth tends to concentrate among the already wealthy, increasing disparities in wealth and therefore power-over. The free flow of capital increases employment but also decreases the security and quality of employment. The net effect on labor rights, working conditions, and the quality of work appears to be especially negative for women and children in the poorest communities. It threatens sovereignty.

It endangers our environment through ever increasing levels of production and consumption, especially in the industrialized north, and through lack of environmental control.

The solution to problems of economic disparity and economic and social development determined by the needs of capital, including globalization, would require a transition to more balanced, less Hobbesian societies: less competition, more cooperation; less egoism, more altruism; less aggression, more nurturing; less isolation, more relatedness. To the "realist" and most economists this is just silly and certainly not scientific. But much evidence suggests that the perception of reality that drives our present dominant and imbalanced economic system is a myth that has been made real and very dangerous. There are so many accounts and analyses of these problems that I need not dwell on them here.[3]

I would say at the outset that I don't think the present trend to globalized capital can be halted in the near future. If it continues at its present rate, however, nature itself will stop it in, perhaps, a cruel and nasty way. The human spirit, human communities, and the ecological systems of our planet can tolerate only so much. If it can't be halted, can globalization be ameliorated to create a sufficient balance to avoid catastrophes and even be developmental? Perhaps. The evidence that leads to my "perhaps" includes the following:

There is growing movement in civil society, outside traditional political systems, that counters in various ways dysfunctional political, economic, environmental, and social trends. Civil society includes women's groups, environmental groups, labor groups, and groups concerned about specific laws, religious issues, political issues, and the like. Many of these network with like-minded and other groups, more and more using the Internet as a means of communion. Civil society has already had considerable success in combatting dysfunctional political systems, especially in the Soviet Union and Eastern Europe, but also in Asia, Africa, and Latin America. Civil society's confrontation of globalization has been evident recently at all the high-level international meetings on globalization and free trade. The serious, nonviolent, and somewhat effective confrontations involve many and diverse groups with a common objective: to stop, retard and/or humanize globalization, to reduce domination, to reclaim space taken by capital.

But concern about these and other fundamental issues of development is not confined to peoples outside the realms of traditional power. The quotation at the beginning of this chapter expressed such concerns by a past prime minister of Canada and his senior advisor—concerns expressed throughout their terms in office. Note also what the past vice-president of the United States said about the dangerous tendencies of the patriarchy, written while he was a U.S. senator, in a book he titled *Earth in the Balance*:

> for the last few thousand years, Western civilization has emphasized a distinctly male way of relating to the world and has organized itself around philosophical structures that devalue the distinctly female approach to life. For example, as the scientific and technological revolution picked up speed, we have seemed to place a good deal more emphasis on technologies that extend and magnify abilities—such as fighting wars—historically associated more with males than females. At the same time, new ways to reduce our scandalously high rate of infant mortality have received far less attention. . . . Ultimately, part of the solution for the environmental crisis may well lie in our ability to achieve a better balance between the sexes, leaving the dominant male perspective with a healthier respect for female ways of experiencing the world.[4]

I like Gore's emphasis on balance and his assessment of the problem in terms of patriarchy. I wonder why he proposes "leaving the dominant male perspective with a healthier respect for female ways of experiencing the world." This could be his assessment of the possibilities in his own country, or simply a problem with expression. Apart from that, it is a radical statement for a U.S. senator and vice-president to make.

But given the dominance of the global economic system and the way its power-over has increased since Gore wrote his book in 1992, even the president of the United States, supposedly the most powerful man on earth, could do little to encourage the change Gore proposes, even if he wanted to.

Nevertheless, evidence that countervailing forces that would improve the balance do exist, not only on the fringes of power, but sometimes near the centres of power, is encouraging.

Even more encouraging is the fact that there are more than three billion women on the planet, that they have power wherever they are, and that more of them are moving into positions of traditional political and corporate power. This in itself should shift the central tendency from power-over toward power-with and move us closer to a natural and developmental balance. And this, it seems, is the only solution that my study of origins puts before me. A move toward "female ways of experiencing the world" and of informing and administering the world is, perhaps, the only way to return to the "conspiracy of love" from which humanity emerged.

Notes

Preface

1. Eisler (1987: 203).

2. By *dominant Western paradigm* I mean the most influential world view in the industrialized West. This dominant view is a rather narrow ideological spectrum within the diversity of Western thought and is the conceptual base for capitalist democracies. I focus on its negative assumptions about human nature and human interactions. It will be defined in Chapter 1.

3. Theodosius Dobzhansky, a founder of the neo-Darwinian theory, sees humanity as *transcending* biological evolution (Dobzhansky 1969: 45). George Gaylord Simpson says that human development breaks away from mechanistic biological determinism and comes under the control of humans as rational, moral, and social (Simpson 1951: ch. 9; 1964: ch. 14), Washburn and Howell (1960: 52) recognize that humans have a unique "technical-social life" which causes biological change. A. I. Hallowell claims that we have not only a capacity for highly complex forms of learning but also "a capacity for transcending what is learned: a potentiality for innovation, creativity, reorganization, and change" (1960: 361). John Hurrell Crook criticizes the authors of popular, "pseudo-biological" works (Ardrey, Lorenz, Tiger, Fox) for their excessive emphasis on genetic factors and claims that "cultural control of society has come to mould not only social change but, increasingly, human ecology as well" (Crook 1973: 436). These major evolutionists are not reductionists; they recognize the emergence of capacities within human evolution which effect new and unique developments that cannot be understood by reducing them to genes and natural selection.

4. Rawls (1971).

5. Nozick (1974).

6. Rawls (1999: 13, 88; 1971: 407 and passim).

7. The dominant Western view virtually ignores women. Where I think it appropriate to call attention to this male bias I will use *man*, set in italics.

8. Thomas Hobbes (1588–1679): "The life of man [is] solitary, poore, nasty, brutish, and short" (1968: 186).

Chapter 1

1. Max Lerner, "Liberalism," *Encyclopaedia Britannica*, 14th ed.

2. *Liberal* is a difficult term. Etymologically it refers to liberty and therefore to any attempt to free the human individual from constraints. Historically this objective took on different forms, depending on the constraints on individual

freedom. For example, many of those within the Soviet bloc who sought freedom from the constraints of Soviet communism were called liberal communists. Today's Western liberal may or may not accept all of Lerner's definition, but is concerned about the freedom of all people to develop within capitalist societies and sees here the need for active state involvement. Lerner's definition now better reflects the view of contemporary conservatives or neoconservatives, who emphasize freedom-from and see the state as a major obstacle to individual freedom; they therefore advocate a minimal state. Whether or not it as an accurate statement of today's Western liberalism, Lerner's definition captures the principles of the dominant Western paradigm that my position counters.

3. Many feel that scholars should refer not to dictionaries, but to other scholars. My emphasis on people in general, rather than on scholars, as the origins of morality, however, justifies some attempt to find more popular definitions. The *OED* is perhaps the best source for general English use of relevant concepts.

4. The all too common use of *moral* as a synonym for *altruistic* deviates from standard use; this will be discussed later.

5. Rawls (1971: 46–53).

6. Wolff (1991: 53).

7. Nozick (1993: 65).

8. For Nozick's elaboration of this see 64ff.

9. Rawls (1971: 408).

10. Paul (1981: 2).

11. See Kant (1952a, b).

12. Aristotle, *On the Soul* (1941: 598).

13. Mill (1955: 13).

14. Rawls (1971: ch. 7, "Goodness as Rationality").

15. Rawls (1985).

16. Freud (1969: 48); Hobbes (1968: 186).

Chapter 2

1. See Tattersall (1998: 84ff).

2. See Lewin (1999: 173ff).

3. Some use the term *consciousness* to refer to this cognitive activity. I use *self-consciousness* to emphasize the reflective nature of this form of knowing and to ensure that it is not confused with simple awareness, perception, or sensation, sometimes also called consciousness, which we share with all living organisms. *Self-consciousness* is the subject of Chapter 3.

4. See Tattersall (1998: 223ff); Jolly (1999: iii).

5. For elaborations of consciousness, intelligence, mind, language, and the brain from an evolutionary perspective see Tattersall (1998); Deacon (1998); Jolly (1999); Miller (2000).

6. A (germinal) mutation is a change in the genetic material of an organism that is passed on to the organism's progeny and could produce a change in that progeny. The mutation could be a consequence of the process of replication of the genetic material or it could be induced by external factors such as chemical reactions or radiation.

7. For an excellent account of this process see Tattersall (1998).

8. De Waal (1996: 67).

9. See Jolly (1999: ch.9).
10. See Lewin (1999: 29ff).
11. Tattersall says: "It's even possible that the human capacity originated at least partly in an epigenetic, developmental event, rather than in a major change in the genetically programmed structure of the brain" (1998: 232).
12. "The early tone of the emerging Synthesis [of Darwin's theory and genetics] was set in 1937 by the naturalist-turned-geneticist Theodosius Dobzhansky, in a book titled *Genetics and the Origin of Species*" (Tattersall 1998: 83).
13. Dobzhansky (1969: 44; see also 1962).
14. Dobzhansky (1969: 45).
15. Darwin (1981).
16. Miller (2000: 4).
17. Darwin (1958: 74).
18. *Fitness* for Spencer refers not to biological fitness but rather to the ability to succeed in the capitalist marketplace—to overpower those who are out to overpower you, as Hobbes had put it. Within his dog-eat-dog society—he obviously didn't read or understand Darwin as quoted above—he sees right as might. He gives primacy to the egoistic individual whose relations to others are contractual and instrumental. See Spencer (1851, 1874).
19. Dobzhansky (1964: 152).
20. For kin selection, see Hamilton (1964); for reciprocal altruism, see Trivers (1971); for more recent studies, see de Waal (1996); Tattersall (1998); Sober and Wilson (1999); Jolly (1999).
21. See Wilson (1975).
22. Jolly (1999: 431).
23. It can be useful for purposes of illustration to focus on a single characteristic such as I do here, but it should be noted that a deeper understanding of selection requires seeing it work on whole organisms and populations. See Tattersall (1998: 99ff). When we speak here of an organism's genes we include both the genes in that organism and those identical genes in other members of its species.
24. De Waal (1996: 5).
25. Buck and Ginsberg (1991: 155, 156).
26. Young et al. (1999).
27. Freud (1969: 48).
28. Estés (1992: 4), emphasis added.
29. For a discussion of "standpoint," see Harding (1993). For discussions of many of the epistemological issues that are relevant to what follows, see Alcoff and Potter (1993). For background on the debate on altruism, see Badcock (1986); Barlow (1992); Boorman (1980), Clark (1991); Colman (1982); Goldsmith (1991); Harcourt and de Waal (1992).
30. Dawkins (1989: 2).
31. See Tattersall (1998: 97).
32. Sober and Wilson (1999: 6).
33. Miller (2000: 292).
34. Sober and Wilson (1999: 237).
35. See Batson (1990, 1991); Batson and Oleson (1991); Buck and Ginsberg (1991); Clark (1991); Colman (1982); Crook (1973); de Waal (1996); de Waal and Lanting (1997); Dovidio et al. (1991); Derlega and Grzelak (1982); Huntingford (1982); Jolly (1999); Miller (2000); Simpson (1951, 1964); Sober and Wilson (1999); Tattersall (1998, 2002); Wilkinson (1990).
36. Buck and Ginsberg (1991).

37. Young et al. (1999).
38. Jolly (1999: 431).
39. Fortey (1998: 58).
40. Margulis (1998: 33).
41. Wilkinson (1990).
42. Hamilton (1964).
43. Trivers (1971).
44. See de Waal (1996: 20ff).
45. Kin selection was introduced in Hamilton (1964). Reciprocal selection was introduced in Trivers (1971). Subsequent discussions of these include Batson (1990, 1991); Buck and Ginsberg (1991); Clark (1991); Colman (1982); Crook (1973); de Waal (1996); de Waal and Lanting (1998); Dovidio et al. (1991); Derlega and Grzelak (1982); Huntingford (1982); Jolly (1999); Miller (2000); Sober and Wilson (1999); Wilkinson (1990).
46. See Miller (2000).
47. Buck and Ginsberg (1991); Young et al. (1999).
48. If bats are now starting to appeal to you, you can read also about the altruistic behavior of the fruit bat in Kunz (1994).
49. Lorenz's *On Aggression* was published in 1963. The better-known popularizations of the Hobbesian view include Robert Ardrey's *The Territorial Imperative* and Desmond Morris's *Naked Ape*, both published in 1967.
50. De Waal (1996: 164).
51. See: Fortey (1998: 58); Tattersall

Chapter 3

1. Tattersall (1998: 188–90); see also Jolly (1999: 26).
2. Tattersall (2002: 78).
3. See Jolly (1999: ch. 9); de Waal (1995, 1996).
4. Frans de Waal analyzes and assesses contemporary primates, especially the chimpanzee and bonobo; see entries in the Bibliography.
5. Deacon (1998: 22).
6. Some apes appear to be self-conscious to some extent, and some of these have been taught to communicate symbolically, using sign language, computers, or printed symbols (see Jolly, 1999: 313ff). No apes have been taught to speak vocally, and they are probably physiologically unable to do so. In this sense they have no language, but have some capacity for symbolic thought.
7. See de Waal (2001).
8. See Miller (2000: passim); Glynn (1999: 50).
9. De Waal (1996: 78ff).
10. For greater elaboration see Dennett (1991: ch. 7).
11. Quartz and Sejnowski (1997). This paper contains a target article, many responses to that article, and the authors' comments on the responses. It provides an excellent view of the state of and diversity within research in cognitive and neural development.
12. Miller (2000: 17, 18).
13. Dennett (1991: 193ff).
14. See Deacon (1998: Part One).
15. See Tattersall (1998: 190ff).
16. Dawkins (1995).

17. Chomsky (1971: 3).

18. The man who experiences has not part in the world. For it is "in him" and not between him and the world that the experience arises.

The world has no part in the experience. It permits itself to be experienced, but has no concern in the matter. For it does nothing to the experience, and the experience does nothing to it.

As experience, the world belongs to the primary word *I-It.*

The primary word *I-Thou* establishes the world of relation. (Buber, 1958: 5)

19. See Tattersall (1998: 211).

20. Haidt (2001: passim).

21. Greene et al. (2001: passim).

22. Buck and Ginsberg (1991: 157).

23. *Symbiosis,* coined in the late nineteenth century, meant an internal, mutually beneficial partnership between two organisms, but now refers to any living arrangement between members of two different species, including beneficial, neutral, and harmful associations.

24. I am not implying that all physical power is power-over and all biological power is power-with.

25. For Hobbes, the energies of more than one *man* can be combined, but in a mechanical rather than organic way. "Therefore to have servants, is Power; To have friends, is Power: for they are strengths united" (Hobbes 1968: 150). "Having" a friend is the same as "having" a servant; each adds to the power-over at your command.

26. Eisler (1988: 3–4, 68); Miller (2000: 309); Mies (1986: 58).

27. Eisler (1988).

28. See Reed (1975); Eisler (1988); Mies (1986).

29. For feminist discussion see Tickner (1992, 8); Offen (1990); Hartsock (1985, 242); Mies (1986, ch. 2); Eisler (1988, 193). For psychological discussion see McClelland (1975); Gilligan (1993); Guisinger and Blatt (1994).

30. Buck and Ginsberg (1991); Batson (1990, 1991); Dovidio et al. (1991); Jolly (1999: 295ff); de Waal (1996).

31. Dovidio et al. (1991).

32. Bar-Tal et al. (1982).

33. See Fiske (1991).

Chapter 4

1. Rawls (1971: 143, 408).

2. Molecular (DNA) evidence indicates that human evolution diverged from that of the African apes between four and eight million years ago (Lewin 1999: 33). The common ancestor at this bifurcation is believed to be similar to the contemporary bonobo and probably would possess the early glimmers of self-consciousness.

3. Deacon (1998: 43).

4. Defined by the *OED* as "a tendency or bent of the mind, will, or desires towards a particular object; disposition, propensity, leaning."

5. David Hume also rejected reason as the source of morality, but his alternative was blind, non-self-conscious feelings that are "nothing but particular pains or pleasures" (MacIntyre 1965: 197).

6. It should be clear that I am not committing the “naturalistic fallacy” (Moore 1903).

7. De Waal (1996: 70); see also de Waal and Lanting (1998: ch. 6) and Jolly (1999: 295ff).

8. Freedom, self-determination, control over inclinations—none of these is absolute. I will assume that the limited and relative nature of these is taken as obvious.

9. Miller (2000: 17).

10. See de Waal (1996, 2001).

Chapter 5

1. Fortey (1998: 61); see also Margulis (1998).

2. Tattersall (1998: 106).

3. Jolly (1999: 408).

4. The etymology of *religion* according to the *OED* is: “by Cicero connected with relegere to read over again, but by later authors with religere *to bind*; the latter view has usually been favoured by modern writers in explaining the force of the word by its supposed etymological meaning” (emphasis mine).

5. De Waal (1996: 173ff).

6. Needs such as association and communication with others have been studied for several centuries. For an early study see Itard (1962).

7. Seligman (1989); Hollon et al. (1992).

8. Hollon et al. (1992: 119).

9. Hollon et al. (1992: 120).

10. See Sampson (1988: 16).

11. Seligman (1975); Garber and Seligman (1980); Montero and Sloan (1988); Hollon et al. (1992).

12. Lefcourt (1980).

13. Seligman (1989).

14. Itard (1962); see also Putnam (2000).

15. Rawls (1971: 476).

16. Carus (1991),133.

17. See Chan (1963: 17, 27).

18. From Auden (1970).

19. Miller (2000: 222).

20. For evidence that a reduction in relatedness—the collapse of community, as Putnam puts it—threatens human development, see Putnam (2000).

Chapter 6

1. Jolly (1999: 408).

2. Aristotle (1941: *Ethics*, II, 1).

3. Ibid.: X, 9.

4. Hobbes (1968: 189).

5. The word “slime” has, of course, a negative connotation, but it has also been used to refer to the molecular mix from which life emerged. The billions of bacterial colonies that comprised life’s first major step can be seen as the slime from which all consequent life evolved. The point to be made is that the

base, primeval stuff might appear disgusting and even evil, but it is interacting energy that is rich in potential for development.

6. See Shue (1980: 5); Eide (1986: 368).

7. For Hobbes, "The Right of Nature . . . is the Liberty each man hath to use his own power, as he will himselfe, for the preservation of his own . . . Life" (1968: 189).

8. Recall our discussion of the psychological evidence for this need in Chapter 5, and see Putnam (2000).

9. Shue (1980: 13).

Chapter 7

1. Rawls (1971: 476).

2. For the sake of simplicity I will include both the value judgment and the judgment of obligation under the term *moral judgment.*

3. This balance would, of course, vary from community to community and also over time.

4. "Southern Africa: The Region: History: Early Humans and the Stone Age." *Encyclopaedia Britannica* (2001).

5. I do not mean to imply that crises are a prerequisite to this development. This is simply one of many reasonable scenarios.

6. See Eisler (1988).

7. See Rawls, (1971: 142).

8. See Gould, (1992: 243ff).

9. Lubbock (1872: passim).

10. See Tattersall (1998: 24).

11. See Eisler (1988).

12. Mies (1986: ch. 2).

13. See Reed (1975).

14. See Eisler (1988).

15. De Waal (1996: 132).

16. Lewin (1999: 34).

17. Included are the lesser apes, which are the gibbons and siamangs from Asia, and the great apes, which are the orangutan from Asia and the gorilla, chimpanzee, and bonobo from Africa. These are tailless primates, quite distinct from monkeys.

18. See Jolly (1999: ch. 9).

19. See Tattersall (2002, ch. 3).

20. See de Waal (1995, 1996); de Waal and Lanting (1998); Jolly (1999).

21. De Waal (1995: 82).

22. De Waal (1995: 88).

23. My own amateur observations of orangutans in captivity indicated very open relationships among females, adolescents, and young. The human in patriarchal society is perhaps closer to the "nasty" end of the spectrum than is the orangutan.

24. Neanderthal already lived in Europe when our ancestors arrived 40,000–50,000 years ago. There is no evidence of Neanderthal after 30,000 years ago. It was once thought that Neanderthal was a sub-species of *Homo sapiens,* in which case they would be *Homo sapiens neanderthalensis* and we would be *Homo sapiens sapiens.* Neanderthal is now considered to be a separate species

(*Homo neanderthalensis*). Recent evidence suggests that Neanderthal was more advanced than earlier believed.

25. Hobbes (1968: 186).
26. Miller (2000: ch. 9).
27. Jolly (1999: 383).
28. Eisler (1988); Mies (1986: ch. 2); Miller (2000: ch. 8).
29. Rawls (1971: 136).
30. Miller (2000: ch. 9).
31. *Reproduction* includes all activities required for the development of the progeny, not only birth and nursing

Chapter 8

1. *Positivism* is the philosophical position that only analytical and empirical propositions are meaningful. A *positive law* is a law legislated by a sovereign state; a *positive right* gets its legitimacy from positive law. A *legal positivist* would claim that the state is the only foundation for rights and law, that is, there is no moral or natural foundation; therefore, there are only *positive rights and laws.* These terms should not be confused with *positive* meaning *not negative.* I see the natural foundations for law to be positive and therefore law itself to be positive—that is, not negative. I am, obviously, not a positivist. To avoid confusion, I will refer to law made by states simply as "law," or use italics, as in "*positive* law."
2. In particular, Jenks (1963); McDougal, Lasswell, and Chen (1980); and Falk (1976, 1989, 2000).
3. See d'Entrèves (1965: ch. 1).
4. Pound (1969: 43).
5. Hobbes (1968: 188).
6. Austin (1954: 1, 4).
7. Hobbes (1969: 228).
8. Aquinas (1947: I-II, Q.94, Art.2).
9. Austin subscribes to rule utilitarianism (see 1954: 49).
10. This, of course, is not a perfectly homogeneous tradition. It contains great variety in emphases on the functions of God, Nature, reason, and authority, and some who are considered members of the school (e.g., Ockham, Bodin) can also be seen as precursors of positivism. My generalization should be interpreted as a central tendency.
11. Grotius (1957: 8).
12. M. P. Golding says that historians of law regard this separation of jurisprudence from theology as epoch-making. He adds that Grotius's identification of natural law with social organization rather than Stoic metaphysics is even more important. See Golding (1967: 6: 259).
13. Kelsen (1970: 64).
14. Kelsen (1971: 137–73).
15. Kelsen discusses the meaning of rights in terms of obligations and, especially, legal obligations; see Kelsen (1966: 7). Asbjørn Eide claims that the concept of human rights makes sense only in the context of the state; see Eide (1986: 367, 369).
16. Aquinas (1947: I-II, Q.94, art.1).
17. See Goodall (1982: 390).
18. Hart (1967).

19. Austin (1954: 10, see also 1–8).
20. Kelsen (1970: 62).
21. Hobbes (1968: 186).
22. Jenks (1963: ch. 4).
23. McDougal, Lasswell, and Chen (1980: 6).
24. The subtitle of their work is *The Basic Policies of an International Law of Human Dignity*. See xvii, 367ff., 452.
25. See Donnelly (1982, 1985); Howard and Donnelly (1986).
26. Falk (1976: 150; 2000).
27. Falk (1989: 27ff).
28. Falk (1989: 95).
29. See Gilder (1981); Goldberg (1977).
30. Eisler (1988: ch. 4).
31. See Mies (1986).
32. See Gilligan (1993); Brabeck

Chapter 9

1. Head and Trudeau (1995: 318). Pierre Trudeau was prime minister of Canada between 1968 and 1984. Ivan Head was Trudeau's closest advisor on foreign policy and relations from 1968 to 1978.
2. See Falk (2000: 89).
3. See Klein (2000). I have noted Putnam (2000) above for evidence of the problems of lack of community.
4. Gore (1992: 212).

Bibliography

Alcoff, Linda and Elizabeth Potter, eds. 1993. *Feminist Epistemologies.* New York: Routledge.

Aquinas, Thomas. 1947. *Summa Theologica.* New York: Benziger Brothers.

Aristotle. 1941. *The Basic Works of Aristotle.* Ed. Richard McKeon. New York: Random House.

Ardrey, Robert. 1967. *The Territorial Imperative: A Personal Inquiry into the Animal Origins of Property and Nations.* New York: Atheneum.

Arnhart, Larry. 1998. *Darwinian Natural Right: The Biological Ethics of Nature.* Albany: State University of New York Press.

Auden, W. H. 1970. *A Certain World: A Commonplace Book.* New York: Viking Penguin.

Austin, John. 1954. *The Province of Jurisprudence Determined.* London: Weidenfeld and Nicolson.

Badcock, C. R. 1986. *The Problem of Altruism: Freudian-Darwinian Solutions.* Oxford: Blackwell.

Badinter, Elisabeth. 1989. *The Unopposite Sex: The End of the Gender Battle.* Trans. Barbara Wright. New York: Harper and Row.

Bar-Tal, Daniel, R. Sharabany, and Amiram Raviv. 1982. "Cognitive Basis of the Development of Altruistic Behavior." In Valerian J. Derlega and Janusz Grzelak, eds., *Cooperation and Helping Behavior: Theories and Research.* New York: Academic Press.

Barlow, Connie C., ed. 1992. *From Gaia to Selfish Genes: Selected Writings in the Life Sciences.* Cambridge, Mass.: MIT Press.

Batson, C. Daniel. 1990. "How Social an Animal? The Human Capacity for Caring." *American Psychologist* 45, 3: 336–46.

———. 1991. *The Altruism Question: Toward a Social Psychological Answer.* Hillsdale, N.J.: Lawrence Erlbaum.

Batson, C. Daniel and Kathryn C. Oleson. 1991. "Current Status of the Empathy-Altruism Hypothesis." In Margaret Sydnor Clark, ed., *Prosocial Behavior.* London: Sage.

Boorman, Scott A. and Paul R. Levitt. 1980. *The Genetics of Altruism.* Toronto: Academic Press.

Brabeck, Mary. 1993. "Moral Judgement: Theory and Research on Differences Between Males and Females." In Mary Jeanne Larrabee, ed., *An Ethic of Care: Feminist and Interdisciplinary Perspectives.* New York: Routledge.

Buber, Martin. 1958. *I and Thou.* New York: Scribner's.

Buck, Ross and Benson Ginsberg. 1991. "Spontaneous Communication and Altruism: The Communicative Gene Hypothesis." In Margaret Sydnor Clark, ed., *Prosocial Behavior.* London: Sage.

Carus, Paul, ed. 1991. *Buddha: The Gospel.* Electronic text. Irvine, Calif.: World Library Inc.

Chan, Wing-Sit. 1969. *A Source Book in Chinese Philosophy.* Princeton, N.J.: Princeton University Press.

Chomsky, Noam. 1971. *Problems of Knowledge and Freedom.* New York: Random House.

Clark, Mary E. 1989. *Ariadne's Thread: The Search for New Modes of Thinking.* London: Macmillan.

Clark, Margaret Sydnor, ed. 1991. *Prosocial Behavior.* London; Sage.

Colman, Andrew M., ed. 1982. *Cooperation and Competition in Humans and Animals.* New York: Van Nostrand Reinhold.

Crook, J. H. 1973. "The Socio-Ecology of Primates: Group Characteristics and Inference to Man." In Ashley Montagu, ed., *The Origin and Evolution of Man: Readings in Physical Anthropology.* New York: Thomas Y. Crowell.

Darwin, Charles. 1958. *The Origin of Species.* New York: Mentor.

———. 1981. *The Descent of Man and Selection in Relation to Sex.* Princeton, N.J.: Princeton University Press.

Dawkins, Richard. 1982. *The Extended Phenotype: The Long Reach of the Gene.* Oxford: W.H. Freeman.

———. 1988. *The Blind Watchmaker.* London: Penguin.

———. 1989. *The Selfish Gene.* Oxford: Oxford University Press.

———. 1995. *River Out of Eden: A Darwinian View of Life.* Toronto: HarperCollins.

Deacon, Terrence W. 1998. *The Symbolic Species: The Co-Evolution of Language and the Brain.* New York: W.W. Norton.

de Bary, William Theodore. 1972. *The Buddhist Tradition.* New York: Vintage Books.

Dennett, Daniel C. 1991. *Consciousness Explained.* Boston: Little, Brown.

———. 1996. *Darwin's Dangerous Idea.* New York: Simon and Schuster (Touchstone).

d'Entrèves, A. P. 1965. *Natural Law: An Introduction to Legal Philosophy.* New York: Harper and Row.

Derlega, Valerian J. and Janusz Grzelak, eds. 1982. *Cooperation and Helping Behavior: Theories and Research.* Toronto: Academic Press.

de Waal, Frans B. M. 1995. "Bonobo Sex and Society." *Scientific American* (March).

———. 1996. *Good Natured: The Origins of Right and Wrong in Humans and Other Animals.* Cambridge, Mass.: Harvard University Press.

———. 1999. "Cultural primatology comes of age." *Nature* 399 (June 17)

———. 2001. *The Ape and the Sushi Master: Cultural Reflections by a Primatologist.* New York: Basic Books.

de Waal, Frans B. M. and Frans Lanting. 1998. *Bonobo: The Forgotten Ape.* Berkeley: University of California Press.

Dobzhansky, Theodosius. 1962. *Mankind Evolving: The Evolution of the Human Species.* New Haven, Conn.: Yale University Press.

———. 1964. *Heredity and the Nature of Man.* New York: New American Library.

———. 1969. *The Biology of Ultimate Concern.* New York: Meridian.

Dovidio, John F., Jane Allyn Piliavin, Samuel L. Gaertner, David A. Schroeder, and R. D. Clark. 1991. "The Arousal: Cost-Reward Model and the Process of Intervention: A Review of the Evidence." In Margaret Sydnor Clark, ed., *Prosocial Behavior.* London: Sage.

Donnelly, Jack. 1982. "Human Rights and Human Dignity: An Analytic Critique of Non-Western Conceptions of Human Rights." *American Political Science Review* 76 (June).

——. 1985. *The Concept of Human Rights.* New York: St. Martin's Press..

Eide, Asbjørn. 1986. "The Human Rights Movement and the Transformation of the International Order." *Alternatives* 11 (July).

Eisler, Riane. 1988. *The Chalice and the Blade.* San Francisco: Harper.

Estés, Clarissa P. 1992. *Women Who Run with the Wolves.* New York: Ballantine

Falk, Richard A.. 1976. "The Role of Law in World Society: Present Crisis and Future Prospects." In W. Michael Reisman and Burns H. Weston, eds., *Toward World Order and Human Dignity.* New York: Free Press.

———. 1989. *Revitalizing International Law.* Ames: Iowa State University Press.

———. 2000. *Human Rights Horizons: The Pursuit of Justice in a Globalizing World.* New York: Routledge.

Fields, A. Belden and Narr Wolf-Dieter. 1992. "Human Rights as a Holistic Concept." *Human Rights Quarterly* 14, 1 (February).

Fiske, Alan Page. 1991. "The Cultural Relativity of Selfish Individualism: Anthrpological Evidence That Humans Are Inherently Sociable." In Margaret Sydnor Clark, ed., *Prosocial Behavior.* London: Sage.

Flack, Jessica and Frans B. M. de Waal. 1998. "'Any Animal Whatever': Darwinian Building Blocks of Morality in Monkeys and Apes." *Journal of Consciousness Studies* 7, 1–2: 1–65.

Fortey, Richard A. 1998. *Life: A Natural History of the First Four Billion Years of Life on Earth.* New York: Knopf.

Freud, Sigmund. 1969. *Civilization and Its Discontents.* New York: W.W. Norton.

Garber, Judy and Martin E. Seligman, eds. 1980. *Human Helplessness: Theory and Applications.* New York: Academic Press.

Gilder, George. 1981. *Wealth and Poverty.* New York: Basic Books..

Gilligan, Carol. 1993. *In a Different Voice: Psychological Theory and Women's Development.* Cambridge, Mass.: Harvard University Press.

Glynn, Ian. 1999. *An Anatomy of Thought: The Origin and Machinery of the Mind.* London: Weidenfeld and Nicolson.

Goldberg, Steven. 1977. *The Inevitability of Patriarchy.* London: Temple Smith.

Golding, M. P. 1967. "Philosophy of Law, History of." In Paul Edwards, ed., *The Encyclopedia of Philosophy,* 6. New York: Macmillan and Free Press.

Goldsmith, Timothy H. 1991. *The Biological Roots of Human Nature: Forging Links Between Evolution and Behavior.* Oxford: Oxford University Press.

Goodall, Jane. 1982. "Order Without Law." *Journal of Social and Biological Structures* 5.

Gore, Albert. 1992. *Earth in the Balance: Forging a New Common Purpose.* Boston: Houghton Mifflin.

Gorz, André. 1989. *Critique of Economic Reason.* London: Verso, London.

Gould, Stephen Jay. 1990a. *Ever Since Darwin: Reflections in Natural History.* New York: W.W. Norton.

———. 1990b. *Wonderful Life: TheBurgess Shale and the Nature of History.* New York: W.W. Norton.

Greene, Joshua D., R. Brian Sommerville, Leigh E. Nystrom, John M. Darley, and Jonathan D. Cohen. 2001. "An fMRI Investigation of Emotional Engagement in Moral Judgment." *Science* 293 (September 14): 2105–8.

Grotius, Hugo. 1957. *Prolegomena to the Law of War and Peace.* Indianapolis: Bobbs-Merrill.

Guisinger, Shan and Sidney J. Blatt. 1994. "Individuality and Relatedness Evolution of a Fundamental Dialectic." *American Psychologist* 49, 2: 104–11.

Haidt, Jonathan. 2001. "The Emotional Dog and Its Rational Tail: A Social Intuitionist Approach to Moral Judgment." *Psychological Review* 108, 4 (October): 814–34.

Hallowell, A. Irving. 1960. "Self, Society and Culture in Phylogenetic Perspective." In Sol Tax, ed., *The Evolution of Man*. Evolution After Darwin 2. Chicago: University of Chicago Press.

Hamilton, W. D. 1964. "The Genetic Evolution of Social Behavior: I and II." *Journal of Theoretical Biology* 7: 1–52.

Hart, H. L. A. 1958. "Legal and Moral Obligation." In A. I. Melden, ed., *Essays in Moral Philosophy*. Seattle: University of Washington Press.

———. 1961. *The Concept of Law*. Oxford: Clarendon Press.

———. 1967. "Philosophy of Law, Problems of." In Paul Edwards, ed., *The Encyclopedia of Philosophy*, 6: 265. New York: Macmillan and Free Press.

Harcourt, Alexander H. and Frans B. M de Waal, eds. 1992. *Coalitions and Alliances in Humans and Other Animals*. Oxford: Oxford University Press.

Harding, Sandra. 1993. "Rethinking Standpoint Epistemology: 'What Is Strong Objectivity?'" In Linda Alcoff and Elizabeth Potter, eds., *Feminist Epistemologies*. New York: Routledge.

Hartsock, Nancy C. M. 1985. *Money, Sex, and Power: Toward a Feminist Historical Materialism*. Boston: Northeastern University Press.

Hawkesworth, M. E. 1989. "Knowers, Knowing, Known: Feminist Theory and Claims of Truth." *Signs* 14, 3: 533–57.

Head, Ivan L. and Pierre Elliott Trudeau. 1995. *The Canadian Way: Shaping Canada's Foreign Policy, 1968–1984*. Toronto: McCelland and Stewart.

Hobbes, Thomas. 1968. *Leviathan*. Harmondsworth: Penguin.

Hogarth, Robin M. and Melvin Warren Reder, eds. 1986. *Rational Choice: The Contrast Between Economics and Psychology*. Chicago: University of Chicago Press.

Hollon, Steven D., Robert J. DeRubeis, and Martin E. Seligman. 1992. "Cognitive Therapy and the Prevention of Depression." *Applied & Preventive Psychology* 1, 2: 89–96.

Howard, Rhoda E. and Jack Donnelly. 1986. "Human Rights, Human Dignity and Political Regimes." *American Political Science Review* 80 (September).

Hume, David. 1965. *Hume's Ethical Writings: Selcetions from David Hume*. Ed. Alasdair MacIntyre. New York: Macmillan.

Huntingford, Felicity. 1982. "The Evolution of Cooperation and Altruism." In Andrew M. Colman, ed., *Cooperation and Competition in Humans and Animals*. NewYork: Van Nostrand Reinhold.

International Human Genome Sequencing Consortium. 2001. "Initial Sequencing and Analysis of the Human Genome." *Nature* 409 (February): 860–921.

Itard, Jean-Marc-Gaspard. 1962. *The Wild Boy of Aveyron*. Trans. George Humphrey and Muriel Humphrey. Englewood Cliffs, N.J.: Prentice-Hall.

Jenks, C. Wilfred. 1963. *Law, Freedom, and Welfare*. Dobbs Ferry, N.Y.: Oceana Publications.

Jolly, Alison. 1999. *Lucy's Legacy: Sexand Intelligence in Human Evolution*. Cambridge, Mass.: Harvard University Press.

Kant, Immanuel. 1952a. *Fundamental Principles of the Metaphysics of Morals* (1785). Trans. Thomas Kingsmill Abbott. In *The Critique of Pure Reason: The Critique of Practical Reason and Other Ethical Treatises*. Great Books of the Western World, ed. Robert Maynard Hutchins. Chicago: Encyclopaedia Britannica.

———. 1952b. *General Introduction to the Metaphysic of Morals* (1785). Trans. W. Hastie. In *The Critique of Pure Reason: The Critique of Practical Reason and Other Ethical Treatises*. Great Books of the Western World, ed. Robert Maynard Hutchins. Chicago: Encyclopaedia Britannica.

Kelsen, Hans. 1966. *Principles of International Law.* New York: Holt, Rinehart and Winston.

———. 1970. *Pure Theory of Law.* Berkeley: University of California Press.

———. 1971. *What Is Justice? Justice, Law, and Politics in the Mirror of Science: Collected Essays.* Berkeley: University of California Press.

Klein, Naomi. 2000. *No Logo: Taking Aim at the Brand Bullies.* Toronto: Random House.

Kunz, Thomas H. 1994. "Allomaternal Care: Helper-Assisted Birth in the Rodrigues Fruit Bat." *Journal of Zoology* 232, 4: 691–700.

Lefcourt, Herbert M. 1980. "Personality and Locus of Control." In Judy Garber and Martin E. Seligman, eds., *Human Helplessness: Theory and Applications.* New York: Academic Press.

Lewin, Roger. 1999. *Patterns in Evolution: The New Molecular View.* New York: Scientific American Library.

Lubbock, John. 1872. *Pre-Historic Times as Illustrated by Ancient Remains and the Manners and Customs of Modern Savages.* New York: Appleton.

Margulis, Lynn. 1998. *Symbiotic Planet: A New Look at Evolution.* New York: Basic Books.

McClelland, David C. 1975. *Power: The Inner Experience.* New York: Irvington.

McDougal, Myres S., Harold D. Lasswell, and Lung-chu Chen. 1980. *Human Rights and World Public Order: The Basic Policies of an International Law of Human Dignity.* New Haven, Conn.: Yale University Press.

Mies, Maria. 1986. *Patriarchy and Accumulation on a World Scale: Women in the International Division of Labour.* London: Zed Books.

Mies, Maria and Vandana Shiva. 1993. *Ecofeminism.* London: Zed Books.

Mill, John Stuart. 1955. *On Liberty.* Chicago: Henry Regnery.

Miller, Geoffrey. 2000. *The Mating Mind: How Sexual Choice Shaped the Evolution of Human Nature.* New York: Doubleday.

Montero, Maritza and Tod S. Sloan. 1988. "Understanding Behavior in Conditions of Economic and Cultural Dependency." *International Journal of Psychology* 23: 597–617.

Moore, George Edward. 1903. *Principia Ethica.* Cambridge: Cambridge University Press.

Morris, Desmond. 1967. *Naked Ape: A Zoologist's Study of the Human Animal.* New York: McGraw-Hill.

Nitecki, Matthew H. and Doris V. Nitecki, eds. 1993. *Evolutionary Ethics.* Albany: State University of New York Press.

Nozick, Robert. 1974. *Anarchy, State, and Utopia.* NewYork: Basic Books.

———. 1993. *The Nature of Rationality.* Princeton, N.J.: Princeton University Press.

Offen, Karen. 1990. "Feminism and Sexual Difference in Historical Perspective." In Deborah L. Rhode, ed., *Theoretical Perspectives on Sexual Difference.* New Haven, Conn.: Yale University Press.

O'Manique, John. 1969. *Energy in Evolution.* London: Garnstone Press / New York: Humanities Press.

———. 1976. "Scientific Objectivity and the Mind-Body Problem." In William R. Shea, ed., *Basic Issues in the Philosophy of Science.* New York: Science History Publications.

———. 1990. "Universal and Inalienable Rights: A Search for Foundations." *Human Rights Quarterly* 12, 4 (November).

———. 1992a. "Human Rights and Development." *Human Rights Quarterly* 14, 1 (February).

———. 1992b. "Development, Human Rights and Law." *Human Rights Quarterly* 14, 3 (August).

———. 1994. "A Marxian View of the Fundamentals of Political Development." *Political Psychology* 1, 2.

———. 1996. "Marx and Activity." In Paul Zarembka and Ajit Sinha, eds., *Latest Developments in Marxist Theory*. Research in Political Economy 15. Greenwich, Conn.: JAI Press.

Otto, Dianne. 1996. "Nongovernmental Organizations in the United Nations System: The Emerging Role of International Civil Society." *Human Rights Quarterly* 18, 1 (February).

Paul, Jeffrey, ed. 1981. *Reading Nozick*. Totowa, N.J.: Rowman and Littlefield.

Pinker, Steven. 1997. *How the Mind Works*. London: W.W. Norton.

Pollis, Adamantia. 1996. "Cultural Relativism Revisited." *Human Rights Quarterly* 18, 2 (May).

Pound, Roscoe. 1969. *Law and Morals*. New York: Augustus M. Kelley.

Putnam, Robert D. 2000. *Bowling Alone: The Collapse and Revival of American Community*. New York: Simon and Schuster.

Quartz, Steven R. and Terrence J. Sejnowski. 1997. "The Neural Basis of Cognitive Development:A Constructivist Manifesto." *Behavioral and Brain Sciences* 20: 537–96.

Raffel, Stanley. 1992. *Habermas, Lyotard, and the Concept of Justice*. London: Macmillan.

Rawls, John. 1971. *A Theory of Justice*. Cambridge, Mass.: Harvard University Press.

———. 1999. *The Law of Peoples, with The Idea of Public Reason Revisited*. Cambridge, Mass.: Harvard University Press.

Reed, Evelyn. 1975. *Woman's Evolution from Matriarchal Clan to Patriarchal Family*. New York: Pathfinder.

———. 1978. *Sexism and Science*. New York: Pathfinder.

Ridley, Matt. 1998. *The Origins of Virtue: Human Instincts and the Evolution of Cooperation*. New York: Penguin.

Rottschaefer, William A. 1998. *The Biology and Psychology of Moral Agency*. Cambridge: Cambridge University Press.

Runyan, Anne Sissom. 1992. "The 'State' of Nature: A Garden Unfit for Women and Other Living Things." In V. Spike Peterson, ed., *Gendered States: Feminist (Re)visions of International Relations Theory*. Boulder, Colo.: Lynne Rienner.

Sampson, Edward E. 1988. "Indigenous Psychologies of the Individual and Their Role in Personal and Societal Functioning." *American Psychologist* 3, 1: 15–22.

Scheffler, Samuel. 1992. *Human Morality*. Oxford: Oxford University Press.

Seligman, Martin E. P. 1975. *Helplessness: On Depression, Development, and Death*. San Francisco: W.H. Freeman.

———. 1989. "Research in Clinical Psychology: Why Is There So Much Depression Today?" In Ira S. Cohen, ed., *The G. Stanley Hall Lecture Series*, vol. 9. Washington, D.C.: American Psychological Association.

Shue, Henry. 1980. *Basic Rights: Subsistence, Affluence, and U.S. Foreign Policy*. Princeton, N.J.: Princeton University Press.

Simpson, George Gaylord. 1951. *The Meaning of Evolution*. New York: New American Library.

———. 1964. *This View of Life: The World of an Evolutionist*. New York: Harcourt, Brace and World.

Sober, Elliott. 1994. *From a Biological Point of View: Essays in Evolutionary Philosophy*. Cambridge: Cambridge University Press.

Sober, Elliott and David Sloan Wilson. 1999. *Unto Others: The Evolution and Psychology of Unselfish Behavior.* Cambridge, Mass.: Harvard University Press.
Spencer, Herbert. 1851. *Social Statics.* London: Chapman.
———. 1874. *The Study of Sociology.* New York: D. Appleton.
Sperling, Susan. 1991. "Baboons with Briefcases: Feminism, Functionalism, and Sociobiology in the Evolution of Primate Gender." *Signs* 17, 1: 1–27.
Stone, Julius. 1984. *Visions of World Order: Between State Power and Human Justice.* Baltimore: Johns Hopkins University Press.
Tattersall, Ian. 1998. *Becoming Human: Evolution and Human Uniqueness.* New York: Harcourt Brace.
———. 2002. *The Monkey in the Mirror: Essays on the Science of What Makes Us Human.* New York: Harcourt.
Tickner, J. Ann. 1992. *Gender in International Relations: Feminist Perspectives on Achieving Global Security.* New York: Columbia University Press.
Trivers, Robert. 1971. "The Evolution of Reciprocal Altruism." *Quarterly Review of Biology* 45: 35–57.
Washburn, S. L. and F. C. Howell. 1960. "Human Evolution and Culture." In Sol Tax, ed., *The Evolution of Man.* Evolution After Darwin 2. Chicago: University of Chicago Press.
Wilkinson, G. S. 1990. "Food Sharing in Vampire Bats." *Scientific American* 262, 2: 76–82.
Wilson, David Sloan. 1980. *The Natural Selection of Populations and Communities.* Menlo Park, Calif.: Benjamin/Cummings.
Wilson, Edward O. 1975. *Sociobiology: The New Synthesis.* Cambridge, Mass.: Harvard University Press.
Wolff, Jonathan. 1991. *Robert Nozick.* Cambridge: Polity Press.
Young, Larry J., Roger Nilsen, Katrina G. Waymire, Grant R. Macgregor, and Thomas R. Isnel. 1999. "Increased Affiliative Response to Vasopressin in Mice Expressing the V_{1a} Receptor from a Monogamous Vole." *Nature* 400 (August): 766–68.

Index

The subject component of this index points only to basic explanations or definitions.